THE POTENTIAL ROLE OF AGROFORESTRY IN COMBATING DESERTIFICATION AND ENVIRONMENTAL DEGRADATION

WITH SPECIAL REFERENCE TO AFRICA

by

Michel BAUMER

D0877541

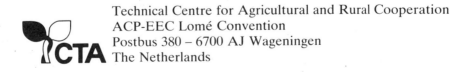

Technical Centre for Agricultural and Rural Cooperation
ACP-EEC Lomé Convention
Postbus 380 – 6700 AJ Wageningen
The Netherlands

© Technical Centre for Agricultural and Rural Cooperation 1990
Printed by GM Drukkerij Giethoorn/Meppel, The Netherlands
ISBN 92 9081 039 4

CONTENTS

ACRONYMS AND ABBREVIATIONS USED IN TEXT

AASS	Atlas of Agrarian Structures South of the Sahara
ACP	Africa, Caribbean, Pacific
AF	agroforestry
ARC	Agronomic Research Centre
BFT	Bois et forêts des tropiques, Nogent-sur-Marne, France
BLACT	Bureau of Liaison for Technical Co-operation Agents, France
CAZRI	Central Arid Zone Research Institute, Jodhpur, India
CERER	Centre for Study and Research into Renewable Energy, Senegal
CILF	International Council for the French Language
CILSS	Inter-State Committee for Control of Drought in the Sahel, Ouagadougou
CNRS	National Centre for Scientific Research, Paris
CP	crude protein
CSIRO	Commonwealth Scientific and Industrial Research Organization, Australia
CTA	Technical Centre for Agricultural and Rural Cooperation, ACP-EEC
CTFT	Centre technique forestier tropical
DM	dry matter
DP	digestible protein
EEC	European Economic Community
ENDA	Environment and development in the Third World, Dakar
FAC	Aid and Co-operation Fund, France
FAO	United Nations Food and Agriculture Organization
FRC	Forestry Research Centre, Cameroon
FU	fodder unit
FWA	French West Africa
GERDAT	Groupement d'études et de recherches pour le développement de l'agronomie tropicale
GTZ	West German Technical Aid, Eschborn
IAEA	International Atomic Energy Agency, Vienna
ICRAF	International Council for Research in Agroforestry, Nairobi
IDRC	International Development Research Centre, Ottawa
IEMVT	Tropical Cattle Farming and Veterinary Medicine Institute, Maisons-Alfort
IFAN	French Institute of Black Africa (Institut fondamental d'Afrique noire), Dakar
IIASA	International Institute for Applied Systems Analysis, Vienna
IITA	International Institute of Tropical Agriculture, Ibadan

IRAT	Institute for Research in Tropical Agriculture and Food Crops, France
ISF	Ingénieurs sans frontières, Paris
JMRDP	Jebel Marra Rural Development Project, Zalingei, Sudan
KARI	Kenya Agricultural Research Institute
kJ	kilojoule
MJ	megajoule
MPTS	multi-purpose trees and shrubs
N	nitrogen
NAS	National Academy of Sciences, USA
OECD	Organization for European Co-operation and Development, Paris
ORSTOM	Office for Overseas Scientific and Technical Research, Paris
P	phosphorus
PRECOBA	Government-initiated community reforestation project in the Groundnut Basin, Senegal
SC	Soil conservation
SCET	Société centrale pour l'équipement du territoire, Paris
SODEVA	Society for the development and improvement of the valley of the Senegal river
UNCOD	United Nations Conference on Desertification
UNDP	United Nations Development Programme
UNEP	United Nations Environment Programme
UNFPA	United Nations Fund for Population Activities
UNIDO	United Nations Industrial Development Organization
UNU	United Nations University, Tokyo
USAID	United States Agency for International Development
WFP	World Food Programme
WMO	World Meteorological Organization, Geneva

NB. This list includes both acronyms and abbreviations. AF is a conventionally accepted abbreviation for agroforestry but we have also used other common abbreviations such as (DP, DM, CP)

NOTE CONCERNING BOTANICAL NOMENCLATURE

For Latin plant names, the international rules on nomenclature adopted by the 7th International Botanical Congress in Stockholm in 1950 have deliberately not been followed. In agreement with EMBERGER (1960) who wrote that decapitalization norms are a regressive form of the scientific language that constitutes nomenclature, we consider that 'like all languages, the language of science is a convention; it is made up of signs conveying meaning, and the more numerous and precise those meanings are, the richer and more instructive it is' (BAUMER, 1975). Specific names have therefore been written with an initial capital where the Latin genitive of proper names or old generic or specific denominations, Latin or not, appear. Specific adjectives have been given a small initial letter, except when the author has used a capital letter in the original description.

The binomial *Faidherbia albida* (Del.) A. Chev. has been preferred to *Acacia albida* Del., for reasons explained by Auguste CHEVALIER as long ago as 1934 and more recently by Henri Noel LE HOUEROU (1979), and which we indicate in section 7.2.1. (See also Appendix 2.)

Albizzia has been spelt with two *z* because the genus is dedicated to the Albizzi family, as recalled by Guy ROBERTY, who himself is related to the family.

Latin binomials are not complete without the name of the author(s). In order to avoid burdening the text, these authors have only been mentioned in a separate list in appendix 1 at the end of the book.

A very recent change has been made in the names of Australian acacia; they are no longer *Acacia* sp. but *Racosperma* Martius (Pedley, 1986-1987 a & b). Consequently where they appear in the text they should be read as follows:

Acacia anuera = Racosperma aneurum (F. Muell. ex Benth.) Pedley, comb.

Acacia Cambagei = Racosperma cambagei (R. Baker) Pedley, comb. nov.

Acacia holosericea = Racosperma holosericeum (Cunn. ex G. Don) Pedley, comb. nov.

Acacia Victoriae = Racosperma Victoriae (Benth.) Pedley Comb. nov.

1. INTRODUCTION

In the strategy to combat desertification in the Sahel, drawn up at the Nouakchott Regional Seminar and refined in 1985 (Club du Sahel, 1985; ROCHETTE, 1985 a and b), several concerned countries expressly mentioned agroforestry in their national communications; for example:

– Gambia accepted 'development of agroforestry in its five strategic priorities', and saw 'a solution to the problems and difficulties of reforestation in an integrated approach: agro-silviculture, associating agriculture, stock rearing and forestry';

– Senegal proposed eight major points for an anti-desertification strategy, among which are 'agroforestry and silvo-pastoral integration';

– Chad intends to 'develop agroforestry (with *Faidherbia albida*)' as one of four principal medium- and long-term courses of action.

These examples demonstrate the interest that exists in agroforestry, a new term which first appeared around 1960 in English, then in French. At the same time they highlight the lack of precision surrounding what is conveniently called agroforestry. For if the word is new, the art is an ancient one.

The term 'agroforestry' is widely used today. Numerous international organizations mention agroforestry in their programmes and support agroforestry projects; for example UNESCO, which has just supported an agroforestry seminar in Gabon, and the FAO, which is fielding thirteen projects in Africa with agroforestry as a major component, plus eight in Asia and seven in Latin America, for an external contribution totalling 26 million dollars.

The Technical Centre for Agricultural and Rural Cooperation, ACP-EEC (CTA) has taken a lead in this field, for example by initiating the present study, and one on the potential role of agroforestry in the ACP countries (BEETS, 1988).

For their part, numerous countries offering bilateral aid (Canada, Switzerland, USA, France, Netherlands, West Germany, Sweden, etc.) have understood the advantage of agroforestry and are backing more and more projects with an agroforestry approach. Non-governmental organizations (NGO) have taken the concept on board and are operating agroforestry schemes in many countries. In literature on Third World development, the term appears more and more frequently, and there are many publications devoted specifically to agroforestry.

Various definitions of agroforestry have been given by many authors; the definition adopted here is the following: 'Agroforestry is a collective term for systems and technologies of land use where perennial woody plants (trees, bushes, shrubs, scrub and, by assimilation, palms and bamboos) are deliberately cultivated on ground otherwise used for crops and/or stock rearing in a spatial or temporal arrangement, and where there are interactions at once ecological and economic between the woody plants and the other components of the system'. These interactions can take several forms, positive or negative, and do not necessarily remain stable in time.

This is the definition drawn up by the International Council for Research in Agroforestry (ICRAF), one of whose tasks it is to establish precise definitions of terms in line with this approach. It also accords with the definition submitted for recognition to the International Council for the French Language (CILF). However, many other definitions have been drawn up. There are a good dozen in an article which appeared in the journal '*Agroforestry Systems*' in 1982. Others have been proposed, no doubt still others are to come, as often happens in a relatively new field which, in addition, arouses considerable interest.

There are, then, some misunderstandings over terminology. For example, there is frequent confusion between agroforestry on the one hand and agro-silvi-pastoralism and agro-silviculture (or agri-silviculture) on the other. These terms denote special types of agroforestry. Agro-silviculture is the combination of woody perennials and cultivated plants, whereas agro-silvi-pastoralism combines woody perennials, cultivated plants and stock rearing. Each of these types can comprise various systems, as shown by NAIR (1985) in an attempt at classification, to which we will return in section 3.2. Taking only arid and semi-arid zones, the following **agro-silvicultural systems** can be distinguished according to their objectives:

a) use of multi-purpose trees and shrubs on cultivated land

    a1) in Brazil, a subsistence economy in which the following species are preserved or planted in the fields:

        Caesalpinia ferrea
        Prosopis juliflora
        Zizyphus Joazeiro

a2) in India, a subsistence economy in which the following species are preserved in the fields, and are sometimes sown or even planted:

Cajanus Cajan
Derris indica
Prosopis cineraria
Tamarindus indica

or a mixed economy (subsistence/market) in which *Zizyphus mauritiana,* horticultural variety – the large-fruited 'ber' is preserved and planted.

a3) in Kenya, a subsistence economy in which the following species are preserved in the fields (for example in the semi-arid parts of north central Kitui district):

Acacia tortilis
A. Senegal
Balanites aegyptica
Commiphora sp.pl
Zizyphus sp.

a4) in Mali, a subsistence or mixed economy, with preservation in the fields of the shea butter tree *Butyrospermum Parkii* for oil production, the African locust tree *Parkia biglobosa* and certain other species like the tamarind *Tamarindus indica* for their forage pods and the pleasant drink extracted from them.

b) use of woody perennials to protect crops from the effects of wind

b1) in Senegal, the tannes (depressions near the northern coastline, that trap rain and contain groundwater from the Quaternary sands) used for market gardening, fruit and food crops are protected by a network of windbreaks approximately fifteen km deep, using cashew gum trees *Anacardium occidentale* (which, because they stand close together to act as a wind shield, naturally do not yield nearly as much fruit as when planted out for fruit-bearing), in turn, these windbreaks are protected from the sea wind by plantations of swamp oak *Casuarina* cf. *equisetifolia*, on the coastal sand dunes.

b2) in the Sudan, hedge windbreaks around irrigated crops in the north, using:

Casuarina cf. *equisetifolia*
Eucalyptus camaldulensis
E. microtheca

c) use of trees and shrubs specifically for producing firewood

c1) in Niger, *Acacia tortilis* and *Faidherbia albida* are preserved in the cultivated fields near Zinder

c2) in Chad, *Acacia Seyal* is preserved, preferably in strips, on periodically flooded vertisols.

Agro-silvi-pastoral systems are equally varied in arid or semi-arid zones, for example:

– in the Sudan (especially in north central Kordofan) traditional multi-purpose gum gardens, unfortunately dying out now because of increased demographic pressures: a crop cycle (primarily millet, also sesame, sorghum, groundnut) followed by fifteen years' bush fallowing with *Acacia Senegal* which produces gum arabic, firewood, cordage and fodder; there is pasturage on the crop fallows and browsing on the shrub fallows. Traditionally, the gum tree, *Acacia Senegal*, is cultivated for a variety of purposes (see later);

– in Spain, the 'dehesa', a sparsely planted deciduous oak woodland, grazed by pigs or sheep, where one or two annual cereal crops are occasionally grown;

– in Kenya, the use of woody perennial hedges (*Acacia horrida, A. mellifera, Commiphora africana, Euphorbia Tirucalli, Zizyphus mucronata*) to provide firewood and latex, and at the same time, serving to keep unherded animals off the fields;

– the noteworthy association of *Faidherbia albida* with food crops (millet and sorghum) or commercial crops (groundnuts) in Senegal, Sudan, Niger, Kenya, etc. to increase yield and provide foliage and the pods much favoured by cattle.

Silvi-pastoral systems are of major importance in arid and semi-arid zones, where they make up the bulk of grazing land covering millions of hectares. These systems have low or very low productivity, basically because of the difficult climatic conditions. The plant biomass is sparse and its growth slow and irregular. In these systems, desertification is often visible and it is here particularly that the most spectacular changes in flora and vegetation were seen following the exceptional droughts of the 1970s. It is in these systems that improvements are most difficult to bring about.

To date it has been difficult to classify these systems as agroforestry because there has been no attempt to deliberately and systematically develop positive interactions between woody perennials and other plants and animals, except on an experimental basis. Examples of silvi-pastoral agroforestry systems include:

- enriching Aristida pseudosteppes in the Sodiri region of Kordofan (Sudan) by planting *Leptadenia pyrotechnica* in 1960;

- protecting *Acacia tortilis* ssp. *raddiana* seedlings to improve the quality of pasture land in the Tanout region (Niger) as part of FAO/NER Project 19, in about 1968;

- systematically introducing Australian acacias to improve grazing land in some regions of northern Ferlo (Senegal), North Cameroon, Niger, Somalia, etc.

2. ENVIRONMENTAL DEGRADATION AND DESERTIFICATION

In 1973, the media drew attention to an exceptionally severe drought affecting the southern Sahara, in the sahelo-saharan and sahelo-sudanian zones, called the Sahel.

SAHEL

The word 'sahel' is an Arabic word meaning 'shore' or 'edge'. It is the word applied to those countries bordering the sea and it is in this sense, for example, that one talks about 'The Algiers Sahel'. The word 'sahel' is also used in North Africa to designate all the coastal plains, as distinct from the 'Atlas' mountainous region, the High Plateaus or the Sahara desert. It is still with the same meaning that one talks of 'al sahel' in Sudan and Saudi Arabia to designate the coastal plains bordering the Red Sea.

The adjectives 'Swahili', used to describe people who live in East Africa, and 'Kiswahili' the name of their language, derive from 'sahel' and come from Arabic: the Swahili people have affinities with the coastal people whose bloodstock and language Arab traders have strongly influenced. The word 'sahel' also denotes countries bordering the desert, so that in Algeria the foothills of the Saharan Atlas which border the desert on the north are called 'Saharan sahel'. The countries bordering the Sahara on the south are also called 'Saharan sahel', and to say 'the Sahel' to describe them is insufficiently precise: to be perfectly logical, one should say 'the South-Saharan sahel'. But if one finds 'sahelian' and 'Sudanian-sahel' side by side it is clear that the sahel meant is the South-Saharan sahel.

The media talked of thousands of deaths and showed pictures of dying children and skeletal remains of cattle. The term 'Sahel' has therefore become for many a symbol of misery, distress, a desperate struggle to survive in a hostile environment. Other disasters (floods in Bangladesh, industrial catastrophes at Seveso and Bhopal, earthquakes, volcanic eruptions, not to mention wars) do not seem to have caught popular imagination as strongly as the exceptional drought in the Sahel (later in other parts of Africa like Ethiopia, where its effects only gradually became known, as governments became willing, or were forced, to admit to it).

14

The food situation of many countries affected by the exceptional drought of the 1970s became such a major issue that the General Assembly of the United Nations, in its Resolution 3337 (XXIX), decided to organize a Conference on Desertification (UNCOD). This was held in Nairobi from 29 August to 9 September 1977, and it brought to the fore the gravity of the situation, without however taking sufficiently wide-ranging appropriate action in response. As Dr TOLBA pointed out in a strongly-worded communication to the International Conference on 'Arid Lands: Today and Tomorrow' held at Tucson (Arizona) in October 1985, the public is still a very long way from grasping all the dramatic consequences of desertification (TOLBA, 1985 a).

2.1 DEFINITIONS AND CONCEPTS

The term 'desertification' has taken on a new significance in the popular language since the United Nations Conference of 1976 (UNCOD) (see box).

Etymologically, desertification is the progression from an arid facies to a hyper-arid facies (=desert), by human action (the word contains the radical -fi-, from the Latin *fieri*, to do, to act). Desertification is the progression from arid facies to hyper-arid facies for whatever reason; in the proper sense of the word it is a group of actions resulting in a more or less irreversible reduction of the plant cover, finally leading to the formation of new desert landscapes in zones which did not before show those characteristics. In the same way, aridization is, in its true sense, the progress from a less arid facies to a more arid one, and aridification is aridization provoked by the action of man.

DESERTIFICATION

The United Nations Conference on Desertification, held in Nairobi in 1977, agreed and propagated a definition of desertification which is in current use, notably in the press and on the radio:

'Desertification is the reduction or destruction of the land's biological potential, finally resulting in the appearance of desert conditions. It is one aspect of the generalized degradation of ecosystems under the combined pressures of adverse and uncertain climatic conditions and overexploitation. This over-use has reduced or destroyed the biological potential, that is to say the plant and animal production for multipurpose use, at the very moment when increased production was needed to meet the needs of growing populations aspiring to development'.

This definition goes to the root of the matter to the extent that it acknowledges that the problems of desertification are inseparable from those of development and, by the same token, tied up with demographic expansion.

'Desertification' is used here in the very wide sense given to the term since UNCOD to describe productivity loss due to plant and soil degradation, even in semi-humid zones which have nothing to do with the desert. Francophone rural geographers have been using the same word for a long time to denote reduction of population density in gradually abandoned rural areas.

Desertification is the most serious environmental problem facing the world, and more especially Africa, today.

In Africa, it is estimated (UNEP, 1977) that south of the Sahara there are more than 75 million people, 15% in towns, 62% mainly in agriculture and 23% mainly in stock-raising. The people living in dry regions are almost all affected by desertification or threatened by it. It is estimated that more than 16 million people are already suffering severe hardship on account of desertification, 7 million of whom (at least 44%) are stock-raisers. Except where there are oases, irrigation, etc., these dry regions are considered to be very low in productivity compared with humid regions, but they still produce enormous quantities of meat, skins, cereals and textile fibres. They are also the cradle of several cultivated plants (wheat, maize, sorghum and barley) and contain a genetic plant and animal potential which has yet to be systematically evaluated.

16

In FAO and UNEP publications concerning desertification, this process is considered as an integrated expression of socio-economic evolution and natural or man-made processes that destroy the balance between natural resources (soil, air, water, and their integrated expression – vegetation) and human needs in areas which suffer from soil and/or climatic aridity. The continuous deterioration of these processes leads to a reduction or destruction of the biological potential, a worsening in living conditions and an increase in desert-like landscapes. In areas not subject to soil and/or climatic aridity, every threatened loss of biological productivity is considered and listed as a degradation risk.

Loss of production capacity resulting from desertification takes any of the following forms:

- a progressive decline in harvests,
- an increasing number of crop failures,
- wind damage to crops, with uprooting or leaf damage,
- deflation of the top layer of humus from the soil and dust storms,
- increase in surface runoff, reduced percolation, formation of erosion channels and gullies,
- shifting sand,
- less biological diversity through loss of species,
- failure of traditional systems which previously functioned well both economically and socially,
- a drop in the water table,
- reduction of surface water,
- insufficient fodder,
- crisis in tree germination,
- harsher living conditions for people, plants and animals,
- soil degradation, etc.

Soil degradation, which generally goes hand in hand with desertification, may take six different forms (RIQUIER, 1978):

erosion by water: sheet erosion, gully erosion, channel erosion, landslides
wind erosion: deflation and accumulation
salification and alkalization
chemical degradation: base leaching and acidification, toxicity other than excess salt or sodium
physical degradation: structure loss, crusting, silting, reduced permeability, drop in aeration, restricted rooting
biological degradation: loss of organic matter, decrease in biological activity

All these processes result in a reduction of soil productivity. Degradation factors are climatic, pedological, topographic or human. Table I shows the physical and biological processes that cause desertification. The fragility of African soils, particularly their structural fragility, leaves them highly vulnerable to degradation, as emphasized by MOULARD, the former Governor General of French West Africa, as long ago as 1948, when he predicted a famine affecting 15 to 20 million people through defective farming techniques, and recommended as the only remedy a massive tree-planting operation in which all Africans would take part: 'We shall plant useful trees, shea butter, African locust, mangoes, palms, forage trees and especially the Faidherbia', and he recommended hedges and an end to shifting cultivation, as CHEVALIER had also advocated more than ten years previously.

One major difference between soil degradation and desertification is that the former is not necessarily continuous; it can occur for relatively short periods, it is reversible and it can happen in all climates. Desertification, on the other hand, is a continuous process, it may occur over very long periods, it rapidly becomes irreversible and it only occurs in arid, semi-arid and semi-humid zones. Degradation of soil productivity, if continuous, can lead to desertification. It should be said that certain important processes in soil degradation (for example, waterlogging, nutrient loss and souring) are not normally taken into account when evaluating desertification. Desertification can, in fact, occur just as well in years of abundant rainfall as in years of drought.

Drought is strictly related to climate. This is not true of desertification. Drought in a region is conditioned by highly complex global climatic mechanisms which sometimes affect the whole world. A drought may occur in a given region as the result of a climatic event originating elsewhere: the climatic system on the earth's surface in one whole system and a modification occurring at any point of that system can cause repercussions a great distance away. Drought is a normal, recurrent phenomenon in all arid zones, as irregular as the famine it often brings in its wake. From this arise two rules that have a bearing on agroforestry:

1) evaluation of production potential in these zones can in no way be based on average rainfall alone;

2) any new schemes for developing these zones must be oriented towards sustainable production, despite the uncertainties of the climate.

On this point, I should like to make the observation that the forecasting of droughts 60 to 80 days in advance (which is beginning to be possible by satellite), although it will enable resources to be mobilized in good time to alleviate famines, could have an inhibiting effect on development: there is a strong possibility that those in authority might be tempted to say to themselves, 'Since my country will be given aid in time if there is a famine, why take so much trouble to create schemes for sustainable production'. Already there are only too many examples of this kind, generated by food distributions for victims of drought.

2.1.1 Types of Aridity

Various attempts have been made to grade and classify the varying degrees of aridity and desertification.

The classification of LE HOUEROU and POPOV (1981) for intertropical Africa's eco-climatic zones combines several criteria. It employs the classification of Emmanuel DE MARTONNE (1928) in tropical zones with a monomodal rainfall distribution and equatorial zones with a bimodal distribution; but monomodal distributions can be found in dry areas (like Lobito Bay in Angola), and even in very dry areas (like the Horn, and particularly the north coast, of Africa), whereas bimodal distributions are to be found in regions of high humidity (such as around Conakry).

Rainy months are those where the average monthly rainfall in millimetres is lower than twice the average monthly temperature expressed in degrees Celsius (BAGNOULS and GAUSSEN, 1953 and 1957) or $P < 2t$.

In West Africa, this formula, like that of PRESCOTT and THOMAS (1949) for bare soil evaporation ($e = 0.4\ E^{0.75}$), or PENMAN's formula ($P < 0.35$ PET) which relates to the water requirements of most African food crops in the days immediately after sowing, agree in fixing the monthly rainfall (1.6-1.8 mm/day) required at the start of the growing season at around 50-55 mm.

In evaluating aridity, it is convenient to use the grading system established by UNESCO (1979). 'The degrees of bioclimatic aridity depend on the relative amounts of water brought by the rains and on evaporation and transpiration losses: the lower the rainfall and the higher the evaporation rate, the greater the aridity'. Following RIQUIER and ROSETTI (1976), therefore, the ratio values $\dfrac{P}{Etp}$ are used to define arid and semi-arid regions, where P is the average amount of annual rainfall and Etp the average potential annual evapotranspiration.

TABLE I

Physical and biological processes causing desertification: problems and solutions

NB - Agroforestry practices are indicated by AF in the solutions column (after UNCOD, 1974)

Factor	Problems	Causes	Solutions
Water	scarcity	low rainfall erratic rainfall distribution poor irrigation management overexploitation of surface and underground reservoirs uncontrolled evaporation losses	improving water supply conservation AF: improved infiltration by increasing deep root systems reducing evaporation by multi-purpose woody plant windbreaks
	poor management of dry soil agriculture	lack of rainfall irregular distribution uncontrolled flow	flow control, cultural techniques soil conservation AF: contour woody plants acting favourably on other crops
	poor irrigation management	use of too much water defects in drainage system imperfect levelling inadequate water distribution imprecise debit measure poor irrigation methods	improved irrigation methods drainage systems salinity control guaranteed water supply AF: reduction of evaporation by multi-purpose woody plants (including screening, hedges, micro-windbreaks)
	floods	irregular rainfall distribution violence of precipitations uncontrolled flow	flash-flood control AF: flow halt by alignments of woody plants in strategic positions
Soil	erosion (water and wind)	reduction of plant cover uncontrolled flow sedimentation and alluviation degradation of soil structure inadequate tillage methods high winds reduced profile thickness loss of water retention capacity	soil conservation soil humidity conservation vegetation planting vegetation conservation fertilizing AF: multi-purpose woody plant windbreaks, hedges, screen shelter, micro windbreaks; contour trees, micro-bowls around trees planted on slopes, nitrogen-fixing trees, trees providing large amounts of organic matter

soil salinity waterlogging	channel alluviation waterlogging poor water quality poor drainage, poor water purification poor irrigation water management defective drainage systems floods	control of irrigation water salinity regularity of water supply control of soil salinity drainage vegetation planting plant conservation flow management cementation of ditches AF: windbreaks along ditches, salt-resistant woody plants like tamarisk, improved value of saline land by halophyte grazing
Plants reduced production	bad land clearance bad plant management over-cultivation over-grazing invasion by undesirable plants uncontrolled wood gathering over-exploitation of forests uncontrolled fires drought	irrigation, flow control water supply soil conservation vegetation planting plant management AF: improved wooded fallow land for multi-purpose use, hedges, planting in avenues, forage trees, tree vigour
Animals reduced production	water scarcity lack of fodder cultivation and food reserves health and nutrition overpopulation	water supply water control management of grazing land stock control soil conservation plant productivity improved strains plant conservation pest control wild animal ranching AF: forage trees and shrubs, reserves of standing grazing, protein-rich woody plants
Energy scarcity and bad use of fuel	uncontrolled wood gathering poor use of available energy sources	reforestation, solar energy, wind energy, energy conservation, biogas AF: use of woody plants valued as firewood or charcoal

The hyperarid zone (A) is characterized by a ratio $\dfrac{P}{Etp} < 0.03$

For arid zone (B) $\qquad\qquad\qquad\qquad 0.03 < \dfrac{P}{Etp} < 0.02$

For the semi-arid zone (C) $\qquad\qquad\qquad 0.20 < \dfrac{P}{Etp} < 0.50$

For the sub-humid zone (D) $\qquad\qquad\quad 0.05 < \dfrac{P}{Etp} < 0.75$

In each of these zones there are sub-zones defined by the average winter temperature t_H (in degrees Celsius)

1	hot	$20 < t_H < 30$
2	temperate	$10 < t_H < 20$
3	cool	$0 < t_H < 10$
4	cold	$t_H < 0$

Then, distinctions are made according to the average temperature t_e in the hot season (in degrees Celsius)

a	very hot	$30 < t_e$
b	hot	$20 < t_e < 30$
c	temperate	$10 < t_e < 20$

By combining these features, types of aridity identified by three features are obtained. In the ACP countries affected by desertification, the following situations are not found: A1b; A2c; A3a; B1c; B2c; B3; B4; C2a, c; C3a and c; C4; D2c; D3a and c; D4.

The situations that are found are given in Table II.

The different types of climate are distributed schematically between the countries as follows:

A1a, *Hyper-arid, warm winter, very warm summer*

Ethiopia	: Kobar Sink depression
Sudan	: Southern Nubian desert, E-NE and SW of Abu Hamad; Red Sea coast north of Ras Abu Shagara
Somalia	: coastal fringe of the Gulf of Aden, north of the Medjourtine massif.

Table II

Distribution of arid regions in the ACP countries of Africa

	Hyper-Arid				Arid				Semi-Arid				Semi-Humid				
	A1a	A2a	A2b	A3b	B1a	B1b	B2a	B2b	C1a	C1b	C2b	C3b	D1a	D1b	D2a	D2b	D3b
Angola								+	+		+		+			+	
Benin			+													+	
Botswana					+					+	+					+	
Burkina Faso							+		+				+			+	
Cameroon																	
Cape Verde								+	+				+			+	
Central Africa				+								+			+		
Chad		+	+		+		+	+	+		+						
Djibouti	+				+												
Ethiopia						+		+		+	+		+			+	
Gambia													+	+		+	
Ghana														+			
Guinea														+			
Guinea Bissau														+			
Ivory Coast														+			
Kenya					+	+		+		+	+						+
Lesotho																	
Madagascar			+								+		+		+		
Mali					+		+		+	+							
Mauritania		+			+	+	+	+	+	+							
Niger		+			+		+			+			+			+	
Nigeria																+	
Reunion						+											
Rwanda						+								+			
Senegal	+				+		+		+		+		+				
Somalia	+				+			+	+				+	+			
Sudan		+	+			+	+			+		+				+	
Swaziland											+				+		
Tanzania													+				
Togo													+				
Uganda														+			
Zaire														+			
Zambia										+						+	
Zimbabwe										+						+	

23

A2a, *Hyper-arid, mild winter, very warm summer*

Chad	: Bodélé, Borkou, Mourdi
Mali	: Hank region, Taoudenit
Mauritania	: Djouf, Hank and Zemmour regions
Niger	: Ténéré
Sudan	: Libyan desert, Nubian desert north of a line Abu Hamad-Bur Sudan, excluding the Arabian desert

A2b, *Hyper-arid, temperate winter, warm summer*

Angola	: extreme SW, Counene
Chad	: region bordering the Tibesti to the north
Mauritania	: around Nouadhibou and Cap Blanc
Sudan	: southern extremity of the Arabian Desert

A3b, *Hyper-arid, cool winter, warm summer*

Chad	: Tibesti

B1a, *Arid, warm winter, very warm summer*

Burkina Faso	: extreme north-eastern point
Chad	: vast area comprising Kanem and Batha
Djibouti	: entire area
Ethiopia	: southern Eritrea and eastern Danakil plain
Kenya	: 'Chalbi desert' and central part of the Somalian frontier
Mali	: central sahelo-saharan strip bounded by a line Diandioumé-Douentza to the south and by a line passing through Timbuktu and Tabankort to the north
Mauritania	: strip continuing the above to the west, northward up to Atar, but excluding a coastal strip of about 100 km and the southern point of the country
Niger	: central sahelian strip bounded on the north by a line running from Agadeni to Tamesna and on the south by a line passing roughly through Diffa, Gouré, Tahoua and Ayorou
Nigeria	: a very small area near Lake Chad
Senegal	: lower Senegal valley up to approx. 100 km from the coast
Somalia	: central part of the country, upper Juba valley and a pocket running along the Kenyan border

| Sudan | : vast area covering: W of Darfur, N of Kordofan, extreme N of the Gezira, Bayuda 'desert', region to the W of Khartoum and up to the coast of Port-Sudan to Ras Abu Shagara |

B1b, *Arid, warm winter, warm summer*

Ethiopia	: western part of the Dankali country, central Chebeli and Juba valleys, E and S of the Ogaden, border strip with Kenya
Kenya	: shores of Lake Turkana and NE of country
Mauritania	: coastal strip to the S of Cape Arguin
Senegal	: very small area at the river mouth
Somalia	: vast area from the Ogaden to the sea

B2a, *Arid, mild winter, very warm summer*

Chad	: W of Ennedi and upper course of Wadi Howar
Mali	: E-W strip running from the river Niger loop to Adrar des Iforas
Mauritania	: E-W strip running from the Mreyye depression to the N of Tagant, to Adrar at Azeffal
Niger	: Air and NW of the country
Sudan	: SW of the Northern Province

B2b, *Arid, mild winter, warm summer*

Angola	: SW coast
Botswana	: extreme SW of the Kalahari
Cape Verde	: whole area
Chad	: central Ennedi
Ethiopia	: N of the Ogaden
Madagascar	: SW littoral
Mauritania	: very small area N of the Bay of Arguin
Sudan	: N of Darfur

C1a, *Semi-arid, warm winter, very warm summer*

Benin	: Extreme northern point
Burkina Faso	: northern half of the country
Cameroon	: extreme north near Lake Chad
Chad	: E-W strip running from the W of Ouadai to S of Lake Chad

Mali	: E-W 'sahelian' strip running from the Dogon country and the Kouri region to the east as far as Bamako, then Kayes and Nioro du Sahel
Mauritania	: extreme S of the country (south of an approximate line Timbedra-Boghe)
Niger	: S of the country (south of an approximate line Zinder-Ayorou)
Nigeria	: N of the country (north of an approximate line Yelwa-Kano-Gombe-Bama)
Somalia	: small area on either side of the middle valley of the river Juba
Sudan	: W-central Darfur, S of Kordofan (except the Nuba mountains) most of Gezira, NE of Bahr-el-Ghazal and extreme W of the Blue Nile Province

C1b, *Semi-arid, warm winter, warm summer*

Botswana	: very small area to the NE near Zimbabwe
Ethiopia	: extreme W of Eritrea
Kenya	: NW of the country and irregular NW-SE strip joining it to SE
Senegal	: coastal strip N of Saloum
Somalia	: SW and W-central part of the country
Sudan	: northern border with Ethiopia
Tanzania	: very small area to the north of the Usambara mountains
Uganda	: extreme NE
Zambia	: valley of the Zambesi and Muchinga mountains
Zimbabwe	: valley of the Zambesi

C2b, *Semi-arid, mild winter, warm summer*

Angola	: inland from the SW coast
Botswana	: almost the whole area
Chad	: northern Ouadai
Ethiopia	: small region in Eritrea and NE-SW highly irregular strip in the SE of the country
Kenya	: extreme south of the Rift Valley
Madagascar	: Mahafaly plateau on the SW of the island
Sudan	: small area N of Jebel Marra
Tanzania	: the largest zone of this type in the ACP countries concerned, basically comprising the Masai steppe

C3b, *Semi-arid, cold winter, warm summer*

Sudan : Jebel Marra

D1a, *Sub-humid, warm winter, very warm summer*

Benin	: small area in the NE of the country
Burkino Faso	: narrow EW strip south of Ouagadougou
Cameroon	: Mandiara mountains to the Maroua region
Chad	: a wide area on either side of the middle Chari as far as the Ouadai neighbourhood
Gambia	: eastern half of the country
Ghana	: a very small area in the extreme N
Mali	: a small E-W strip in the SW of the country
Nigeria	: two small regions W of the river Niger near the NE border with Benin and N of the upper course of the Bénoué
Senegal	: the SE of the country
Sudan	: a thin NW-SE strip on the banks of the upper and middle Bahr-el-Ghazal as far as the upper course of the White Nile; Jebel Marra at Darfur

D1b, *Sub-humid, warm winter, warm summer*

Burkina Faso	: SW and SE
Ethiopia	: extreme western point and the Rift Valley
Ghana	: SE coast and northern third
Guinea	: a very small area to the N-NE
Guinea Bissau	: a tiny area to the NE
Ivory Coast	: a very small area in the extreme NE
Kenya	: the southern coast
Rwanda	: a small part of the Akagera
Sudan	: a N-S strip running along the central Ethiopean border to the border with Uganda
Togo	: N and coast
Uganda	: the NE and shores of Lake Mobutu Sese Seko
Zambia	: a small NE-SW strip following the line of the Muchinga mountain

D2a, *Sub-humid, mild winter, very warm summer*

Central Africa	: very small area S of the middle Chari
Madagascar	: small strip in the middle of the west coast
Tanzania	: SE and coast

D2b, *Sub-humid, mild winter, warm summer*

Angola	: SE third and a pocket in the NW
Botswana	: in the NE near Zimbabwe
Benin	: small areas in the S and N
Burkina Faso	: SE and SW
Central Africa	: very small region in the extreme NE
Ethiopia	: a few areas in the west-central part
Gambia	: central region
Ghana	: extreme SE
Madagascar	: region in the SW
Nigeria	: small north-central region
Reunion	: extreme SW of the island
Swaziland	: almost the entire country
Zambia	: extreme W and a few small areas in the S and NE
Zimbabwe	: most of the country

D3b, *Sub-humid, cool winter and warm summer*

Lesotho	: the western half of the country

The UNESCO map also supplies details about periods of drought and rainfall patterns. The patterns relevant to the ACP countries are:

I   A pattern of dominant summer drought and winter rains sometimes retarded towards the spring. This is comparable to the Mediterranean pattern, and typically Mediterranean plants sometimes occur. A single region is indicated on the map, the coastal fringe of the Red Sea, from the Egyptian border to northern Eritrea. My observations (BAUMER, 1968) lead me to suggest including the northern extremity of the Kordofan and the southern Libyan Desert where the rains, when they come, occur more often in winter than in summer.

II   A pattern of predominantly dry winter and summer rains sometimes delayed towards autumn. This is the most widespread pattern in the ACP countries affected by desertification; it is found:
a) in Madagascar and Reunion,
b) from Lake Victoria and central Tanzania as far as Botswana, Lesotho and Swaziland,
c) in the extreme NE horn of Somalia,
d) but principally throughout the whole sahelian strip (in the widest sense) from Cape Verde to western Ethiopia.

III A pattern of predominantly dry winter and two rainy seasons, one towards the end of the spring, the second at the beginning of autumn. Summer drought is less pronounced and shorter than the drought in the winter. This pattern is found in the south of Benin, Ghana and Togo, and from the SE of Tanzania and the Masai steppe to Uganda, Ethiopia's south-east region and Somalia.

IV A transitional pattern of two rainy seasons, one in summer, one in winter, such as occurs in the Djibouti area.

V An irregular transitional pattern of haphazard, unpredictable rains, along the northern coast of Somalia.

All these data should not make us lose sight of the fact that it is variability – more particularly variability in rainfall – which is the feature of arid and semi-arid regions, rather than the small amount of rainfall. Monod wrote (1973): 'It should be remembered that, given the extent of annual variability at any given point, the seemingly so precise isohyets on our maps only represent approximate guides: the 100 mm curve in Mauritania, which passes 'on average' through Nouakchott and Adrar, occurred 300 km further north in 1951/52 but 300 km further south in 1941/42, giving a positional discrepancy of 600 km. Trees do not move themselves to suit these episodic fluctuations, but it is nonetheless true that, for the nomad and his animals, the steppe-desert boundary makes a broad sweep hundreds of kilometres wide.'

2.1.2 The Risk of Desertification

It is possible to evaluate the risk of desertification from the map drawn (UNEP/FAO/UNESCO/WMO, 1977) at the time of the United Nations Conference on Desertification.

According to the criteria adopted in the making of this map, the following ACP countries have no part of their territory under visible threat of desertification:

– The Caribbean and Pacific countries,

– Benin, Burundi, Central Africa, the Comoros Islands, Congo, Ivory Coast, Gabon, Gambia, Ghana, Guinea Bissau, Equatorial Guinea, Lesotho, Liberia, Mauritius, Rwanda, Seychelles, Sierra Leone, Swaziland, Togo and Zaire.

Eight ACP countries have true deserts within their territorial boundaries: Angola, Chad, Ethiopia, Mali, Mauritania, Niger, Somalia, Sudan.

Four countries have their territory 100% affected by desertification characteristics:

- Cape Verde, at high risk basically from the gullying of its hillsides.
- Djibouti, situated in an arid climate, at high risk principally from scouring of the topsoil by deflation; the territory totals 21 990 km^2, of which 12 566 km^2 are desert and 9 424 km^2 are arid (LE HOUEROU and POPOV, 1981).
- Mauritania, approximately half of which is in a bioclimatic desert zone and almost all the rest in an arid zone, at a high risk, basically because of sand movements but also to deflation and, locally, to gullying; with a small area near Nouakchott at extremely high risk because of salification and alkalization; according to LE HOUEROU and POPOV (1981) the 858 748 km^2 of territory comprises 385 684 km^2 of tropical desert, 343 500 km^2 arid land, 120 525 km^2 semi-arid land and only 9 039 km^2 semi-humid land.
- Lastly Somalia, more than three-quarters of which lies in a bioclimatic arid zone, and where over approximately 35% of the territory the risk of desertification is high or very high from a combination of animal pressure with deflation and sheet erosion in the centre, and with salification in the south; over only 15 to 20% of the area is the risk of desertification considered to be moderate. According to LE HOUEROU and POPOV (1981), the 627 306 km^2 can be divided up as follows: 238 974 km^2 equatorial desert, 219 059 km^2 equatorial arid, 126 125 km^2 equatorial semi-arid and only 39 829 km^2 equatorial semi-humid. In addition, 3 319 km^2 semi-arid land is subject to frost risk on account of the altitude.

In all the other ACP countries, the risk of desertification is very variable. It has been evaluated as moderate, high or very high. The dominant factors and processes leading to desertification have also been indicated:

H   human pressure (and mechanization)
A   animal pressure
W   movements of sand by wind
R   stony and rocky surfaces subject to deflation scouring or sheet erosion; extreme erosion results in the formation of desert pavements, laterized horizons or rocky outcrops

Table III

Risk of desertification in ACP countries
(Source: UNEP/FAO/UNESCO/WMO, 1977; FAO/UNEP, 1984)

	very high	high	moderate	low or nil
Angola	0.2 (WH)	2.6 R	11.4 V & W	85.8
Benin	0	0	21 (W)	79
Botswana	0	0	61 W, S, U	39
Burkina Faso	0	0	58.3 RH	41.7
Burundi	0	0	0	100
Cameroon	0 (VA)	0	5.1	94.9
Cape Verde	100 V	0	0	0
Central Africa	0	0	3.4	96.6
Chad	9.6 VA, RA	39.7 W, S, R, VH	28.9	21.8
Comoros	0	0	0 (W)	100
Congo	0	0	0	100
Djibouti	2.7	6.9 R	90.4	0
Ethiopia	4.4 RA, WA, R	15 R, (S)	36.2 V	44.4
Gabon	0	0	0	100
Gambia	0	0	56	44
Ghana	0	0	4.4	95.6
Guinea	0	0	2.5	97.5
Guinea Bissau	0	0	1.2	98.8
Kenya	1.7	21.0 R, S	64.3 V, (R)	13
Lesotho	15.9	0	57.2 W	26.9
Liberia	0	0	0	100
Madagascar	0.1 VA, W	2.4 W	6.1 V, R	91.4
Malawi	0	0	5.5 (R)	94.5
Mali	36.1 RH, WA	6.0 W, R	45.1 V A, R, W	12.8
Mauritania	54.4 S	23 W, V, R	17 W, R, V	5.6
Mauritius	0	0	0	100
Mozambique	0	0.1	20.1 W, R	79.8
Niger	29.1 WH	52.9 W, R	17.9	0.1
Nigeria	0 WH, VA	5.8 W	31.4	62.8
Rwanda	0	0	0	100
Senegal	0 (WH)	1.3 (W)	R, W 72	26.7
Seychelles	0	0	0	100
Sierra Leone	0	0	0	100
Somalia	1.2 SA, RA	34.2 R, W	56.7 V, R, S	7.9
Sudan	24.4 WH, RH	7.7 R, W,	V, W 33.8	34.1
Swaziland	0	0	30.4	69.6
Tanzania	0	1.2	V, R 33.4	65.4
Togo	0	0	0	100
Uganda	0	0.6	(V) 19.2	80.2
Zaire	0	0	0	100
Zambia	0	0 (R, V)	2.9	97.1
Zimbabwe	0	5.8	V, 55 W, R	39.2

The main desertification factors are indicated by a letter: W for sand movements, R for wind scouring of rocks, V for water erosion, S for salification and alkalization, H for human pressure, A for animal pressure (cf. text). Where several factors are involved, the code letter of the factor affecting the greatest area is underlined; brackets indicate that a very small area is involved. The figures show the percentage of territory affected.

V   alluvial or residual surfaces subject to soil scouring and accelerated rainwash, to slope gullying and/or sheet erosion of flat deposits

S   surfaces exposed to salification and/or alkalization

The map also shows the distribution of hyperarid, arid, semi-arid and sub-humid bioclimatic zones. There is no direct correlation between the bioclimatic zone and the risk of desertification.

It is possible to list, as shown in Table III, the 25 ACP countries affected by desertification or threatened by it. All are African countries.

We should recall here that it is the African continent that has the most widespread extreme risk of desertification, with 5.7% of its surface affected, i.e. 1 725 165 km². In addition, 16.2% (or 4 910 503 km²) are classified as high risk (against 22.4% in Australia and 16.5% in Asia), 12.3% (3 740 966 km²) as medium risk (against 48.3% in Australia and 12.8% in Asia), while 20.4% (6 177 956 km²) is already desert (against only 3.6% in Asia). Africa therefore has 16.5 million km², or 54.6% of its surface area already desert or threatened with desertification. Although not having any true deserts, Australia has 74.7% of its surface area threatened with desertification, but a lower population density, greater affluence and more advanced technology mean that the problem is less worrying and more under control than in Africa.

2.2 AFFECTED ACP COUNTRIES

As regards biomes, the great majority of ACP countries come within the domain of tropical Africa; but there is equal concern for a very small part of the Indo-malaysian domain (Seychelles), the Oceanian domain (countries of the Pacific) and the neotropical domain (Antilles). Six of the fourteen principal biomes corresponding to the earth's major ecosystem groups (UDVARDY, 1975) are represented:

1. the lake and river system (notably the Great African Lakes and Lake Chad);

2. the island system, an appreciable part of which is represented by ACP Caribbean and Pacific countries, the remainder being essentially made up of the other Antilles and New Guinea;

3. the mixed mountain and highlands system, with complex zoning, basically affecting Burundi, Ethiopia and Rwanda, but also Cameroon;

4. the desert and hot semi-desert system, forming an irregular continuous arc from Mauritania to Tanzania and also affecting Angola and Botswana;

5. the forest system with dry or deciduous forests, which form an arc inside the above and also cover the greater part of Madagascar;

6. the tropical rain forest system, which takes in central and western Africa on either side of the Equator, and the east coast of Madagascar;

Although desertification – in the sense used by UNCOD – is not limited to arid zones, it occurs frequently in zones that are dry.

Terminology to define the dry regions of Africa varies. Specialists have different criteria for defining the different ecological zones, and hence there are several systems of classification. Indeed, the great extent of arid and semi-arid zones in the world, and especially in Africa, explains the diversity of terminology. The different ecological factors often vary imperceptibly but continuously over wide areas, creating a wide diversity of series usually in a sequence without precisely defined limits. Depending on the criteria being considered, it might be said, for example, that this sequence occurs:

– between the hyper-arid and semi-humid, if climate is the consideration,

– between the desert and the forest, if vegetation is the consideration,

– between regosoils and humisoils, if pedology is the consideration,

– between the domains of the addax and the buffalo, if fauna is the consideration, etc.

But all arid and semi-arid zones are characterized by a deficient water supply, because of long dry season and the irregular and variable rainfall. The dry period may cover one season of the year (monomodal regime) or two well-defined seasons (bimodal regime).

There are dozens of definitions of drought. The simplest is the one

33

which says that drought is a situation where the need for water in a biological community cannot be met. This is a clear demonstration that drought is relative. It is evident that in a gradual development of an environment from a humid stage to a less humid one, drought levels will not be the same for the hippopotamus, which must keep its hide wet to survive, the ox, the dromedary or the addax, which can go without water other than what it finds in plants for several months at a time. The same is true of crops: each has its own water requirement, which varies greatly with the physiological cycle of the plant.

Meeting the water requirements for human beings depends not on the amount of water present but on the availability and quality of that water. The amount of available water not only consists of the water that falls out of the sky. In arid zones, concentrating the water collected over a vast catchment onto a small area under cultivation makes dry-farming possible: a region with 100 mm average rainfall receives 2×10^6 1/ha; if this water is concentrated onto 20% of the surface area, as in the Nabatean method (EVENARI et al., 1971, 1975) small areas are created where available water is the equivalent of 500 mm of rainfall. There are many techniques for making the best use of water (BAUMER, 1977, 1978): collection of rainwater, runoff farming, collection of atmospheric humidity, salt-water irrigation, water recycling, etc. The Incas knew how to gather water from sea mists over the coastal desert of Peru; the Kababish nomads of Kordofan know how to make the most of 'gizzu', the fragile desert vegetation which grows thanks to unseen condensation from humid winds from the Mediterranean which have first crossed the entire Libyan desert.

2.3 PROCESSES OF DESERTIFICATION

Desertification generally starts with unthinking crop expansion into ecologically fragile zones and poor soils not suitable for sustained cropping, and formerly used by herders or acting as a buffer zone between farmers and herders. This crop expansion results in:

- a rapid loss of soil fertility which of necessity leads to shifting cultivation;

- erosion of soils, mainly by wind because, particularly after the harvest, they no longer have permanent protection from a plant cover, however sparse;

- reduction in grazing areas, leading to an excessive concentration of animals and over-grazing.

Although there is general awareness of this process, and although many speeches on desertification and even efforts to combat it are made, it is noticeable that few governments have taken and applied the first of the measures necessary to halt the advance of desertification, which is to ban agriculture everywhere where it is out of place and incapable of ensuring in good years and in bad the survival of the group of people practising it.

The diagram of the desertification process in Fig. 1, illustrating the case of northern Kenya, is generally applicable to arid and semi-arid zones. There are other processes. For example, it can happen that in semi-humid zones over-extended agriculture leads to the destruction of all woody vegetation on sloping soils liable to erosion; if such fields are only cultivated from time to time, within a system of shifting with a long cycle, the plant cover can reform and the environment accommodating this regime will not suffer too much. But if, for instance because of population increase, the cycle is shortened or if cultivation is even repeated without application of anti-erosive growing methods, erosion will set in, the wind will carry the soil away as dust, surface runoff will increase, the surface humus layer of the soil will disappear, cracks and gullies will appear and, little by little, all loose soil will be removed. Or else the hammering of the denuded earth by drops of rain will lead to a hardening of the surface, preventing water infiltration, causing the water table to fall and the vegetation to die. Rainwash will increase, triggering downhill water erosion if more friable soils are present, or increasing the risk of flooding. Water erosion often assists wind erosion by forming deposits of loose materials easily picked up by the wind. In irrigated soils, desertification consists in soil salification or alkalization through insufficient salt leaching and/or excess of salts in irrigation water on soils of low permeability. On soils temporarily flooded, leached salts tend to be deposited on the surface of the soil when the water evaporates. On non-flooded irrigated soils, when evaporation is high, saline solutions tend to run back up the irrigation furrows towards the ridges separating the furrows, or to evaporate, leaving salt deposits.

The processes of desertification are varied. Desertification does not advance like an invading force spreading in from the desert; it has many and varied forms, and it makes its advance on the earth's surface rather like a skin disease, with blotches of desert appearing here and there, together or singly, and always on the increase. But the processes of desertification can be reduced to the following four:

wrong exploitation and/or over-exploitation of land under cultivation,

deforestation,

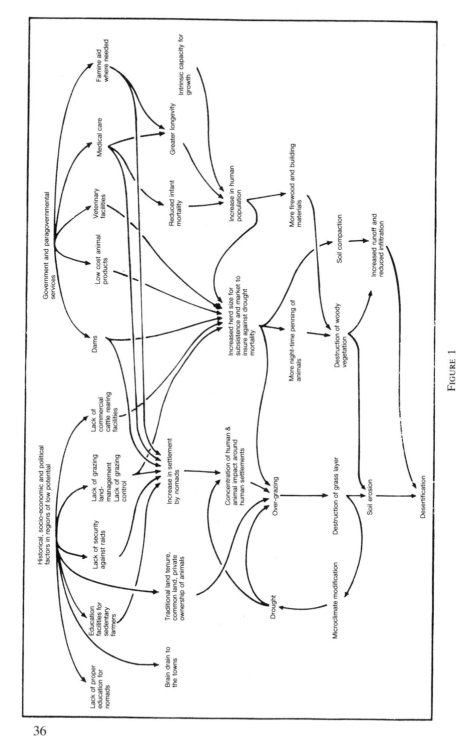

FIGURE 1

Some of the factors responsible for the encroachment of the desert in northern Kenya (according to LAMPREY, 1978)

over-grazing,

bad irrigation practices.

These processes are often interlinked and have multiple consequences. Thus deforestation often results in a fall in harvests, as illustrated in Fig. 2.

One consequence of desertification is the loss of productive soils and hence a reduction in the amount of food produced. Over the whole planet, the number of hectares available for cultivation was approximately

1.42 ha/person	in 1800
0.82	in 1900
0.50	in 1950
0.34	in 1970
0.27	in 1980

and in 1999 we shall probably have to make do with 0.18 ha to feed every person in the world. These disturbing figures – even if they share the weakness of all generalized statistics and need to be treated with caution – signal a worrying development in the ratio of cultivated ground to inhabitants of the planet. It is true that only 11% of the area of developed countries is under cultivation. Table IV shows the distribution of land among the continents and the population density per hectare cultivated. In 1970, every inhabitant of the planet had available to him in theory 3.5 ha, divided as follows:

cultivated land	0.34 ha (or less than 10%)
grassland	1.09 ha
forest not regularly managed	1.28 ha
forest under management	0.05 ha
bare	0.83 ha (or 23%)

There are considerable inequalities in distribution: for example 65% of Denmark, but less than 15% of China and less than 10% of Egypt is cultivable. This notion of 'cultivability' is only an average notion, and therefore only approximate, since that characteristic is of course a function of the amount of resources that can be put into cultivation: Libya has demonstrated this over the last decade by cultivating at great expense thousands of hectares of desert and stabilizing huge areas of dunes with the aim of making them productive (forage, firewood).

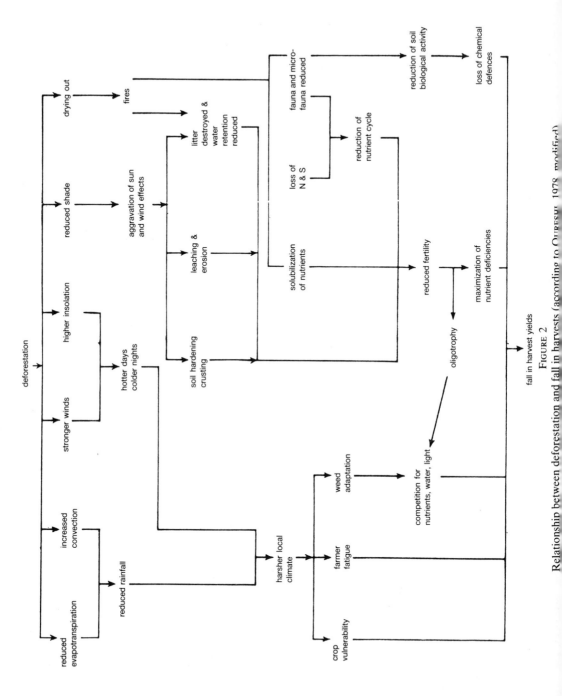

FIGURE 2

Relationship between deforestation and fall in harvests (according to Ourbesy, 1978 modified)

TABLE IV

World distribution of cultivated land
(from FAO, Annual Statistics)

	A total area (10^6 ha)	B actually cultivated (10^6 ha)	C potentially cultivable (10^6 ha)	D people per ha cultivated	ratio C/B
Central America	272	36	75	3.3	2.083
South-West Asia	677	69	48	2.1	0.695
South-East Asia	897	272	297	4.5	1.09
Central & Southern Asia	1116	113	127	8.4	1.12
South America	1770	124	819	2	6.60
Africa	2886	168	789	2.5	4.69

The table shows that Africa, and even more Latin America, still only utilize a relatively small proportion of the land that it would be theoretically possible to cultivate. By contrast, South-West Asia is already cultivating land unsuitable for regular and sustained crop production. Among the 90 developing countries, 17 (which together contain half the world's population) already have 90% of their cultivable land under cultivation. By the end of the century the lack of land will have become critical for about 2/3 of the people in the developing countries.

In theory, the area under cultivation world-wide could be doubled by drainage and irrigation. However, agriculture is hampered by various causes, the principal obstacles being:

for 28% of soils   dryness
for 23%   chemical problems, among them salinity
for 22%   shallowness
for 10%   excessive humidity
for 6%   frost

Erosion is another factor in reducing agricultural production. It will mean that if massive protection measures are not taken, foreseeable production losses between 1975 and 2000 will be 25% for Africa and 10 to 20% for the Caribbean countries and the Pacific. (This includes irrigated and non-irrigated agricultural production as well as that of grazing land. In the same period, the capacity to support the population will be reduced throughout tropical Africa, by more than 50% in the Sahelo-Saharan zones and in the arid regions of southern Africa and Madagascar, and by at least 15% over more than half of intertropical Africa. However, major efforts are being made in the direction of soil conservation: in Ethiopia alone, the World Food Programme spent more than 175×10^6 dollars between 1972 and 1985, and the European Community will have put in more than 100×10^6 US dollars in 1984, 1985 and 1986.

MABBUTT and FLORET (1980) give excellent analyses of cases of desertification, particularly from the Eghazer and Azawak regions of Niger.

Desertification can be measured in different ways. Among the criteria generally adopted are:

reflectance (which is affected more by overcropping than by overgrazing),
rainfall amounts,
frequency of sand storms, amount of dust in the air,
depth of arable soil, degree of erosion, amount of sedimentation,
soil fertility and primary productivity of the plant biomass,
soil and water salinity,
depth of water table,
distribution and frequency of plant species,
net plant primary productivity,
plant production,
poverty and misery of populations.

In this context it should be remembered that the primary productivity of the flora is the quantity of organic matter created by photosynthesis. The net primary productivity is the quantity of carbon dioxide taken in by plants over and above the organic matter they use for their metabolism (it is estimated for dry bushes at 10 to 250 g dry matter/m^2/year with a world average of 70 g). Production is the fraction of the net primary productivity that can be harvested without destroying the basis for productivity; i.e. sustainable production.

2.4 CAUSES OF DESERTIFICATION

Desertification is the result of interaction between human activities and a difficult environment. As MAINGUET (1982) says, according to A. DAVY: 'Desertification is a broad and complex concept describing the degradation of landscapes as a result of the combination of a wide spread of processes occurring in regions where the climatic, geomorphological, pedological and biogeographical conditions are in precarious equilibrium.' Quite rightly, MAINGUET sees among the causes:

- the natural environment and the limits to which its fragility can be pushed,

- the climate and its variations,

- man and his life styles,

and among the mechanisms:

- onslaughts suffered by the plant cover (grazing, fuel gathering, agriculture, bush fires),

- worsening of natural mechanisms by external forces (water and wind erosion),

- deterioration of soil structure (rapid mineralization of humus, loss of organic matter, destruction of the structure and excessive soil loosening,

- deterioration caused by irrigation and traumatizing technologies (salinization, alkalization, waterlogging, accumulation of toxic substances).

As for the consequences, they are essentially the lowering of water tables and reduction in available water on the one hand, and on the other hand wind erosion, which takes the form of soil removal and excessive sand deposits.

41

Desertification is not a new phenomenon. Some of the major symptoms were already being identified by Auguste CHEVALIER in 1950, when he pointed to:

'. . . rivers and streams dried up for six months of the year, where water flowed permanently 50 years ago . . .;

'The lakes in the Timbuktu region (Faguibine, Horo, Daounas) have shrunk to the point of being unrecognisable compared with their shapes when I saw them in August-September 1899 . . .;

'(In the Senegalese tannes) the lakes are gradually disappearing . . . They are not even respecting any more the artificial forest of Casuarina planted between 1905 and 1914 . . .;

'There is no doubt that within the confines of the southern Sahara and over the sahelian and sudanian zones there is a climatic drying off due to natural causes, such as occurred in Europe in the Quaternary period; but this dessication and advance of aridity would be very slow if present-day man did not exacerbate matters by intense deforestation of the country, allowing bush fires to spread, and if farming and forestry methods, often empirical, were not spread without preliminary scientific study. The agricultural system of Africans in former times, subsistence farming, was primitive, not very scientific, but it conserved the soil and plant life . . . (The) farming methods (of the African native) with trees and shrubs retained through the fields was far from being ridiculous. They left fields to recover a long time . . .'

MOURGUES (1950) took up the ideas of HUBERT (1921) who had drawn attention to the increasing scarcity of water, the drying up of springs, the disappearance of permanent pools, and those of HARROY (1944), who maintained that desertification is due to climatic causes but exacerbated by man and his herds.

There was much discussion at UNCOD (HARE, 1977), which still continues, about the part played by climatic variations in the causes of the exceptional drought which hit Africa in the 1970's. In the first place, occasional weather distortions should not be confused with other variations.

Table V defines the terminology for variations. In 1977, most climatologists and meteorologists considered that the exceptional drought was no more than a repeating pattern: Africa experienced droughts of at least equal severity around 1880, from 1910 to 1915 and in 1940-42, but the

TABLE V

Terminology of climatic variations
(according to LANDSBERG, 1974)

Name	Duration	Known or possible origin
Climatic revolution	$> 10^6$ years	Geotectonic activity (continental drift, orogenesis, major changes in relative distribution of land and water). Possible solar variations.
Climatic change	10^4 to 10^6 years	Aperiodic or periodic changes (10^4) in solar activity. Changes in extraterrestrial insolation due to gradual changes in orbital factors (orbital eccentricity, inclination on the ecliptic, precession of the equinoxes).
Climatic fluctuation	10^1 to 10^4 years	All other climatic variations of more than 10 years' duration, – either aperiodic: volcanic activity – or semi-periodic: changes in solar emission (sun spot cycles), cycle of magnetic declinations. Deep slow currents in the oceans. Terrestrial mechanisms, repercussions of the above.
Repeated climatic pattern	10 years or less	Short-term quasi-periodic natural variations. Quasi-biennial oscillations (2-3 years). Possible earth/atmosphere/ocean interactions.
Climatic distortion	less than 10 years (?)	Anthropogenic causes with effects on different levels: – Global: increase in atmospheric concentration of CO_2, NO_x, carbon and halogen compounds, dust particles – Regional: energy production, industrialization, urbanization, destruction of plant cover – Local: urbanization, agriculture, (land clearance, ploughing, drainage, irrigation), grazing, reservoirs, deforestation, reforestation, wars.

consequences were not so marked because the population was smaller, and they were less publicized because communications and the media were far less developed; furthermore, two of these droughts coincided with World Wars which comandeered the information services. In fact, Africa is not alone in experiencing exceptional droughts; in 1982 Australia had 60% of its farming severely affected by the most devastating drought for half a century; in 1983, Spain experienced a very severe drought, Italy lost half its crops in the south, and in France cattle only survived with the aid of artificial feed and imported cereals.

Climatic fluctuations are a recognized fact. For example, the climate of western Europe was much colder between 1600 and 1850 than in the 20th century and frost has caused crop loss and famine on several occasions. In Africa the finds of palynologists, particularly on the shores of Lake Chad, and dendrochronological analysis provide evidence for these kinds of variation. Much reliance has been placed on the fact that no increase in aridity is

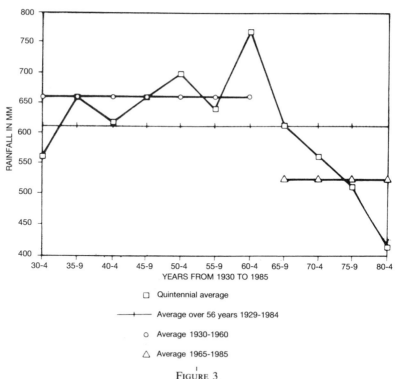

FIGURE 3
Average quintennial rainfall measurements at Zalingei (Sudan), 1930-1984
(DARNHOFER, in BAUMER et al., 1985)

discernible from the meteorological data from the oldest stations around the Sahara (which has been a desert for at least 2500 years and as long as 5000 years at most), suggesting that the climate had not varied until 1977 since 1838 in Constantine, 1843 in Algiers, 1855 in St Louis, Senegal, 1860 in Jerusalem and 1887 in Dakkar. But other analyses show that the regions bordering the Sahara are entering a dry period:

- In Tripoli (Libya), the ratio of mean annual rainfall totals for 1957-1985 compared to 1892-1985 is of the order of 0.7

- In Agadez (Niger), four consecutive years (1969, 1970, 1971 and 1972) had rainfall of less than 100 mm, whereas the statistical probability of such a sequence was estimated at 1/2400

- In Zalingei (Sudan), the drop in rainfall is dramatic, as shown in Fig. 3 drawn up by T. DARNHOFER.

Man's activities, when they are badly managed, whether they be bad farming, deforestation, over-grazing or badly managed irrigation, aggravate the consequences of drought.

Whatever the root causes, worldwide approximately 200,000 km^2 of additional land are affected by desertification each year in such a way that their yield becomes zero or insignificant. This represents a loss to be recouped of more than 25 million dollars per year. As Dr TOLBA, executive director of UNEP, said in 1982: 'There can be no doubt that the process of desertification is accelerating, and millions of hectares of arable land are disappearing every year'.

3. SYSTEMS OF PRODUCTION AND AGROFORESTRY IN ARID AND SEMI-ARID ZONES OF AFRICA

3.1 GENERAL PRINCIPLES

In systems analysis, a system is a physical grouping of components, linked or connected in such a way that they form a unique entity and/or act as such.

Systems function by interacting, as shown in Fig. 4

Land systems can be graded according to the intensity of cultivation, by using the land-use factor (ALLAN, 1965):

$$L = \frac{C + j}{C}$$

where the factor L is a function of the number of years of cultivation, C, and of the number of fallow years, j. The following theoretical series is then obtained:

	L
Nomadic cultivation	10
Recurrent cultivation	
long cycle	7-10
medium cycle	5-7
short cycle	3-5
Semi-permanent cultivation	2.5-3
Permanent cultivation	2

The problem arises: 'What is the best utilization of an area of land? For whom? From what point of view? In what perspective?' Use may vary with time. Thus for more than a century the High Plateaus of Algeria were considered to be 'bled-al ghanem', the domain of the sheep. Then came the Algerian war of independence, when they were abandoned and became a battlefield. When peace returned, it was decided that they must be opened up to large-scale cereal cultivation.

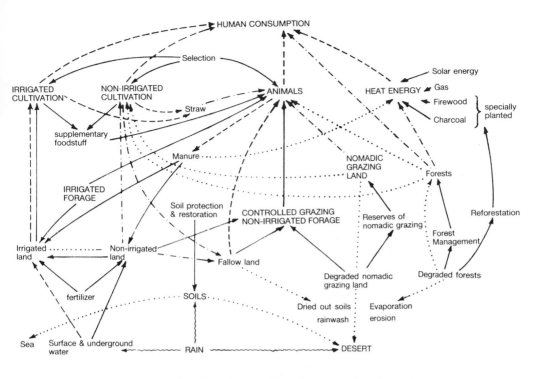

HUMAN CONSUMPTION

Selection

Solar energy

IRRIGATED CULTIVATION

NON-IRRIGATED CULTIVATION

ANIMALS

HEAT ENERGY

Gas

Straw

Firewood

specially planted

supplementary foodstuff

Charcoal

Manure

NOMADIC GRAZING LAND

Forests

IRRIGATED FORAGE

Soil protection & restoration

CONTROLLED GRAZING NON-IRRIGATED FORAGE

Reserves of nomadic grazing

Reforestation

Forest Management

Irrigated land

Non-irrigated land

Fallow land

Degraded nomadic grazing land

Degraded forests

fertilizer

SOILS

Dried out soils

Evaporation

rainwash

erosion

Sea

Surface & underground water

RAIN

DESERT

- - - - - at present used and can be considered as normal and ongoing
- ·- ·- ·- actually used, but needing control or modification
.... at present used and should be stopped
————— do not exist or hardly exist and should be introduced or utilized further

FIGURE 4

Model of how systems work: methods of land exploitation in arid and semi-arid zones

Use can vary depending on the users: for example, in Kenya sedentary farmers are increasingly taking over semi-arid territory that for centuries had been used by herdsmen like the Masai, who maintained the biological balance. The best utilization can vary, too, depending on the intention: the same semi-arid region may be suitable for stock-raising management, for establishing a National Park or a military training area, depending on the circumstances, political choices, or the relative power of different pressure groups.

From the standpoint of land utilization, the value of agroforestry is that it aims to establish systems of stable but flexible production with the minimum of external resources.

47

Intensification of production is often linked with a high population density, as can be seen in Nigeria, where traditional methods of land use are in the process of being replaced (1984) by more intensive systems in which production per unit of land is increased while at the same time attempts are made to conserve the capital that natural resources represent. From this it must not be concluded that we have to do with inevitable evolution, nor that the main themes of the Nigerian development (support for the development of small farms, settlement of nomadic herdsmen and development of private and para-State farming enterprises) are applicable everywhere. Indeed, two sets of constraints may impose different solutions: political and ecological. Governments may choose other paths for political reasons; for example, if they want to encourage State capitalism, or to aim at an egalitarian sharing of revenues. This is not the place to discuss the consequences of all the different options. But there are also ecological constraints which may force other choices: Nigeria for instance, may have the advantage of good soil on the whole and the irrigation capability to support a large population and to adopt intensive production systems, but the same is not true everywhere in Africa: many countries, notably those subject to desertification, have very limited capacity for change, because of their poor soils, hostile climate and lack of water resources. This may mean that they must sacrifice economic and political independence (but does that exist always and everywhere?) to accept solutions for intensification of production.

Agrarian production systems can be classified in many different ways. A first distinction can be drawn, for example, between the various traditional and transitional systems on the one hand, and modern systems on the other, with their local variants. Modern systems are proportionately more important in eastern and southern Africa than in West Africa. In fact, traditional systems and small farms are more suited to agroforestry than modern systems and large farms, although these can also derive benefits from the agroforestry approach.

Among traditional systems, the one that perhaps most strongly evokes Africa under threat from creeping aridization, although it is not unique to Africa but also found in Asia, is nomadism. It is the most extreme form of pastoralism, where populations and their herds move round on vast grazing routes not clearly determined in advance, in search of fresh grazing or trading opportunities (the Toubbou nomads, for example, do not hesitate to travel a good thousand kilometres across Chad in order to sell animals at a better price in Sudan, at Geneina or preferably at Kutum, or to go west to Mali), and, in former times, on pillaging raids. This way of life has virtually disappeared under the dual pressure of drought, which has rendered numbers of wells in the desert dry or unreliable, and, above all, of war. War has forced many groups to settle, or at least to stop wandering, because they are no longer safe in the vast domains they used to frequent.

Another form of pastoralism is semi-nomadism, where only a part of the human group moves off with the herds and where movements are less continuous than in nomadism. For example, the whole group will move off to find good pasturage, and, if water is plentiful, a camp will be established where the women, young children and old men will be installed, to look after the young animals unable to make long journeys. So as not to exhaust too quickly the always too meagre pasturage, the adult animal herd will be sent as far away as possible: for example, a few vigorous men, will go off with the dromedaries for several weeks or several months, looking for a new pasture. So in the Sudan, the Kababish nomads used to send out scouts in winter in the direction of Wadi Howar, the fossil wadi that cuts across the southern Libyan desert from the Ennedi towards the Nile: between 1930 and 1955 in about 2 years out of 5 winds from the north laden with moisture blew from the Mediterranean in winter and condensed on the sand at night, allowing a fleeting germination of 11 plant species, among which the Rosacae *Neurada procumbens* predominated. During those years, several thousands of adult dromedaries were sent for 1, 2 or 3 months to these pasturages called 'gizzu' (from the Arabic 'gizzein' = strike camp), where they had nothing to drink except dew and plant sap, the few camel drivers accompanying them living exclusively on milk, dates, a little millet flour and, very rarely, gazelle meat. Between 1973 and 1984, the 'gizzu' did not reappear.

While the dromedaries leave for distant parts, the small ruminants, herded by adolescents and a few adults will move round in big loops, during the rainy season when the water supply problems are not so acute. These routes bring them back to the encampment after several days, after successively using the various grazing around the camp. From time to time the camp is moved if the water supply or forage availability run too low.

Transhumance is a particular form of semi-nomadism. The main core of the population generally remains in an encampment or village and the herds move round according to the seasons, following predetermined routes. In the Sahel, herds move en masse from the south towards the north during the dry season. Transhumance is widespread outside Africa.

Pastoralism has been defined as 'the combination of all the arts and sciences brought to bear on improving the living standard of husbandmen (social objective), increasing the profitability of extensive rearing (economic objective) and on the maximum regular and sustained production and utilization of all kinds of forage resources (technical objective), within the framework of the harmonized integral development of a country's natural resources' (BAUMER and REY, 1974).

Strictly speaking, then, it does not include two other forms of animal husbandry: semi-sedentary hubandry and sedentary hubandry.

As its name indicates, sedentary husbandry is practised by fixed populations whose exclusive occupation is the rearing of sedentary animals. It is the absolute exception in Africa, as most often the sedentary populations are farmers as well as rearers, and these systems are classified as mixed production (agriculture/husbandry). There is, for instance, President Mobutu's model farm at N'sele, or the Belgravia Dairy farm at Khartoum. But these are exceptions, albeit on the increase, particularly in the semi-humid urbanized zones, under pressure from investors.

Semi-sedentary rearing is the system of animal husbandry practised by a sedentary population using herdsmen to take the flocks a few days' march from base. On the face of it, this seems very like semi-nomadism, but here the main core of the human group does not move, but lives in a village or town. It is very rare for people practising semi-sedentary husbandry not to be engaged in another activity. For the most part, they have an additional secondary occupation, perhaps something other than farming: there are not a few civil servants, for example, who are semi-sedentary stock rearers, particularly since the last exceptional drought in the Sahel, when their privileged positions sometimes enabled them to buy back animals from genuine husbandmen at a good price, and then entrust their herds to herdsmen who take them out to graze a few days' march away from the town outskirts.

In mixed farming cropping systems it is shifting cultivation systems, from the most primitive to the most sophisticated, that have the highest land use factor. Integral shifting systems have, like nomadism, almost disappeared. They consist, for example, of clearing a patch of forest or burning it down and growing crops in the ashes as long as the ground is fertile. When the soil is exhausted the field is abandoned and new ground found elsewhere. The fertilizer value of bushes in shifting cultivation is considerable: they produce far richer ashes than do grasses, being especially rich in calcium, magnesium and phosphorus. Experiments have shown that biological fixation of nitrogen in forest soils without leguminous plants is second only to that of leguminous plants and grasses, (HAUK, 1971). The period for which fertility is sustained is often very short (three or four years); by contrast, in pristine shifting cultivation, the surrounding vegetation's invasion of the abandoned field and its development last for long periods before the same farmer, or more often another, uses the same

50

ground again. For example, one might have:

duration of cultivation (in years)	duration of non-cultivation (in years)	L
3	25	9
3	30	11
3	40	14
4	30	8
4	50	13
5	45	10

There is agreement (OKIGBO and GREENLAND, 1977) that values of 10 and above for the land use factor correspond to shifting cultivation systems we call the Phase I type. When the factor is between 5 and 10, one talks of Phase II, and between 2 and 4, of Phase III: at this stage we are talking of a rudimentary sedentary cultivation. Take the case of 'gum gardens' in Sudan, which are an agro-silvi-pastoral system (cf. 3.2.2.7): if the fallow period enriched by *Acacia Senegal* is a long one, that can be Phase II: for instance, if the shrubs are cut down after 32 years and the plot cultivated for 8 years, with a system of rotation as illustrated below, where

C = cultivated plot
1 = plot regenerating with gum shrub (1-8 years)
2 = plot of young gum shrubs (8-16 years)
3 = plot of mature gum shrubs (16-24 years) browsed
4 = plot of old gum shrubs (24-32 years) browsed and used for firewood and gradually thinning out naturally, to permit grazing

8-year Rotation

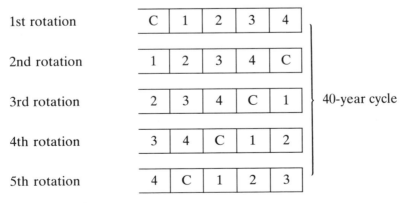

1st rotation   C 1 2 3 4

2nd rotation   1 2 3 4 C

3rd rotation   2 3 4 C 1   } 40-year cycle

4th rotation   3 4 C 1 2

5th rotation   4 C 1 2 3

This system has not been operated for at least 25 years because:

51

– it put out of action too much fallow land improved with gum shrubs (4/5);

– the gum shrub becomes less productive after 25 years;

– since the soil was poor and its fertility insufficient after 8 years under cultivation, it had to be left fallow in the 5th and 6th years or, more accurately, half a plot in the 5th and half in the 6th, but that did not matter very much because the farmer's fields used to be far bigger than they are today.

It appears (VIDAL-HALL, pers. comm.) that in about 1930 a shorter rotation was adopted

6 years	C	1	2	3	4

which gave better results. Then, because of the pressure of increasing population and a growing need for land, the shrub phase was reduced again relative to the cultivated phase and reversals began to occur:

– the shrubs no longer have time to reach their age of maximum production,

– the amount of available forage is insufficient,

– there is a lack of firewood,

– soil fertility no longer has time to recover,

and the final result is reduced agricultural productivity, insufficient food and forage is grown, and dearth of fuel for burning; this is a sad example of desertification. A sustainable system has been replaced by a system in which supply can no longer meet the demand. This example also shows that the index of land use is not linked to the quality of soil utilization; the soil is not necessarily used better the lower the index. When the rotation time is reduced to 6 years, as in this example, the index is 3, also corresponding to a Phase III shifting cultivation and tending towards Phase IV. The index for the old system, however, a quarter of a century ago was $\frac{8 + 32}{8} = 5$, corresponding to a Phase II shifting cultivation which did not entail exhaustion of the soil.

Shifting cultivation should not be condemned on all counts. When a farmer has no means of buying fertilizer it is logical to cultivate different plots of land so as to find soils fertile enough to stand up to the one or more years of debilitation entailed in producing harvests. Soil regeneration is helped by invasion of the fallow land by woody perennials, and reconstitution can be accelerated by introducing fast-growing species that can improve the soil. This technique can even help reduce the fallow time.

BEETS (1982), has analysed the multi-cropping systems associated with shifting cultivation.

In Africa, production systems were traditionally oriented towards subsistence farming. Food crops still dominate, but they are increasingly being grown alongside other crops which open the door to commercial agriculture for the African small farmer. In the early days of colonialism, it was spices, then sale of wood, that procured for the farmer the money resources he needed to buy goods, services and resources for his farm. Over the last decade and with the worldwide, and even local, expansion of industrialization, cash cropping has become increasingly important (cotton, peanut, rubber, cacao, oil . . .). A fair number of industrial products produced by the African farmer come from woody perennials (coffee, cocoa, tea, oil palm, gum shrub, date palm, etc): so already we have in cash cropping one of the indispensable elements in an agroforestry system: the woody perennial.

Although traditional systems are highly diverse, as much on account of ecological variability as multi-crop cultivation, they display some fairly constant features that are of great importance for the application of agroforestry technologies. Since the land is poor and the small farmer does not have enough income to buy fertilizer, much importance is attached to fallowing. Because the origin of the fields is various (land clearance by communal consent, acquisition by marriage or purchase, inheritance, exchange, etc.) the farm plots are usually very scattered, which entails time and energy spent on reaching all the fields and makes efficient supervision difficult. But around or close by the dwelling there is a garden plot, under permanent and intensive cultivation, which constantly receives fertilizer in the form of household waste and often also human excrement: both annual and perennial crops – tobacco, for example – are grown in a complex mix, often linked to one form or another of agroforestry, as there are often one or more trees in this plot, for fruit, forage, etc. Particularly in humid zones, these household gardens often have a multi-storey structure, as with the Chaggas of Kilimanjaro (FERNANDES et al., 1984).

Useful woody perennials are very often retained in the fields and sometimes transplanted or even sown or planted there. Among the most common are:

in semi-arid zones: 'haraz', African locust, shea butter tree, 'heglig'

in semi-humid zones: mango, shea butter tree

in humid zones: oil palm, *Pentaclethra macrophylla, Irvia gabonensis*

So here, too, we find the first of the components indispensable to any agroforestry system – the tree.

Remember this

Where there are trees, there is always life.

When the climate makes agriculture difficult, the tree is there to help the farmer if he knows how to make use of that help.

The trees and perennials – those which remain alive from one season to another – allow the farmer to have a measure of control over the harsh climate. To cut them down or misuse them is a serious error which can put the existence of the field at risk.

Looking after them, maintaining them and managing them is a sure way to intensification and modernization of farming.

In tropical climates, associating trees with annual cultivated species is a way of guaranteeing the future of farming.

(DUPRIEZ and DE LEENER, 1983)

Among other frequent characteristics of African farms are the following:

– there are no properties, only farms; ownership of the soil falls to the clan, the village, the tribe, in many cases recently replaced by the State; usage rights vary considerably depending on the ethnic group, but roughly speaking, one can say that

 – it is recognized that whoever clears and prepares the land has the right to farm it;

– on the other hand, whoever plants a tree is not always sure to harvest the fruits of his labours; this is an obstacle both to conventional reforestation and to agroforestry.

– There is little mechanization, even less motorization, but cultivation with oxen has been on the increase, very slowly unfortunately, for half a century. This has important consequences for the agroforestry approach:

– fodder is needed for the draught animals,

  – these animals produce manure.

– Crops are often mixed on the same unit of land, or in relays or in sequences. Monocropping is rare (except for cash crops).

– The division of labour is highly organized, by sex and by age group. This often accentuates the acute problem of labour shortage at the busiest time on the farm, further exacerbated by the rural exodus and by children having to attend school during peak times. There are two important points in this from the agroforestry point of view:

  – woody perennials often have a more flexible yield than annual crops (firewood, forage, for example) and because they are therefore less restricting they are well regarded by farmers;

  – certain tasks attached to growing woody perennials, such as digging holes prior to planting, trimming and natural pruning can all be undertaken at slack times for the farmer.

– The vast majority of farms possess animals; however, from the point of view of utilization, the agriculture/husbandry combination is not fully exploited; it is sometimes replaced by a juxtaposition of a husbandry system, without interpenetration or only very superficial combining of the two systems. This is what happens near Jalalaqsi in Somalia, in an irrigated plain fringed by dunes, where the animals graze freely on the dunes, resulting in sand shifting. An operation to stabilize the dunes was agreed and in order to carry it out cattle were banned. They were moved into the irrigated area, but this did not lead to the start of a genuine mixed agriculture/husbandry economy. The herds grazed the tracks and road sides, corners of fields and small plots at some distance away which did not form part of the irrigated network. There has been no attempt to combine these two activities, agriculture and animal husbandry, for mutual benefit. The cattle dung is not systematically used to manure the fields and the crop residue is not systematically used to improve forage.

55

However, relationships, often complex and formal, do exist between farming populations and animal husbandry populations, as described, for example, by ASAD (1970), DUPIRE (1962), DYSON-HUDSON (1972), GALLAIS (1972), HOROWITZ (1972) and JAHNKE (1982). MONOD (1975) points out that even the Tuareg nomads of the Sahara have always maintained trading relations with the oasis dwellers . . . and not only when they wanted to trade in slaves. Also, in areas of low humidity, soil fertility is often so low that the presence of animals is essential for the survival of the agriculture. There is, in fact, an increase in cattle numbers almost proportionate to that of the population. The animals provide milk more commonly than meat, they constitute a savings bank, they derive benefit from the farming and household by-products and, perhaps most importantly for many populations like the Woodabe of Niger, the Masai of Kenya and the Dinka of Sudan, they play a social and cultural role.

Rapid changes are taking place in these traditional production systems: introduction of new crops, population increase and reduced available area of land per head, adoption of cultivation using oxen, acceptance of new techniques. But it is noticeable that these changes are greater in the more humid zones with a higher potential than in the drier zones with less potential. The changes are oriented towards crop specialization and intensified production, and require additional resources, tools, technology and capital. It is also undeniable that they are drawing Africa increasingly closer to world capitalist systems. And it is debatable whether the resources needed for these new types of production will ever be available to the most deprived regions, often those ravaged or threatened by desertification. Who would dare to invest there in the hope of seeing some financial return? And if financial profitability is a very remote chance, what other reasons would there be for investors to be interested in those regions? Certainly, agroforestry cannot solve the problems of threatened or abandoned areas, but it can make a very significant contribution, specifically because the agroforestry approach is sparing of outside resources and because it tries to respond to needs as the populations concerned understand them.

3.2 FEATURES OF AGROFORESTRY SYSTEMS

The agroforestry approach rests essentially on the considered interactions between perennial woody vegetation on the one hand and other products of the land, whether animals or vegetable. Even if for people who have remained close to the soil there has never been any divide between the different components of their environment, the same was not true of the peoples influenced by Greece and especially Rome. Roman law, which has had such a profound influence on every aspect of Western thought, the arts and technology, has led to a clear distinction between 'ager', the space

56

cultivated, 'saltus', the area grazed, and 'sylva', the place where trees grow. The word 'forest' itself, as BECHMANN reminds us (1984), comes from the latin 'forestare', to put outside, to throw far away. LITTRE explains that 'the forest was originally an area placed under a prohibition, forbidden to farming and habitation in the interests of the seigniorial hunt'.

DEFFONTAINES (1933), pointed out that 'It would be wrong to always talk of forest and fields as opposites'. Describing the situation in bygone days in Europe he wrote: 'These two landscapes previously co-penetrated (in Europe), there were types of transition and even association. Primitive agriculture had to adapt to the proximity of trees and often even meet peremptory demands of the forest for its needs. The field exhausts the fertility of the soil, it needs restoring with manures. For a long time farmers were ignorant of the use of manure, and besides, they did not possess sufficient animals. Man had to look to the forest to fertilize his fields.'

Soil fertilizing practices involving burning off the forest are not unique to tropical countries. Wood ash was the first agricultural manure in a large part of the world, everywhere, in fact, where over the centuries the forest has given way to agriculture, as in Western Europe. This process, called burning over, is only possible where there is low population density. The part worked each year after burning of the woody vegetation as it stands is only a very small part of the area used by the farmer in his lifetime, since he prefers to burn over plots where the vegetation is woody, in order to have the greatest possible amount of ash and since it take years for woody vegetation to spread; but the European farmer of former times did not change fields every year, no more than his African counterpart does today. The field was used for several years to get the most return on the considerable amount of strenuous effort put into clearing the land and to give certain non-annual crops the time to develop – i.e. for as long as it was fertile enough to yield a harvest.

The use of fire, called burning over (also clearing, even grubbing, though these terms apply more generally to the destruction of vegetation by whatever means, machine or fire), was thus as dear to European peasants of bygone times as to the African small farmer today. It may not be easy to change the habits of these people today, but nor was it easy either in Europe yesterday. DEFFONTAINES recounts how the practice was so deeply ingrained that in 1835 it was declared that 'trying to suppress it would be cutting off the means of subsistence to a working people'. The primary forest may be dificult to clear and burn but this is not so with the secondary forest, where fire can often spread along the ground without the necessity of cutting the branches, and this has prompted farmers to burn off the same plot again to make the task less arduous, but this has led to a loss of soil fertility, an impoverishment of natural resources and even desertification. It seems highly probable that even if very slow, progressive, but fairly widespread climatic changes have taken place in the historic past and initiated changes in vegetation, it is the action of Man which has completed the replacement in Africa of primary forests by secondary forests, the shrinking of these through lax forestation, and then the formation of savannas, which can thus be classified as anthropogenic.

However, at the same time as he destroyed, Man became aware – but not sufficiently – of the importance of the tree for agricultural production. He conserved trees to meet the needs of agriculture, whether the trees directly produced food (fruits principally, also leaves and flowers . . .) or improved the soil by fertilizing it, or provided forage, or because as a group trees had a beneficial effect on the agriculture. Instead of random burning over, he turned to certain parts of the forest for mulch or ash, which he transferred to his permanent fields, instead of moving the fields; the enormous hedges or 'cheintres' which surround the cultivated plots of Morvan, in France, creating 'enclosures', are still drypruned every five or six years to burn the branches and spread the ash on the soil.

The similarity in behaviour of African and European small farmers when it comes to the tree is also found in the domain of animal husbandry. The Sahelian shepherd is criticized for cutting down branches to feed his animals but at the beginning of this century, in the Grésigne forest in the Albi district of France, 'the shepherds even cut down trees so that the young shoots could be browsed' (DEFFONTAINES, 1933).

The purpose and raison d'être of the majority of agroforestry systems consists of optimizing positive interactions in order to obtain a higher, more diversified and more sustained total production, using available resources and existing ecological, technological and socio-economic conditions.

As a science, agroforestry is the study of interfaces and their variations in time and space between perennial woody vegetation and other animal and/or plant crops.

Agroforestry is neither the exclusive domain of agriculture, nor of forestry. Without claiming to be a panacea for combating desertification and for managing arid and semi-arid zones, it can contribute to their amelioration. The policies and strategy of the International Council for Research in Agroforestry (ICRAF) are particularly concerned with the need to make those affected participate fully in measures to combat desertification, right from the initial stages of programme and project conception.

58

Agroforestry strengthens solidarity among farmers (as the village producer groups in Senegal are intended to do), regulates their incomes to make them less dependent on weather variation, especially by better conservation of water and soil resources, and by a combination in space and time, and to their mutual benefit, of woody perennial crops and other products.

Agroforestry is thus readily applied – but not exclusively so – to small or medium-sized projects involving indigenous initiatives rather than to grand schemes imposed from 'above'.

So it fits very well a definition of development given by LEBRET in 1951: 'development, for a given population and the sub-populations that comprise it, is the series of transitions, at the fastest possible pace and the least possible cost, from a less human way of life to a more human one'.

This definition takes account of the cultural wealth and the aspirations of each people and each human group and does not suppose the adoption of an exogenous model, from which only a privileged few – mainly urban dwellers –benefit in the end, bringing no benefits to the great majority of the people.

Agroforestry systems relate to mixed cropping rather than monocropping. Monocropping, however, is not without its advantages. It can be very productive, and since on a single plot of land it produces a greater quantity of a single product than does mixed cropping, it facilitates commercialization. It requires strict management: one small error in planning supplies, for instance, can have fearsome consequences: an entire harvest can be destroyed because a fungicide or insecticide has not been applied in time. The same is certainly true of mixed cropping; its management is perhaps even more complicated because not one product only but several have to be managed; but a management error more often only has consequences for one of the products, and thus the agricultural risks are more widely spread. One of the advantages of agroforestry is that it is intended to produce a variety of crops. This allows them to adapt better to weather variations, to be more resistant to pests and diseases and be safer for the farmer than single crops; both because their economic value is more broadly based and because they provide a huge range of lasting social benefits. In addition, all the root systems of the different species comprising an agroforestry system on the one hand, and the total leaf systems on the other, make possible a more intensive exploitation of the environment they inhabit: each different foliage has its own requirements in sunshine intensity and duration, is at different heights off the ground and so the available light energy is better exploited: the roots, also situated at different levels, exploit the soil more completely and more deeply, both for moisture and for nutrients, and are more effective in combating erosion.

Compared with other production systems, agroforestry systems present to varying degrees a certain number of advantages:

- They contribute to the supply of firewood better than monocropping (except for certain types of tree monocropping.

- Thanks to their deep roots, woody perennials are less affected than herbaceous plants by temporary water deficit, and hence agroforestry systems make it possible to increase directly (for example, *Faidherbia albida*/millet) or indirectly (for example, woody shrub windbreaks or browse/grazing trees) the production of food, both in quality and quantity, notably by greater product diversity.

- Through this product diversification, they often also contribute to increased stability in the food supply.

- Their effect on the environment is positive and lasting; they contribute to the maintenance and fertility of soils, to reducing wind speeds, to creating micro-climates favourable to crops and to load capacity.

- Woody perennials in agroforestry systems are chosen not only because they give wood; they can also provide many other products such as forage, fruits, cordage, tannin, flowers, medicines, dyes, etc. etc.

- By intensification of a balanced soil utilization, with fertility preservation in mind, agroforestry systems contribute to the improvement of economic and social conditions in rural areas, not only by increasing profitability, sustainability and crop security, but also by creating jobs.

- Agroforestry systems encourage cultural exchanges by combining traditional experiences with advanced technologies and by researching modern solutions that are compatible with the socio-cultural customs of the populations concerned.

However, agroforestry does not have exclusive rights on these advantages, any more than it is a panacea for the problems of rural development, but it combines many advantages and may in many cases contribute to an improvement in standard and quality of life in rural zones.

The deliberate association of woody perennials with other animal and/or plant production from the earth is a very ancient practice: witness, for example, the cereal crops associated with olive trees found all around the Mediterranean, or systems that involve felling trees to clear land for cultivation in tropical forests, where certain chosen trees are deliberately retained where they stand. What is new is awareness of the these interactions between the woody plants and other productions, the attempt to understand the mechanism of these interactions and the increasingly numerous and systematic attempts to utilize interactions intelligently towards better, more intense and above all more sustained yields. Agroforestry is a concept which for the first time tries to synthesize practical ancestral experience and the technical expertise of the last decade in the fields of agronomy, ecology, forestry, pedology, sociology and rural economy. It is a scientific approach; it is a sort of concept or state of mind that leads on to tackling the complex problem of interfaces between woody perennial and other production, not from the point of view of a single science or single technique, but from an overall standpoint trying to intergrate all the specialist approaches. Among the interactions in question, we have, for example:

- The effect of shade on the yield of crops that trees overhang. This can be studied by the climatologist interested in the relationship between leaf density and intensity of light, by the forester interested in the relationship between pruning, light intensity at the soil surface and woody perennial production, or by the agronomist or the physiologist interested in the relationship between light intensity and plant growth under tree cover;

- the relationship between the presence of nitrogen-fixing bacteria, nitrogen supply to the tree and the crops surrounding it, or the relationship between the presence of micro-organism in the soil (inside or outside the roots, in contact with them or very close), which permits or facilitates mineral activity (domain of the physiologist) and influences not only the yield of woody perennials (domain of the forester) but also often that of crops that are associated with them (domain of the agronomist), and possibly their mineral composition, their taste . . . and their market price (domain of the economist . . . and the consumer).

The agroforestry approach to these interactions will not be that of the physiologist, the forester, the agronomist or the economist, but will be an overall approach which seeks to integrate every point of view. That is why, for example, ICRAF personnel comprises not only agronomists and foresters (they are in the minority), but also geographers, sociologists, econo-

61

mists, horticulturalists, pedologists, meteorologists, etc.

It is a fallacy to believe that

$$agroforestry = agronomy + forestry$$

although this fallacy gives rise, it is true, to the word 'agroforestry'. Agroforestry has to do with forestry insofar as it only applies when woody perennial plants are involved; it has to do with agronomy insofar as it deals with production techniques. But it also has to do with production systems, which links it to multiple disciplines like rural economics and sociology.

An agroforestry system will therefore present the following features (LUNDGREN and RAINTREE, 1983):

- it will involve at least two living plant species, one of which will be a woody perennial;

- there will always be a biological and/or economic interaction between the woody species (one or more) and the other species (one or more);

- it will yield at least two products;

- it will have a cycle of more than one year;

- it will always be more complex ecologically (by its structure and functions) and economically than a monocrop system.

Agroforestry is particularly important for small low-income farms, but its merits are sometimes dangerously exaggerated, as LUNDGREN and RAINTREE (1983) reported; when some people affirm subjectively and presumptuously that agroforestry is *a priori* a better approach and inevitably more successful than any other, they can only harm the development of agroforestry. It has an important role to play, but it is not necessarily or everywhere the best of all possible solutions. The 'D and D' approach developed by ICRAF (see section 8.3) enables the feasibility of an agroforestry solution to be evaluated objectively.

3.3 COMPONENTS OF AGROFORESTRY SYSTEMS

Numerous production factors are involved in agroforestry systems. The most important include: plants, water, animals, soil, and so on. How plants and animals considered as a resource contribute to agroforestry systems is examined below.

3.3.1 *Plants*

In agroforestry systems, as in all systems of agricultural production, an increase in plant production can be achieved mainly by:

- better use of water,

- judicious use of fertilizers,

- systematic control of pest and diseases,

- reducing/recycling agricultural waste,

- protecting and enriching the genetic capital contained in plants.

Some of these measures also work towards other objectives; for example, the use of artificial fertilizers may be considered from different angles:

- soil: because they alter the soil's composition and therefore its growing capabilities,

- plants: because they have an effect on their growth which can be positive or negative according to the amounts used,

- animals: because they alter soil biotopes, acting on the composition of the fauna in the soil, (notably earthworms and bacteria), which leads to further alteration in soil formation; and because the health of animals, and especially domestic or wild herbivores, depends in part, through the plants they ingest, on soil composition (presence or absence of trace elements, for example);

- water: because in certain cases *water* can be the vehicle for certain toxic elements associated with fertilizers, as around phosphate-processing plants in North Africa (which almost always contain up to 5% fluoride ions);

– transfer of knowledge: the education of small farmers and the training of fertilizer specialists.

Increased productivity per farmer is sometimes a myth. Certainly, in countries said to be developing, as in the industrialized countries, such an increase may be real. However, it is not always as great as statistics suggest, when, for example, it is contended that the work of an African peasant farmer only feeds himself, whereas the Russian peasant farmer feeds a dozen people and the American farmer nearer fifty. One should also count among agricultural producers the manufacturers of tractors, of fertilizers, pesticides and packaging, the mechanics, repairers, sellers and distributors of these products and materials, if one really wants to make a fair comparison. When other statistics show that it takes a peasant farmer in the Sudanese zone five days to produce 50 kg of grain when it only takes five minutes for a farmer in the American Middle West, this does not give due weight either to the different ecological conditions or to the effects on the environment, which are again totally different. This is perhaps the most disturbing aspect of a certain kind of farming modernization, when it may bring with it wastage and damage to the environment which may be irreversible. More important than modernization of agriculture for its own sake is the search for sustainable production systems that do not destroy the capital which the environment represents, and an improvement in the status of small farmers, especially those in developing countries, who already contribute considerably to production but whose potential for increasing their contribution to national, economic, social and political development is even greater. Agroforestry can often help achieve these objectives.

In some circumstances, looking to increase productivity, which is a logical response to the need to increase production, can also create environmental problems that are better acknowledged from the very start of any programme. For example, using high-yielding varieties of cultivated plants inevitably entails higher fertilizer consumption and pesticide use. The repercussions of this may include: deterioration in the quality of groundwater, making it unfit for consumption; eutrophication of surface water; multiplication of aquatic vectors of certain diseases. If the application of fertilizers and pesticides is mechanized, the result may be increased air pollution and higher energy consumption (often accompanied by an outflow of hard currency).

Regarding energy, there is a close link between the inputs of energy dedicated to food production. Thus from 1945 to 1970 in the USA, the energy devoted to maize production rose by 33%, from 5.6 kJ/kg to 7.5 kJ/kg, whereas production in the same period increased by 138%. But there is a saturation point beyond which supplementary input becomes lost or excessively dear and can cause serious environmental damage. The replacement of the 22 million mules and horses owned by the USA in 1901 and the 3.5 million in the United Kingdom in 1920 by 4.4 million and 500,000 tractors respectively fifty years later was not accomplished without damage to the environment, especially if one takes into account the consumption of fossil fuels required by mechanized agriculture: so that, to grow an acre of grain maize in North Central USA it takes 6.1 gallons of diesel and 2.1 gallons of petrol (COMMONER et al., 1975). In the same region, and for the same crop, the cost of inputs (ammonia, diesel, petrol, electricity, etc.)rose by 80% between 1970 and 1974, but in the same period the product price rose by 119%. In that price rise for the product, the increased energy cost only accounts for 2% and represents 13% of the increase in total variable costs.

Table VI shows in schematic form the environmental risks of different technologies that can increase plant productivity, and how recourse to an agroforestry approach could reduce those risks.

Plant resource management

When properly managed, agroforestry can optimize the plant resource. The components of an effective strategy include the following:

- Control of forest and bush fires; in particular, the use of agroforestry of woody plants resistant to fire or plants suitable for fire-breaks (e.g. cacti);

- Evaluation of the potential of the principal plant systems and in particular of their ability to tolerate certain ecological constraints (drought, for example, which requires that the plants be hardened off in the nursery before planting out and the use of drought-resistant species);

- Collection and conservation of endangered species and primitive cultivars; development of centres for preserving genetic resources, including cereals, forage plants, fruit trees, forest trees and micro-organisms. On a practical level, particular care should be taken in agroforestry not to introduce species known to be invasive where they could become a nuisance, and not to impair the local genetic heritage by the incautious introduction of exotics that could hybridize with indigenous species or even replace them;

- Protection of biotopes; vital for those with high productivity e.g.

TABLE VI

Potential of agroforestry regarding the environmental risks inherent in increased plant production

Technology	Main environmental risks	Potential of agroforestry
A. Irrigation, especially of deserts and arid zones	1. Possible climatic changes (the consequences of changes in the albedo, which would be very important here, are little known)	Tree, shrub & bush tops reflect less than bare soil Essential role of multi-purpose tree windbreaks
	2. Possible risk to fauna, e.g. if a dam destroys swamps that may be necessary to the reproduction of certain fish, for example, or that act as a feeding ground for migratory birds	Well planned & well distributed clumps of trees, even isolated bushes, can shelter wild game which could well be considered a resource and exploited rationally
	3. Soil salification, especialy by too rapid evaporation, or by use of saline, carbonated gypseous water	Use (notably for forage and fuel) of woody plants which 'pump' salt, e.g. the Tamarisk and halophytic shrubs
	4. Development of certain human and animal diseases, water-borne or from water-loving insects: malaria, onchocerciasis (African river blindness), filariasis, bilharzia	Increased numbers of woody plants used against these diseases or carriers in indigenous medicine
	5. Risk of erosion	Planting of suitable woody perennials.
	6. Danger of water wastage	Avoiding where possible woody plants which consume large amounts of water (willows, poplars, eucalyptus) . . . which are recommended, however, for drainage

B. Use of suitable species and varieties	1. Danger of uncontrolled introduction, especially of self-propagating plants or harmful invasive colonizers	There are cases (on hyperarid ground, for instance) where it would be good to find useful colonizers (*Opuntia, Prosopis*)
	2. Danger of loss of valuable genetic potential by mono-cropping, crop clearing or destruction of biotopes	Using mixed species wherever possible. Agroforestry contributes to keeping genetic variety
C. Use of fertilizers	Risk of water pollution. Potential depressive effect. Danger of acidification, alkalization or toxicity	Use of nitrogen-fixing shrubs, that do not have these drawbacks. Use of woody plants to purify water (Jahn, 1985)
D. Control of productivity-reducing pests	1. Risk of toxic accumulations in the soil, water, plants and food	Use of the woody plants with insecticidal properties, such as neem
	2. Depressive or lethal effect at certain doses or certain use frequencies, reducing germinating ability, growth or fruit formation (particularly seeds) or fibres (cotton, jute, raffia)	
E. Reduction of waste products and utilization of waste	Risk of soil and water pollution by certain waste products	Agroforestry advocates composting of organic waste
F. Protection of existing plant resources	Endangered species Endangered biotopes	In agroforestry, it is expressly indicated to use endangered species in species mixtures, and agroforestry can help to reconstitute biotopes close to those threatened by extinction

67

estuaries, marshes, some deltas. Establish reserves (especially biosphere reserves), national parks, and more simply set up collections of local woody species, particularly multi-purpose ones;

– Specific programme of fodder selection and production for grazing-route plants; a special effort to select forage Capparaceae for *sensu lato* arid zones;

– Fermentation and other processing of organic waste: composting, distillation, etc., with possible production of biogas.

– Preference given to species and varieties suitable for providing green manure, enriching the soil with a large amount of organic matter (leaves, branches etc. which rot down quickly) and reducing or complementing the use of chemical fertilizers;

– Pest control, with particular emphasis on rodents and food plants, beginning with rice, sorghum and maize; special research into woody perennials with insecticide properties, such as neem;

– Research into manures and fertilizing agents (nitrogen-fixing bacteria, for example, associated with woody perennials);

improving their efficiency,

'better targeting' by concentrating the effect on single species to be encouraged,

finding formulations that liberate active ions just when the plant to be fertilized needs them.

However, certain shortcomings require attention if the plant resource is to be optimized.

– Insufficient agricultural varieties (not only cereals but also protein and vitamin-yielding plants) are well adapted to different local conditions, where woody perennials are plentiful;

– The links between climate, farming methods, growth, incidence of pest and diseases and the phenology of woody perennials are poorly understood;

– Current world networks of ecological information, meteorological forecasts and warnings are inadequate;

- Models incorporating food crops/woody perennials/climatic factors, which would make it possible to optimize sowing, harvesting and the various tasks of the labour force, are lacking or inadequate.

- There is insufficient clean and certified, or at least good quality, seed of known provenance and origin.

3.3.2 Animals

Table VII attempts to show how agroforestry could help reduce the environmental risks attached to techniques for increasing animal production.

Animal resource management

The strategy should include:

- Speeding up the ratification and implementation of the conventions on wildlife protection, which in some cases could become an important component of silvo-pastoral systems in arid and semi-arid zones.

- Taking into consideration the problem of aquatic mammals which can, especially in tropical estuaries, help to control harmful aquatic plants and adapt very well to mangrove plantations or hydrophilic shrubs.

- Obtaining a whale oil substitute, encouraging cultivation of jujube in arid zones which suit it but without losing sight of the fact that potential markets for its wax are few.

- Using projects set up purely for the purpose of developing controlled wild game hunting, in the first instance to protect species or re-introduce them (addax, oryx, falcon, monitors, gazelle, deer, ostrich, crocodile . . .) and to then integrate them into the silvopastoral production systems of arid zones.

- Improving knowledge about wildlife economy, particularly with a view to determining under what conditions the management of wild animals can be combined with (or given precedence over) raising domestic animals (productivity in weight and in proteins), chiefly by developing grazing resources within production systems.

- Greatly intensifying of all forms of aquaculture, in fresh water and

TABLE VII

Potential of agroforestry regarding the environment risks inherent in increased animal production

Technology	Main environmental risks	Potential of agroforestry
Protection of species	Risk of permanent extinction of some wild or domestic species; to be considered particularly for their importance in balancing ecosystems and their economic importance: aquatic estuary mammals, birds of prey, crocodiles and turtles in the water, and on the land greater ungulates, reptiles and . . . useful microbes	Shelter role of trees, copses and forests
Use of suitable species and varieties	Conservation of animal genetic potential and especially rare or disappearing domestic species. Better adaptation of species and varieties of animals to the environment; avoidance of catastrophic introductions; selection for hardiness and adaptation.	Contribution to safeguards by maintaining or creating appropriate ecotopes. Importance given to wildlife, which is ecologically adapted. Preference given to indigenous species when their production is satisfactory.
Feed improvement and use of growth stimulants	Risk of animal tissue changes, especially fats, by using unsuitable feed and hormones, with serious dangers to humans at the end of the food chain.	Qualitative and quantitative increase in potential forage (including food for bees).
Pest control and other factors reducing productivity	Risk of toxic accumulation in water, but also in the soil and animal tissue, by unconsidered use or misuse of certain pest controls.	Insecticide properties of some woody plants. Provision of shade and temperature reduction. Improved humidity of the air.
Reduced production of waste and use of waste	Risk of pollution from certain waste. Some, however, is very useful and has many purposes: manure, slurry, opotherapy products, bonemeal, dried blood, horn and shell, hides and skins, etc.	
Special case of Man Security and quality of life Satisfaction of basic needs	Numerous	Contribution to production of food, fuel, logs and timber, medicines, fibres, fibres, dyes, tannins, resins, gums, etc. Establishment of stable systems of production.

along the coast, not only to bring about a rapid increase in protein production, but also to help take more effective action to save endangered aquatic species or those on the point of becoming so, and to help reduce the number of domestic animals on grazing land which is already overcrowded almost everywhere.

– Giving preference, especially in Third World countries, to the use of hardy animals, adapted to local conditions and feeding off the local woody flora.

– Improving conditions where stockrearing is practised; in particular, providing protection from wind and heat.

– Planting cordons of woody perennial plants (hedges, windbreaks, plant enclosures) to facilitate cattle management.

3.4 Types of agroforestry systems for combating desertification

Nair (1985 has studied and classified the various types of agroforestry systems.
Such systems can be classified according to how they are structured. A distinction can therefore be made between systems related to agro-silviculture, silvo-pastoralism, agro-silvi-pastoralism, api-silviculture, etc.
Woody perennials play different roles in the different utilization methods.

The relative arrangement of the components can be taken as a basis for classification. The arrangement can be considered spatialy:

– densely mixed systems, such as the household garden;

– scattered mixed systems, such as fields jointly planted with shea butter (*Butyrosperum Parkii*) or African locust (*Parkia biglobosa*) or vène *Pterocarpus erinaceus*;

– strip systems, such as contoured wooded strips on bench terraces or terraces;

– edge systems, such as a line of trees bordering a grazing plot.

Or, one can consider the arrangement in time instead of in space. Systems are then coincident, concomitant, intermittent, interpolated, overlapping or in relay, as shown in Table VIII.

TABLE VIII

Arrangement in time of the components of agroforestry systems
(according to NAIR, 1985)

Temporal arrangement	Schematic illustration	Examples
coincident		coffee trees under shade trees
concomitant		taungya
intermittent (predominantly spatial)		annual crops under coconut palms
interpolated (predominantly spatial and temporal)		household gardens
overlapping		hevea and pepper plant
relay		bush fallow

——— woody plant component
--------- non-woody plant component

One can also base the classification on the kinds of components in the systems. Figure 5 shows such a classification of systems and sub-systems.

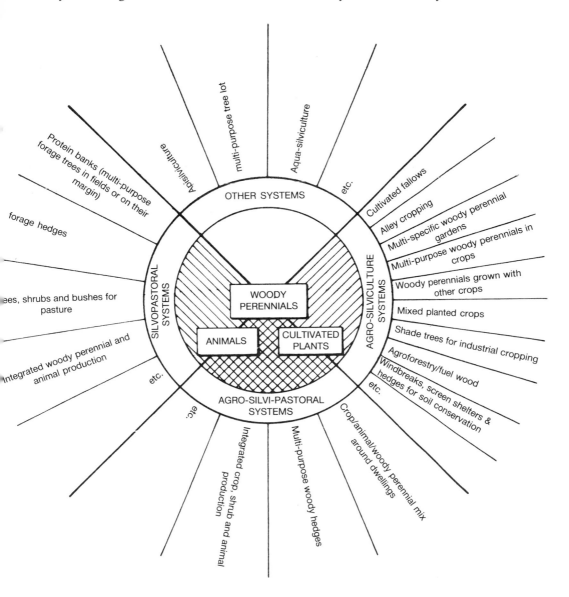

FIGURE 5
Classification of agroforestry systems and sub-systems according to the nature of their components (according to NAIR, 1985 adapted).

Such systems of classification help in the planning of forestry operations. This is how the various roles that woody perennials could play in some types of soil utilization in the Zalingei region of Darfur (Sudan) were classified; the recognized types of utilization were:

A1 Wadi Azum valley irrigated and sometimes flooded
A2   ,,   irrigated but not flooded
A3   ,,   non-irrigated although on alluvia
B1 plateau with *Balanites aegyptiaca* and crops
B2   ,,   without crops
R grazing land
M mountainous area

Role of woody perennials	A1	A2	A3	B1	B2	R	M
Improved fertility		+	++	+		+	
Soil conservation	++		+			+	+
Dendro-energy	+			+	+	+	
Logs							+
Timber	+			+	+	+	+
Forage						++	
Fruit and food	+		++	+	+		+
Fencing	+	++	+	++	+	+	
Textile fibres			+	+			+
Medicines					+	+	++

By way of example, Table IX shows the principal features of some agroforestry systems in arid or semi-arid zones of Africa.

3.4.1 *Traditional dry zone cultivation in Africa*

In their perceptive study of tropical African agricultural land, DUPRIEZ and LEENER (1983) describe the traditional dry region cultivation system, taking as an example a field at Sine Saloum, Senegal, on flat sandy soil, with 500 to 700 mm of rainfall from July to October, the hot season.

'The number of trees growing in the fields depends also on the amount of rain falling during the rainy season and seeping into the soil. To survive the dry season, the trees must share the soil's water reserves. If the reserves are plentiful, the number of trees can be high; if they are low, the number of trees will fall.

'The farming areas around the villages are strewn with trees which have been preserved by the farmers: they are mostly baobab, locust, shea butter, kadd and other species of thorny legumes. The number and quality of trees scattered through the fields vary from place to place, depending on how the villagers act: some do not pay much heed to the role of trees and only see in them the profit they can get from selling the wood; others, on the other hand, know what part trees play and watch over them.

'Here we have millet growing. You can see that under the tree it is growing a little faster. It is a little damper and less hot there'.

'During the whole of the dry season, the soil will remain bare, since the natural vegetation which follows the peanut harvest has been weeded off. Only trees provided the field with a little shade. The soil is all the barer for the peanut haulm having been collected in heaps and taken away for cattle forage.

'After two seasons of cultivation during which the seeds (millet and peanut), forage (peanut haulm), wood, pods and other products from trees have been taken away with all the food they contain drawn from the soil, the earth is exhausted. That is the way it is left **fallow** for two years.

'Note, however, that certain species are permanently present; the trees. They are able to sustain life from one season to the next in an aerial milieu, particularly the kadd (*Faidherbia albida*) which remains quite green during the dry season. Its leaves and pods are valuable forage for cattle'.

3.4.2 *Traditional humid zone cultivation in Africa*

The same care to reserve a place for woody perennials is also found in the traditional farming system in wet forest regions. The same authors describe a farm in eastern Cameroon. After clearing the land, the farmer goes on to do the following:

- in the first year, he plants a cleansing crop like cucumber, but plants banana here and there, the leaves of which provide shade for the cucumbers;

- in the second year, he plants a maize crop between the young banana trees;

TABLE IX

Some features of agroforestry systems in the arid and semi-arid zones of Africa
(after NAIR, 1985, adapted)

System	Sub-systems and practice	Main function	Place	Socio-economic production type	Main woody species	References
Agrisilviculture	MPTS on crops	Food, forage, fuel, etc. Soil conservation, sustained production	Mali	subsistence	*Butyrospermum Paradoxum Parkia biglobosa*	
		ditto	Central Africa	subsistence	*Adansonia digitata Balanites aegyptiaca Borassus aethiopum*	YANDJI, 1982
		Woody plant strips on terraces, food, forage	Kenya (Machakos District)	subsistence	*Cajanus cajan Balanites aegyptiaca Prosopis juliflora Acacia* spp.	
	Dendro-energy	Firewood, charcoal	Sahel	subsistence	*Acacia tortilis Acacia* spp.	VON MAYDELL, 1984
	Windbreaks & screen shelters	Crop protection, wood production	Sudan (N. province)	subsistence	*Tamarix aphylla Propopis juliflora*	
		ditto	Niger (Maggia)	subsistence	*Azidarachta indica Acacia scorpioides A. Seyal Prosopis juliflora*	RICHARDS, 1985
	Bank protection	Soil conservation posts, firewood	Sudan (JMRDP)*	mixed	*Eucalyptus camaldulensis*	BAUMER et al., 1985
Silvopastoralism	Live hedges	Crop protection, firewood, beekeeping, forage, fruit, firewood, 'incense', windbreaks	Sudan (JMRDP)* Somalia	subsistence mixed	*Acacia mellifera Balanites aegyptiaca Commiphora africana Zizyphus mucronata*	BAUMER et al., 1985

System	Practice	Description	Location	Scale	Species	Reference
					Acacia spp. *Eucalyptus gomphocephala*	
		Reduced water expenditure for hedges, reduction in watch-man requirements	Kenya	subsistence	*Parkinsonia Commiphora africana*	Hoekstra et al., 1985
	Mixed hedges	Crop Protection food, firewood, fodder	Cameroon (Mounts Mandara)	subsistence	*Zizyphus nauritiana Cassia Siamea Acacia Sp. pl.*	
	Woody plants for grazing land	Forage reserve	Sahel	subsistence	*Acacia toritis Faidherbia albida Tamarindus indica*	
		id.	Kenya	subsistence	*Prosopis pallida Faidherbia albida Zizyphus sp. Balanites aegyptiaca*	Hoekstra et al., 1984
Agro-silvipastoralism	MPTS on fields grazed after harvest	Forage, soil fertilisation, firewood, and with associated farming	Sahel Sudan	subsistence	*Faidherbia albida*	
		id.	Chad	commercial	*Acacia sp. pl. Salvadora persica Combretus sp. pl. Combretaceae*	
	gum gardens	Gum production, forage, firewood in rotation with crops	Sudan (Kordofan) Mauritanisa Senegal	mixed or subsistence	*Acacia Senegal*	
	Annual harvest of forage on grazing land and field edges	Forage, (quantity, quality, availability)	Kenya (Machakos District)	subsistence	*Prosopis pallida Leucaena leucocephala Acacia saligna Stylosanthes scabra*	Hoekstra et al., 1984

*JMRDP = Jebel Marra Rural Development Project

– in the third year, he plants crops (e.g. peanuts) between the now tall banana trees, and plants macabo (*Xanthosoma sagittifolium*), with second generation maize from the seeds that fell on the ground during the preceding harvest, and some stands of tobacco; he parcels the field, planting one plot with coffee, one with cacao, another with pineapples and another with cassava (*Manihot esculenta*), giving two parcels in all over to orchards of woody perennials.

'The young coffee and cacao stands were planted out along with the first peanut crop. The rains were heavy at the time and assisted the striking of the young plants. These benefited from the shade created by plants in the higher vegetation storey, whether macabo, banana or tall forest trees left unfelled.

'During the following seasons the young trees develop in the shade of the growing numbers of banana palms and a few forest trees. Gradually, the banana grove will disappear through age and the coffee trees occupy the entire space, leaving no room except for low grass cover. The tall forest trees which have not been felled will also remain.

'On parcel B, the cacao follows the same development as the coffee on parcel A. However, it eventually smothers the low grasses beneath it almost entirely. When the trees come into full production the field is five or six years old'.

After the third season's harvest, or at the start of the fourth, the farmer planted other useful plants, such as oil palm which, from the fifth season, will be protected to the detriment of the other crops and will continue to grow despite the regrowth of wild species.

This system of farming therefore associates:

– short-lived plants with long-lived ones,

– plants either sown, propagated by cuttings or planted out,

– plants which are labour intensive and those which 'grow on their own',

– species which grow in groups and others which grow as isolated individuals.

Each plant plays a particular role in the association and the farmer knows perfectly well how to combine them, what attention and care they need to obtain the best diversified and staggered harvests, while still protecting the soil from erosion and maintaining its fertility. The small farmer is thus acting in the spirit of agroforestry, by planting on the basis of reciprocal interactions between woody perennials and other products of the soil, and on their ordering in space and time.

Seven other traditional agroforestry production systems practised in Africa are described in Appendix 3.

4. NATURAL WOODY VEGETATION IN DRY ZONES

The density of woody vegetation is highly variable over the whole *sensu lato* arid zone. This vegetation includes many more bushes, shrubs and underbrush than trees, especially in arid and semi-arid zones. However, the many positive effects that it has on the environment and the numerous products that man obtains from it make it desirable that there should be more of it wherever ecologically feasible. One way of increasing the number of woody plants is, of course, to plant them, but that is not always possible or achievable at an acceptable cost.

Another solution springs to mind: the management of natural woody vegetation. Unfortunately, much less attention has been paid to this than to the management of tropical rain forests or temperate forests, and few cases are reported in the literature. Furthermore, management in the proper sense of the word is in most cases not possible, because of the lack of statistical data and satisfactory surveys. Given this state of affairs, one must make do with general directives.

4.1 MANAGEMENT AND DEVELOPMENT

Management comprises three phases: it must cover all practices and, in the light of a *survey*, realize a *potential* within the framework of a *time cycle*. The survey is an inventory detailing the quality, quantity and geographic distribution of the different components of the vegetation carpet or ground cover, and related data: climate, soil, sociology, economic activity, etc. The survey therefore includes investigations of every kind. Good examples are the series of reports by the Mauritanian RAMS Project, evaluating rural resources and manpower, or the resource surveys conducted as part of the Jebel Marra Project for integrated rural development in Sudan.

As far as vegetation is concerned, the inventory of the plant and ecological features of the components of the vegetation carpet, makes it possible to organize these coverings according to groups developing in time, called plant groupings or vegetation series. A map of the vegetation seen in this manner should therefore make it possible to draw up both a current inventory (type, state of distribution of plants and their groupings) and a potential inventory ('dynamic' aspect of vegetation series). Some countries have realized the value of a survey conducted on these principles. In 1970, the Department of Agronomic Research's Plant Ecology Station in Morocco recommended that four series of maps should be compiled (ION-

NESCO, 1970 a and b). The first two of these illustrate the survey phase of management:

type (A): Actual occupation of the land (types of vegetation, their forms, etc). Map showing the components and a synthesis, drawn up on the basis of aerial photographs and soil tests. Examples: maps of vegetation types in TOTHILL (1954), BAUMER (1968).

type (B): Plant ecology: plant groupings, formations, series and their dynamics, ecological groups, bioclimates, desertification factors, human and animal pressures, etc. A correlative, very detailed map. Examples: LE HOUEROU (1968), BAUMER (1962 a), BERNUS (1980).

To the pastoralist, potential, the expression of the productive capacity of an area put under grass, defines the annual quota of croppings, by animal or tool, in area or in volume for grassland. In one year a population grows by a certain volume: management defines potential, depending on that growth. The result desired by the planner in a given circumstance will be the preservation, increase or reduction of the population volume, or else its transformation.

In other words, 'potential' represents what can be taken from the soil each year, what part of the vegetation it supports can be removed without reaching the limit, without diminishing the capital, avoiding erosion, over-grazing, damaging cutting and all other forms of overexploitation. The (C) and (D) types of map from the Moroccan Plant Ecology Station are concerned with defining potential:

type (C): Pastoral resources, special map (BAUMER, 1962 b) or inter-pretative map using the data in the (A) and (B) type maps and requiring a complementary investigation into pastoral value, wealth of forage, load capacity and seasonal varia-tions of these.

type (D): Capabilities (development, urgent intervention, interven-tion costs, etc.). Map giving overall picture of zones of equal potential, to be used as a basis for management.

The information given by estimation of potential can be displayed on a map. Consequently, the most rewarding way to use a vegetation map is to use it to define bio-geographical groupings, characterized by the territorial extent of the same 'landscape' type, taking that term not only in its traditional sense of 'appearance', but also and more importantly giving it a synthetic significance, combining four groups of variables.

1. The stage of physiognomy reached by the plant cover on the way to dynamic evolution of a vegetation series (type (A) and (B) maps)

2. The nature, intensity and effectiveness of human pressure on the environment ((A) type maps)

3. Relationships between ecological conditions (climate and soil), natural vegetation and the use made by man of both these ((B) and (C) type maps)

4. The amount of effort required to achieve the chosen economic target, from a point of departure doubly defined by its ecology and its dynamic state ((D) type map).

In this way, the idea emerges of various zones of equal potential and therefore justifying the same type of management. This is a much more fertile notion than that of 'natural region', because the static description of a landscape is augmented by a biogeographical explanation and an indication of the environment's evolutionary trends. The main outline of a management plan can then be sketched in, in full awareness of this triple formula.

The geographical demarcation of zones of equal potential presents another concern, that of providing a sure guide to the setting-up, organization and discussion of experiments and trials that will explain management methods more effectively.

Once the conditions governing geographical distribution of relationships between life and the environment within any one zone of equal potential are known, it becomes possible to set in motion an efficient research package, positioned at key points on the ground, each with precise reciprocal objectives and whose results can be used in controlled extrapolation, with the underlying guarantee of the validity of the equipotential zones.

Such a process of development of 'in-depth' research, exploring in time what the notion of zones of equal potential already expresses in space, is fundamentally different from the 'pilot sectors' or 'control zones' method so frequently adopted. These can only be meaningful in terms of management if they fit into a dynamic perspective. In reality, the idea of the pilot zone can only be applied to development questions, that is to say, at a level where the notion of time is much less important: 'there is in fact (REY, 1962) all the difference of a time cycle between management and development'.

The third term – and perhaps the key one – in management, the time cycle, defines a duration: the time that passes between two successive harvests on the same spot, or that which has been 'fixed for the realization of the entire material' (PLAISANCE, 1961).

It would seem logical that at the conclusion of this time cycle it would be possible, by a correct estimation of potential, to come up again with the initial survey. The reality is usually different, in the wake of an intentional or unintentional disharmony between the annual increase in resources and the vigour with which they are exploited. The basic inventory, or at any rate the comparison of two states, makes it possible to draw up a balance sheet and to judge the operation. Measurement of forage units, of load capacity, of grazing value, of woody perennial production, of biomass, etc., all carried out before and after the management operation, enable the level and cost of that management to be evaluated.

This basic aspect must be respected in every type of management; if this term is to keep any real value, calculations of profitability can only be truly meaningful if they take sufficient account of the difference in potential separating the two inventories, before and after a time cycle (or at the very least a 'rotation', a stage limited in time to the periodicity of harvests on one plot). For example, the profitability of a hydroelectric scheme means nothing if the disruption or alterations to the biological balances or the silvopastoral upheavals it has caused are left out of the calculation.

The profitability of any rural management scheme must take into account erosion, the risks of soil exhaustion, and the biocenotic changes of all kinds that an intensive 'development' of the land all too often entails. This is in no way to denigrate or reject all efforts of this kind, but it is quite obvious that a correct assessment of the balance sheet at the conclusion of the time cycle is absolutely essential for a healthy conception of the very notion of management. And it is here – and in many fields – that mapping the vegetation and the accompanying measures and survey work can play a leading role, for example in defining zones of equal potential or zones which are isodynamic, or even investment profitability.

It is obviously not possible to carry out management schemes in the complete and conventional sense of the term in arid, or even semi-arid, zones, because:

– most of the time, there is no available qualitative and quantitative inventory, at least in the *sensu proprio* arid zones. Where an inventory does exist, it is rare for it to have been made from a management perspective, and so it often lacks the real 'forestry' or 'pastoral' data particularly necessary when one is looking towards an improved silvopastoral system;

– the more arid the environment, the less well defined and distinct from agricultural space in the wide sense (agriculture and stockrearing) the forest space; consequently, if there is management, it must be an integrated management concerned with the whole space (in the same way as it is perceived, incidentally, by its habitual users).

In practice, rather than real management, it will be a question of directives on exploitation and management and on how to proceed in developing vegetation, woody or otherwise.

4.2 Characteristics of natural woody perennial vegetation in dry zones

Dry regions have highly diverse types of vegetation, sometimes incorrectly grouped together under the name savanna. In its true sense, a savanna is a grass formation more than 1.30 m in height, composed mainly of perennial broadleaved graminaceous plants. If this formation is lower, it is known as low savanna. When the grasses are less than 80 cm high they are generally also more widely spaced, annuals are more prevalent than perennials and the leaves are narrow, rolled up or bent over: this is then known as pseudo-steppe (the same physiognomy as the true steppe in Russia, but dormant period caused by lack of water and by heat rather than physiological dryness combined with cold).

Savanna, low savanna and pseudo-steppe normally succeed each other from the humid towards the arid. Savanna, low savanna and pseudo-steppe can be modified by the presence of trees, bushes or shrubs. These forms will be called, respectively, 'treed', 'bushed' or 'shrubbed'. Without entering into too much detail the qualifications 'densely', 'moderately' or 'sparsely' will be added to denote the apparent density of the woody vegetation. If this is distributed irregularly, in some places forming copses, in others small woods where, locally, the tops touch, these formations will be called 'wooded': for example, 'wooded savanna'. If the woody plants are in the great majority thorny bushes or shrubs, they will be referred to as 'thorny savanna (or pseudo-steppe)' and if the formation is predominantly thorny, the term 'thorn thicket' will be used.

So, wooded low savanna and wooded savanna gradually change into

84

thin forest when the woody plant density increases, when the cover tends to close and when the majority of the plants are trees. Woody formations in dry zones are often of medium height or even low or very low (e.g. salt pseudo-steppes with Chenopodia). But the customary rule in temperate countries that the height of a tree above ground is the same as the depth of its roots is not applicable here. Generally, the underground parts are much more developed than those above ground. So in one-year-old *Acacia Senegal* plants on deep sand, the main root may reach a depth of 7 m. FERLIN (1981) reports that the root of *Prosopis cineraria* might grow to a depth of 50 m. The root of the kadd can go down to 30 or 40 m. Although too few studies have been done on the root systems of woody perennials in arid zones, it is evident that the strength and length of their root systems enable them to tap deep sources of water and minerals.

Woody perennials possess all kinds of adaptation to their environment and in particular to drought. Some of them are better able to resist fire than others, either because there is no, or hardly any, natural combustible vegetation at their base, often owing to the presence of phyto-toxicity (as seems to be the case with many Eucalyptus), or because they have a very thick corky bark. The seeds themselves often present special characteristics that ensure their extended preservation in a hostile environment. There is little information on the viability of indigenous species which have, on the whole, been studied far less than the exotics, but it is clear that many seeds with a hard cuticle remain viable for several years. This is what happens in nature with many very hard acacia seeds. They are so hard that to make them germinate they have to be subjected to special treatment, scarification or soaking in an acid solution, or most often, a period soaking in freshly boiled water – and even for *A. sieberiana* in actually boiling water; in nature the seed only germinates when it is softened at length by humidity as in the digestive tract of small ruminants; but the seed can also retain its germinating ability for several years and only start to germinate in a year of high rainfall. Other seeds (e.g. of *Azadirachta indica* are surrounded with a protective mucillage, which is usually dissolved in water to facilitate seed germination: the remaining solution is effective as an anti-mosquito spray.

Many acacia seeds frequently used in dry regions have the advantage of pretreatment before they are used; a general survey of these is given in Table X, an extract from a study done by the CSIRO for the FAO (DORAN *et al.*, 1983).

4.3 OBSTACLES TO REGENERATION

Natural populations have difficulty in regenerating because they are under far too much pressure almost everywhere from fire, animals and

TABLE X

Recommended pre-treatments for the seeds of some dry zone acacias (from the 'Guide to the seeds of dry zon acacias, FAO, 1983, by DORAN et al.)

Species	Recommendations[1]	References
A. aneura	Plunge seeds in boiling water for 5-30 seconds, or pour boiling water onto them and leave in the water until it cools to the ambient temperature.	Preece (1971) Hall et al. (1979) Turnbull (unpubl.)
A. Cambagei	Fresh seeds often need no pre-treatment; more mature seeds can be treated like A. aneura.	Hall et al. (1975)
A. Caven	Soak in concentrated sulphuric acid for 120 minutes.	Galleguillos (comm. pers.), Turnbull (unpubl.)
A. farnesiana	Soak in concentrated sulphuric acid for 40-120 minutes. The optimum time varies with each batch of seeds.	Kumar & Purkayashta (1972), Turnbull (unpubl.)
A. holoserica	Treat as for A. aneura.	Delwaulle (1978), Turnbull (unpubl.)
A. nilotica	Fresh seeds with soft integument need no pre-treatment. Immersion in boiling water as for A. aneura is sufficient, but if the seeds are hard, soaking in concentrated sulphuric acid for 60-120 minutes is recommended.	FAO (1974a), NAS (1980), Turnbull (unpubl.)
A. pruinocarpa	Treat as for A. aneura	Hall et al. (1981b)
A. Senegal	Fresh seeds with soft integument need no pre-treatment. More mature seeds can be immersed in concentrated sulphuric acid for 3-15 minutes, or plunged into boiling water for 5 seconds.	Kaul & Manohar (1966) Cheema & Qadir (1973) Giffard (1975), NAS (1980), Turnbull (unpubl.)
A. tortilis	Soak in concentrated sulphuric acid for 20 minutes. The optimum time varies with different batches of seeds. Immersion in boiling water as for A. aneura can also be effective.	Karschon (1975), Carr (1976), Pathak et al. (1980, NAS (1980), Turnbull (unpubl.)
A. Victoriae Acacia albida = Faidherbia albida	Treat as for A. aneura Fresh seeds with soft integument need no pre-treatment, or may be soaked in cold water for 23 hours before planting. More mature seeds can be soaked in concentrated sulphuric acid for 20-60 minutes[2].	Hall et al. (1981 a) West (1950) Wickens (1969) Giffard (1971) FAO (1974a, 1974b) Elamin (1975) and Turnbull (unpubl.)

(1) Manual scarification is the most effective pre-treatment for all species.

(2) The pre-treatment methods found in the literature for A. albida are contradictory. The reason for this seems to be that the state of development of the integument has a great effect on the relative success of any treatment given for this species. Clearly, the age of the subject is also crucial.

man. But the ability to regenerate is very elastic and very often, as in the case of reconstitution of wildlife in arid zones, effective protection over several years will be sufficient to see woody vegetation recover strength and start to spread.

Around permanent water sources, as in all areas of high cattle concentration, the plant cover, particularly grass, is frequently greatly reduced, even to bare ground, and one talks of pronounced vegetative degradation. The reality is often more complex: it may be true that the earth is bare, encouraging erosion, particularly wind erosion, and that aerial photographs reveal circles of degradation centred around these areas of concentration, but the potential for regeneration is far from always being zero. If a sector of such a circle is protected from all grazing, by fencing it off, for example, the first rains often see the return of abundant plant life, frequently greatest at the centre of the degradation circle. This is because the soil, enriched by animal dung, often contains a large quantity of seeds brought there by the animals and which will germinate when given the chance. Degradation is therefore only on the surface, there is no loss of regenerative ability but only temporary obliteration. However, if several years of drought have occurred, the animals no longer leave the forage, and the climax plants are progressively replaced by species with a shorter cycle offering less resistance to erosion, as BOUDET showed (1972); for instance, on the sandy soil of Niger, *Aristida mutabilis* is replaced by *Boerhavia repens* and *Tribulus terrestris,* which cattle do not eat.

When protected from fire and browsing animals the regenerative capacity of the vegetation, particularly the woody perennials, is great. So great that it sometimes explains why common pasture is set alight, especially when the woody plants are of the type least favoured by the cattle. In 1958, we installed an enclosure in the north of Kordofan between Mazrub and Sodiri in an Aristida low savanna very thinly bushed with *Combretum cordofanum* and very thinly shrubbed with *Acacia orfota,* in order to study the development of the protected plant cover there: to our great surprise, within two years the vegetation was a quite impenetrable thicket of acacias with four Combretum, although the nearest Combretum was 220 m from the enclosure and the nearest acacia 240 m away.

Overexploitation and bad exploitation take different forms, notably excessive lopping, uncontrolled fires, overgrazing, damaging land clearances in areas that ought not to be cultivated, either because of the poverty of the soil or because rainfall is too often insufficient to guarantee a reasonably regular or rewarding harvest. Fundamental to all these malpractices is lack of balance between the resource, which is limited, and the demand, which is ever increasing on account of demographic pressure, which shows no sign of slowing down. The United Nations Conference on Desertification pointed clearly to the relationships that exist between over-exploitation of plant resources, deforestation in particular, and desertification, considered as biological degradation.

Despite ill-treatment, woody vegetations generally maintain themselves fairly well. Clearly, in places there have been major reductions in woody perennials due to exceptional drought: as in Mauritania, where the gum trees disappeared between Moudjeria, Boutilimit and Khorifa during the great drought of 1972-1976. A hypothesis was offered (BAUMER, 1981) that if the trees had not been so severely stripped of their bark in order to produce a little more gum, at least some of them could have survived. The dead fallen trees formed small impenetrable thorny clumps beneath which a few grasses appeared during the rains, but advantage was not taken of these natural shelters to dibble in more gum seeds, some of which at least might have germinated and grown to maturity. Several years went by before the gum garden was restored; the dead trees had rotted or ended up as fire-wood, the shade from their branches no longer existed and it was necessary to undertake costly planting with artificial protection.

The regenerative capacity of woody plants is, as has been emphasized, considerable. Thus the 'forest' of Bled Thala (in Arabic, 'Thal' means *Acacia Seyal*) only existed on the map; but following independence, goats were strictly excluded and a well-developed acacia grove with a closed canopy grew up.

Many woody perennials in arid zones are able to reproduce vegetatively. This helps them to perpetuate the species and resist fire, lopping and heavy browsing. Many of the Mimosas are much used in agroforestry systems because of their readiness to sprout from the stump, produce suckers and respond to layering, notably *Acacia Seyal*, *Faidherbia albida* and *Prosopis juliflora*. Other agroforestry species have these same abilities – the neem, Cassias, the bell mimosa, *Dichrostachys cinerea*, eucalyptuses, *A. Senegal*, mitragyna, the African locust, the date palm, *Piliostigmas* sp.pl., *Salvadora persica*, *Sclerocarya Birroea*, *Stereospermum kunthianum*, the tamarind and the jujube trees. Others grow easily from cuttings and this property is often used for making hedges or living fences, as with *Commiphora* sp.pl., *Boswellia papyrifera*, *Euphorbia* sp.pl. It has been noted that in certain species, such as *Pterocarpus angolensis*, repeated cutting or browsing of the aerial branches has not prevented the continuous development of the root system until it forms, from its now more powerful roots, a sprout that is stronger than the rest and which escapes browsing or chopping down (HAIG et al., (1958).

We still have very few precise data on the biomass production of natural vegetations, but the figures given by GOUDET (1984) according to the average annual rainfall (P) may be taken as a preliminary indication:

P < 400 should produce 0.01 m³ biomass/ha/year (saharan and sahelo-saharan zones)

400 < P < 600	0.1	(sahelian zone)
600 < P < 800	0.18	(sahelo-sudanian zone)
800 < P < 1000	0.24	(sudano-sahelian zone)
1000 < P < 1200	0.29	(sudanian zone)
1200 < P < 1300	0.35	(sudano-guinean zone)

In addition, it is estimated that industrial plantations can give approximately

1.5 to 3 m³ biomass/ha/year with P = 600 mm
3 to 5 m³ biomass/ha/year with P = 800 mm
6 to 10 m³ biomass/ha/year with P = 1000 mm

In practical terms, economically speaking, this means that industrial plantations have very little chance of ever becoming profitable when the average annual rainfall during at least the early years of the population does not exceed 800 mm. There is a tendency to call the 800 mm isohyet 'the FUGALLI line', after one of the first foresters who had the courage to say aloud what many were thinking to themselves. Family or private plantations can in principle give better results than industrial plantations under state control, given the same amount of rainfall, because:

– problems posed by the constraints of the environment are resolved better and on a case-by-case basis,

– the interest is all in home consumption and therefore very direct,

– it is easier to practise agroforestry and intercrop woody perennials with food crops,

– at a pinch, one can use the stand as crop for private profit.

Below the 800 mm isohyet it seems clear that the natural vegetation, especially if it is correctly managed, is capable of giving as much wood and at less cost than the plantations. This is even true in wetter climates when soil constraints become apparent. For example, in the Kinshasa area, at an altitude of about 400 m, with a rainfall of the order of 1400 mm, only 3 dry months, relative humidity varying between 69 and 83% and mean monthly temperatures between 17°C (lowest of the minimum temperatures) and 30°C (highest of the maximum temperatures), on the very poor sands of the Bateke plateau, the most that could be obtained was 12 m³/ha/year with *Acacia auriculiformis*, whereas the fallow with a ten year growth, treated from the eighth year, had a surface area of 14.98 m²/ha and an average height of 8.75 m, giving a production of 13 m³/ha/year (BLANCHET, pers. comm.). The industrial reforestations of eucalyptus in semi-arid zones of Senegal have not achieved a higher average annual production than the natural formations that were replaced at great cost.

Of course, one of the chief obstacles to regeneration and good growth of woody perennial vegetation in arid zones is the aridity itself.

The socio-political obstacles to the development of woody perennials are significant. Since the majority of lands are public property or owned collectively, everyone pillages them without caring what will become of them. Now, whether it is a question of wood production, forage or whatever, it holds that the only way to bring a little organization to bear is to hand responsibility over to the users. If the area is to be productive on a regular and sustained basis, it must therefore be recommended that funds be allocated to individuals. Declaring, for example, that pasture lands belong to all, cannot but lead to the destruction of these lands, if the people are not aware of the need for a management strategy or are unable to implement such a strategy.

There is a general lack of awareness among the populations most directly concerned of the importance of keeping the woody plant cover productive and developing it. It is probably this fact, and the absence of political will of governements, that forms the greatest obstacle to conservation and development of woody plants in arid zones. There are, however, exceptions, usually when the situation has become critical and the solution hard to find. The example of northern Ivory Coast (Ferkessedougou, Siemantaly, Korhogo) is significant in this regard. In the country as a whole there is little concern over the question of firewood. Increased oil production, covering 125% of national consumption, the start of exploration for off-shore gas and the opening of a highly sophisticated oil-cracking plant give many people the impression that the problem of rural energy will be largely resolved by gas. However, in some regions the problem of supplies of fuel for burning is rapidly becoming very serious. Around Korhogo, where people burn millet stalks and cow pats for lack of wood, in Ferkessedougou and in Siemantaly, where some thorough research (Dosso *et al.*, 1981) has revealed the precise extent of the problem, the situation is acute. Twenty years ago firewood was plentiful in these regions, but today the villagers have to walk 3 km in search of wood. What will happen in a few years, when the wood-gathering circles of the different villages overlap, bearing in mind that the villages are, on average, 8 km apart? The problem is equally acute for those who, instead of going to gather it, buy wood, as do many state employees. The price of wood and charcoal is rocketing and is becoming a heavy burden on the family budget, especially in large urban centres, Abidjan in particular, where the price of a useful therm from firewood is as much as 440 CFA Fr. whilst it costs only 45 CFA Fr. at Bouake.

4.4 MEASURES AIMED AT MANAGING NATURAL WOODY PERENNIAL VEGETATION

The most useful step that can be taken is first of all to protect existing vegetation. The difficulty here is that this often comes down to saying to the people: 'Die, but don't use these shrubs either for your animals or for cutting firewood', which is naturally received very badly. It is necessary to be able to offer some compensation. This proved impossible at the time of the last exceptional drought in the Sahel; would the situation be any better today? And yet it was a golden opportunity to take advantage of the massive reduction in numbers of cattle to begin proper management of grazing land. Instead of this, priority was given to speeding up the replacement of cattle, and wells were dug, resulting in the further depletion of underground water reserves. At first sight, everything happens in arid ecosystems as though the maximum human carrying capacity had been reached in the absence of any rational controls and as if, at the same time, a rational control method could not be embarked upon without reducing the human load. How, indeed, can protection and supervision be exercised over such vast areas where the woody vegetation is often very sparse? Forestry department resources cannot normally stretch to this, except in the relatively most humid or least degraded parts of the area, where relatively dense wooded areas may still exist; but in such cases, where the forests are often listed, the forester has frequently found himself in a difficult position *vis à vis* the population.

This situation must change and, as Mr. FLORES-RODAS, former Director of the FAO Forests Department, said at the 7th meeting of the Tropical Forests Commission (Rome, 10-12 June 1985), the forester must broaden his outlook and approach to rural development still further. He must no longer continue to set himself apart from the population.

Traditionally, foresters have first and foremost devoted themselves to preserving the national heritage. For this they must be thanked, for without them desertification would have advanced still further than it actually has. Today, foresters must put themselves at the service of the largest group of clients in every nation affected by desertification – the peasant farmers. Strategies, policies, actions must all be realigned to serve the needs of that clientele. This will not be easy, because violent antagonisms sometimes exist and the people will probably need a little time to realize that foresters wish to become their friends and benefactors.

On this subject Mr Nampa SANOGO, Director General of Forests in Mali, declared in April 1983:

'. . . land agents in the forestry service come up against numerous difficulties which explain the slow pace of the processes of evolution: I do not even speak of the inadequate resources available to them, which are a serious handicap for anyone wishing to take action. The biggest problem lies in a certain barrier of incomprehension, mistrust, even hostility between forestry agents and those to whom the forestry service wants to give the benefit of its aid and knowledge, that is to say the people',

and, not content with making a diagnosis of what is wrong, he went on to suggest a remedy:

'. . . Our agents have to be accepted by the people: to achieve this they need to prove that what they say is true, to prove their competence by practical demonstration, to explain what they are doing and even what their policies are, and to educate and heighten the awareness of the population. This can only be done in conjunction with the other services working alongside us'. (KEITA, 1983).

The lack of understanding is often very real, as the following lines of NAJADA (1980) relate: 'It may be that with the sedentary farmers it is relatively easy to explain the usefulness of the tree in a field and the importance of retaining it, both for its immediate exploitation (products) and for the beneficial effects (increase in productivity), but it is very difficult to persuade a 'Bororo' or 'Targui' herdsman not to top a young Acacia or a Balanites (10-15 years old) with a few slashes of his constant companion, the axe or chopper.

Indeed, the nomadic shepherd (in particular) is extremely stubborn and his bearing borders on the insolent. 'Even if you imprison me for 20 years, the day I am released I will start all over again'. Many foresters, (even armed) have had these words from the mouth of herdsmen caught in the act, when they attempt to intimidate or reason with them in order to dissuade them from some extreme form of environmental destruction.

'This explains (without perhaps always justifying) why acts of ill-treatment (handcuffing, corporal punishment) are committed in their turn by nervous agents who have been unable to retain their composure in the face of such defiance', and the author concludes that there is a certain impermeability of mental attitude among users of soil and forest products.

I believe that an erroneous conception of forest space is largely to blame for the mistrust, not to say hostility, felt by populations with regard to the forester. It is because they have kept a separation between the forest, the cultivated area and the grazing area, that foresters have aroused the enmity of farmers and herdsmen. It is a division which is all the more artificial because traditional African usage, which is largely a consequence of ecological conditions, does not lend itself to the Roman distinction between *ager* (the cultivated area), *saltus* (the grazed area) and *sylva* (the forest). In fact, there is only one space, an agro-silvipastoral space, which is used in rotation or simultaneously to produce food and wood and to keep cattle. Shifting cultivation, transhumant stockraising, nomadism and gathering do not lend themselves to fixed land allocation. The directors of the Sahel forestry services, meeting in Dakar in 1976, understood this very well (CILSS, 1976) when they insisted on the point that grazing land fell within their province and, in principle, within their competence.

It is, however, quite clear that space must be perceived as extending far beyond the limits of the forest in the ecological sense (continuous population of trees). If not, one could end up considering that there are sahelian countries with no forestry problem, as COULIBALY (1983) might lead one to suppose; 'Present forest formations throughout all countries are man-made. There are no natural climatic forests. Continual exploitation of trees and the introduction of new species of exotic origin are contributing to the establishment of a particular landscape only faintly resembling the forest formations of tropical Africa as defined in Yangambi'.

A change of attitude is taking place, it would appear, with regard to soil use. The forester is beginning to understand that to be a manager (his most apposite title, in fact) he cannot remain in his ivory tower, behind the increasingly ill-defined frontier of his forest, in a physically arid environment and a human environment in a state of rapid change. The forester must be a manager of grazing land, he must be an agroforester. It is a fact that cattle browse, i.e. consume woody vegetation, as much as they graze, i.e. consume grass. The importance of woody plants in the cattle diet is very great, and it is extremely regrettable that so few efforts have been made by foresters, at least in West Africa, to get to know their woody perennials and propagate forage species. It has even been estimated that in arid zones 80% of digestible proteins consumed by animals during the three driest months

93

come from the woody plants of a single family, the Capparaceae. What do foresters know about the physiology and propagation of the Cadabas, Capparis, Crataevas, the Maeruas, etc.? Yet, a study of these can prove most instructive: it was in this way that *Boscia senegalensis* (Pers.) Lam., generally considered unpalatable, has become, in certain regions of Senegal at least, the species that husbandmen are most eager to see propagated by the foresters (BAUMER, 1981 b). Foresters also tend to close forests to animals, whereas a controlled use of the grassy layers is possible and helps to reduce the fire hazard, which is so damaging.

The forester must no longer limit himself to the forest. He must come out of the woods to see the trees and take charge of them, trees in all their many functions: as producers of wood, but first of all shade, fruit, edible leaves, barks for medicinal use, dyes, forage, and as shelters from wind, etc.

Where intervention in natural formation of woody perennials is concerned, one can do no more than propose guidelines of a general kind, since local conditions vary considerably.

In any steps that may be taken towards intervention, it must be remembered that the environment is particularly fragile. So the motto is 'tread softly and avoid harsh measures'.

Despite an appearance of homogeneity, soils are often patchy, so that what works well on one spot may very well fail ten metres further on. The results of a study done in Guiring (Cameroon) are a good example of this. Table XI shows how four provenances of *Eucalyptus camaldulensis* and five other species reacted to four types of soils (sandy alluvial soil on clay; clayey alluvial soil on sand; clayey vertisol; compacted planosol on alluvia with a surface-impoverished sandy horizon) with a completely overlapping mosaic.

High mortality was observed on the 'compacted' soils, good eucalyptus growth on vertisols and the best growth of all in clay on sand.

Water is nearly always a limiting factor. Rainfall is highly erratic. Therefore there must be flexibility in any instructions for stand management, so that a planned operation can for example be brought forward or delayed so as to coincide with the right climatic conditions.

Since the high cost precludes any chance of forestry services doing all that should be done, it is absolutely essential to have massive participation on the part of the local population, clear definition of ownership of the trees and shrubs planted, ('trees belong to whoever plants them?') and, in an

94

TABLE XI '

Reactions of some woody species to different types in a soil mosaic in Cameroon

	No. of plants	Compacted soil		Sand/clay		Vertisol		Clay/sand	
		H (m)	% success	H (m)	% success	H (m)	% success	H (m)	% success
Eucalyptus camaldulensis									
81/3302 N	189	3.65	44	4.25	70	4.8	61	–	–
80/2865 N	352	3.25	66	3.55	74	4.35	85	4.70	100
78/2148 N	352	3.15	40	2.60	48	4.00	59	5.20	100
80/2810 N	352	2.70	40	3.00	65	4.10	49	5.60	100
Cassia Siamea	28	3.20	17	–	–	–	–	3.45	90
Azadirachta indica	73	2.35	65	–	–	1.90	84	2.90	89
Dalbergia Sissoo	55	2.00	69	–	–	–	–	2.95	95
Khaya senegalensis	23	1.15	75	–	–	–	–	1.40	82
Tamarindus indica	16	–	–	–	–	–	–	0.55	100

certain number of situations, mobile brigades on call to work the ground by machine, for example when the soil is too hard to allow the pre-planting preparation to be done manually.

A question that often arises concerning woody plant vegetations is whether they consume too much water in arid zones, where water is so deficient. One might well ask whether from the standpoint of optimal use of resources it is not preferable to have a grass cover or a woody perennial cover. Trees do indeed require more water and evapotranspire more than grasses. Although few data are available for arid zones, figures for optimum tree cover have sometimes been advanced: the Revised National Forest Policy of 1952 in India recommended that 20% of the territory should be wooded. But as the arid zones of India are subject to a high degree of wind erosion, some authors have recommended that the figure should be increased to 30% and the *ad hoc* Committee for stabilizing the Rajputana Desert, formed by the Indian Government, even proposed a figure of 50%. However, optimum use of resources requires that the needs of the people are met. It is not enough to say that the aim must be to encourage a utilization that produces most while causing least damage to the soil: the greatest production may not be the one that best meets the need of the people; there is a lack of the consideration of quality. Only by asking whether the desires and customs of the people are being satisfied, and the agricultural practices and other local conditions best being met, can the question of choice between wooded cover and grass cover be approached. In the case of Rajasthan, three very important factors were taken into consideration:

– there is a greater fire risk with a grass cover than a wooded cover;

– there are remnants of primitive forests, such as those around the Hunjhunu sanctuary, where the principal species found are *Prosopis spicigera, Tecoma undulata, Capparis* sp.pl., *Salvadora oleoides* and *S. persica:* beneath these forests the soil is thick, more humiferous and in a better condition than anywhere else;

– apart from a few sanctuaries, not an inch of ground is left uncultivated during the rainy season.

Both the wooded and the grass solutions were therefore judged to be impossible and it was logical to turn to an agroforestry solution which consisted of helping the peasant farmers to develop *Prosopis spicigera* in their fields. This species has a very deep root system which does not compete with the crops (millet, maize, beans, etc.), fixes oxygen from the air and enriches the soil with nitrogen, which helps the associated crops instead of creating competition; lastly, it is tolerant of pruning and, because its pods are particularly protein-rich, it feeds a flock of goats which are vital to the peasant farmer for their milk, but also for their hair, hides, horns and meat. This solution, which is the one the people had found for themselves, is comparable to that which the Serer of Senegal have adopted in planting 'kadd' in their fields of millet. It remains to decide on the number of trees to the hectare per age category, which is where research work comes in. Green fences of *Euphorbia royleana* are also planted round field edges to make a sort of windbreak network; this species was chosen because the young *Prosopis* that can be planted there grow through the hedge quite easily towards a place in the sun.

4.5 FOREST SPACE

Forest space in the new expanded sense in which it will be understood from now on cannot be separated from agricultural space. Gathering supplies an important part of the food for rural populations. In the Sahel, at least thirty plant species are currently used in human food, among the best known of which are baobab, jujube, shea butter, African locust. In times of famine, gathering may account for up to 80% of all food, whereas it only provides a small percentage in a normal year. Wild game is also much prized and a very important part of food gathering. Despite its greater resistance than domestic animals to drought, its adaptability to difficult conditions, disease resistance, the protein-rich meat it affords, and in many ecosystems, particularly very arid or very wet, its productivity, very little effort has been made by foresters to develop it. It is true that there is a serious problem with parasites from game meat, but little has been done to overcome this. The supply of wild game to feed people is less vulnerable in times of drought than is the supply of domestic cattle. Lastly, unlike conventional stock, wild game can re produce in difficult ecological conditions without causing damage to the environment.

However, forest space cannot be dissociated from the agricultural milieu for another, even more important reason. The forest protects the soil and maintains the fertility of the land, not only over the areas that it occupies but also over a vast area which is protected by its influence. One could even say that on generally fragile soils like those of arid zones, the fertility of the territory cannot be maintained without disproportionate expense except by retaining some wooded cover to protect the soil. There is a danger that this measure – or lack of it – will soon be illustrated in the Ivory Coast where, since February 1983, considerable areas have been destroyed by bush fires or at least swept by these fires (ten times more, it appears, than in the previous years). Change in the albedo brings a high risk of drawing southwards the hot, dry winds from the north (harmattan) and it is then that one might see the advance of desertification from the induced effects of degradation of the plant cover.

However, perhaps the most important role of the forest is to maintain biological diversity in an unpolluted state. The forest is a complex ecosystem, whose biocenosis comprising trees, other plants, animals and, naturally, man, is in constant interaction with the physical environment. Man, or rather human society, is without doubt the most active and most important factor in the system. That ecosystem in constantly evolving. Its different components and their relationships vary with time. Change in a single component affects many others. In the present state of knowledge and despite great strides made by science, we are a long way off from being able to predict the global effects of change in one element in an ecosystem. If one considers the principal (by virtue of being the most active) component in the ecosystem, man, one has to take account into all his relationships, some intraspecific (socio-economic, physiological, etc.) and others interspecific (with the other elements of the forest) This is the totality that needs to be comprehended.

Forest spaces remain among the chief areas where a complex ecosystem that is much less altered by man than other ecosystems is maintained. In the light of what has been said above, it seems to me a wise precaution, not one that can be quantified economically, to preserve them for future generations. It is not a question of moral duty, but more a necessity. Despite all the progress of technology, life on our planet remains dependent on the action of chlorophyll. This simple fact should give us pause for reflection on our own helplessness. We have no reason to believe that we would be shielded from unexpected major disruptions of the equilibrium, which present technology would be powerless to respond to.

When giving instructions for the management of natural woody perennial vegetations in the dry zone, the role of plants and woody plant vegetations as windbreaks should not be forgotten. Even undergrowth helps to slow the wind, as is often seen by the accumulations or even the micro-barkhans that form at the base of small bushes only 20 to 30 cm high; if the wind is swirling and the sand abundant, these windward sandy formations are sometimes completed to leeward by tapered triangular tongues pointing in the direction of the wind. If the undergrowth is very crowded, the micro-barkhans join up, forming sand barriers which gradually build up . . . and bury the bushes; but some perennial woody species adapt well to invasion by sand and continue to develop their aerial system above the surface of the sand while the stem is buried, sometimes under several metres of sand: examples are to be found in *Leptadenia pyrotechnica, Retama Raetam,* even *Acacia tortilis* and *Salvadora persica* in which there have even been reports of adventitious roots forming on the part of the trunk buried in the sand.

It should be remembered that it is the water available in the soil and not the total water which it contains that is the important factor in plant nourishment. In practical terms, the same amount of water is more available in sand than in clay to most plants (since they do not all have the same physiology). The water balance of dunes has been studied to find out in which part of the dune the greatest amount of available water for plants lies and consequently where vegetation, natural or introduced, has the best chance of growing. In shifting dunes with a gentle slope to windward and a steep slope to leeward, the greatest mass of available water is generally found under the thickest part of the dune and nearer the leeward than the windward side, which is understandable because the windward side undergoes a higher rate of evaporation because of that very wind. In the example of agroforestry based on *Prosopis spicigera* already mentioned for Rajasthan, each tree acts individually as a windbreak and it has been observed that on fields not planted with Prosopis a thicker veil of sand is deposited than in the shelter of those that are treed. What remains to be determined – and that depends on local conditions: sand granulometry, abundance of sand source, wind speed, etc – is the ideal number of trees per unit of surface area, when attempting to reconcile the following opposing functions:

too many trees: leave insufficient light or space for growing crops,

not enough trees: make inefficient windbreaks and do not provide sufficient browsing to maintain the goats, which are essential.

It is generally accepted, as for *Faidherbia albida* in Senegal, that about forty mature trees per hectare is the maximum and twenty-five the optimum number; but younger plants must also be included, to ensure renewal. Finally, it should be noted that in the case of the Rajputana 'Desert' the windbreak effect of Prosopis in the middle of fields is appreciable when all the fields are planted with trees, whereas a single planted field has no appreciable windbreak effect.

The effects of woody perennial formations on the regulation of water systems and on halting erosion are well known. By contrast, far less is known about their role in overall air temperature; in a tree's shade the heat is less, but is there less heat in a landscape covered by forest? Nor has any possible role in increasing rainfall yet been proved and it seems reasonable to accept the conclusion of GOLDING (1970): 'The maximum effect that can reasonably be attributed to the forest represents only a 5% increase in rainfall, and that only under particular conditions'.

In establishing directives for the management of perennial woody vegetations, one must not lose sight of the part they play in human health and in the oxygen/carbon dioxide balance, although this latter aspect is only meaningful in terms of Planet Earth. However, man will only ensure his well-being if he acts in unison with the rest of mankind. It does not appear that the total complement of wooded formations currently existing on earth can generate enough oxygen to compensate for the disturbing rise in the carbon dioxide content (HOFFERT, 1974). This increase certainly activates the photosynthetic process and therefore the release of oxygen, but lack of phosphates and nitrates limits plant growth. However, net primary productivity of the sylva is 13 t/ha/year, hardly less than that of swamps (15 t/ha/year) and more than that of all the other terrestrial ecosystems (DUVIGNEAUD, 1974). The role of the forest in atmospheric composition is underlined by the following data:

- the inhabitants of a town with population of 100 000 have an oxygen requirement equivalent to the production of 3 000 ha of forest,

- in one flight a Boeing 747 flying between Paris and Bamako (Mali) consumes more oxygen than the forest of La Faya (S.E. of Bamako) provides in one year.

It is a question of order of magnitude and one cannot generalize. As for their role in matters of health, perennial woody vegetation has not received much attention from researchers and it is only really when it is dense that any such work has been considered. The forest plays a role in the health of man; this is true at least on a psychological level, even if it has not yet been proved scientifically beyond any doubt.

It is often asserted that the air is purer in a forest than anywhere else and that it does the body good to be in a forest. This is really an old wives' tale. It is true that there are fewer sources of pollution in a forest than in a town, also less noise, but it is also true that much of the taller vegetation that is found in the forest produces phytoncides. Very few results have yet been obtained on the effects of these products in nature: LAKHNO (1972) published a monograph on the importance to health of the phytoncides; Soviet researchers have probably done the most work in this field, among them TOKIN who wrote (1963): 'Plants at a distance can halt or stimulate germination in other plants . . . They play a role in the mutal relationships between organisms within biocenoses'.

5. PROBLEMS PRESENTED BY DESERTIFICATION

5.1 THE EFFECTS OF WIND

The wind is an important climatic factor in the desertification process. It is a mechanical agent, direct or indirect, and it affects the physiology of plants.

The direct mechanical action of the wind results in bent stems and torn leaves. If the wind is very strong, it may uproot plants, especially tall trees. A moderate wind, especially when it is constant, can cause tearing of leaves; in the irrigated regions of Somalia which are not far from the sea and exposed to two monsoons as well as to sea breezes, a considerable number of broad-leaved crops (banana, maize, sorghum, millet) have their leaves torn by the wind. A plant having its leaves shredded in this way loses some of its photosynthetic capacity and its production is reduced.

The wind acts mechanically in an indirect way by hurling particles (grains of sand) against plants; this sometimes damages them sufficiently to kill them, and in every case reduces their yield.

But the most harmful action of the wind is, without doubt, the increased evapotranspiration it causes in plants. In the Sahel, in particular, the harmattan, a dry wind from the north east which blows almost constantly from November to February/March, causes great dessication of soils and vegetation.

Finally, the wind is the driving force behind wind erosion. Millions of tons of sand and dust are shifted by wind action. The less hard rocks are worn away, they disintegrate and blow away as dust particles. Soil deflation has to be balanced against wind deposits; the total is positive or negative, from the quantitative point of view, but from the qualitative standpoint there is always a loss, either because the elements deposited as a whole have little agronomic value (for instance the Nubian sandstones eroded by the wind in Egypt and propelled towards Sudan and Chad), or because the transported soils are destructured and their components deposited erratically so that a soil is not reconstituted (a great many very fine particles carried south from the Mediterranean pass right over the Sahara without being deposited, and fall into the Caribbean Sea).

The more friable the soil, the more pronounced the erosive effects of

101

wind. The most effective protection against wind erosion is a fairly dense plant cover that is continuous in time and space. This is impossible on cultivated soils which are of necessity denuded, at least partially, at harvest time. The fragility of agricultural soils is increased once the harvest has been lifted: at that moment the soil is bare and unprotected. This becomes more significant when population density outstrips the limit of its capacity, for then the whole land area is cultivated and, since there are not normally any green hedges and still less any windbreaks, wind erosion takes place on a grand scale, unhampered by any obstacle. Around Zinder in Niger, where the population is more than $70/km^2$ or almost double the acceptable level, agriculture is continually pushing northward, since the Government has not persisted in applying its sensible legislation forbidding domestic agriculture north of the 400 mm isohyet. The result has been a fall in the average production of staple cereals (especially millet) from 599/ha to less than 499/ha in the last twenty-five years and, less visible but more dangerous, scouring of the surface horizons least poor in organic matter: impoverishment of the soil causes loss of productivity and the situation worsens, following a vicious circle, since reduced productivity means a reduction in the amount of organic matter returned to the soil.

Wind even has an undesirable effect on animals, increasing their transpiration rate and their water requirement. Dessicating winds of great strength, so laden with grains of sand, loam and dust that groundlevel visibility is no more than a few metres, such as the 'habub' in Sudan which sometimes blows for several days at a time, can be very harmful and even cause deaths among animals, especially sheep (nearer to the ground than cattle), as in Kordofan in 1960. The animals grow thin, they are blinded, wounded, they dare not move, burying their head in the fleece of another animal in an attempt to protect themselves, and they can die of thirst and dessication if the 'habub' blows for a long time. Even sheep with a high drought tolerance, needing water only every four days, such as the 'kababish' or desert sheep, can suffer major losses. In Dar Maganin, in Kordofan, shepherds have even been known to get lost in a 'habub' and to die of thirst.

Constructing networks of curtain shelters, windbreaks and mini-windbreaks is the solution that springs to mind for combating the effects of wind. The terms denoting these structures are imprecise and I propose to apply the term 'windbreak' to a line of trees, bushes or shrubs in single or double rows, either of one or several species, arranged in such a way as to reduce wind speed, generally perpendicular to the prevailing wind or the wind most harmful to the crops or animals to be protected. For our purposes, a curtain-shelter is a wooded strip, much wider than a windbreak, which may be anything from several dozen to several hundreds of metres deep. I shall call a mini-windbreak a linear wind barrier of small plants, not necessarily woody perennials, generally located within cultivated plots, not round the edges, as these plots may themselves be protected in turn by windbreaks. It is also theoretically possible to have a network of shelter with three different meshes: a wide mesh of curtain shelters, a second mesh of windbreaks and a third of mini-windbreaks. But in talking of windbreaks in general this includes windbreaks in the strict sense, curtain shelters and mini-windbreaks.

Three points should be borne in mind with regard to windbreaks:

– there is very little way of measuring their impact in regions subject to desertification;

– the wind can also be slowed down by scattered trees, if there are enough of them;

– the effect of the windbreak can be negative, either because it creates whirlwinds if it is badly constructed (particularly wind blowing under a windbreak made of trees whose canopy is high off the ground), or by raising the already often very high daytime temperatures, especially in arid and semi-arid zones.

Mini-windbreaks are often made with Gramineae: *Andropogon gayanus* in the Kano region in Niger, *Sporobolus festivus* or *Setaria pallide-fusca* formerly in Darfur, *Oxytenanthera abysinica* in the Nuba Mountains. They can be particularly useful in irrigated crops; since the soil is better there than elsewhere, the peasant farmer often hesitates to plant proper windbreaks which will necessarily occupy some of the land, whereas he is less reluctant to plant a mini-windbreak which takes up little space, especially if it is fast-growing and provides needed products, such as *Oxytenanthera* stems for making hurdles or for stakes (haricot beans, cowpeas, tomatoes, aubergines . . .). A large number of low, very thin obstacles are enough to slow the wind down appreciably, so that the mere act of digging over a cereal field after harvest without turning the clods over, leaving the straw standing upright, constitutes an appreciable check to wind erosion. In addition, the stubble helps water infiltrate into the soil.

Among the first windbreaks planted in Africa south of the Sahara, those in North Cameroon, first planted in 1955 with *Cassia Siamea* have given remarkable results, and the network of windbreaks there is literally shaping the landscape, (e.g. north of the Kapsiki Mountains) into a kind of farmland enclosure.

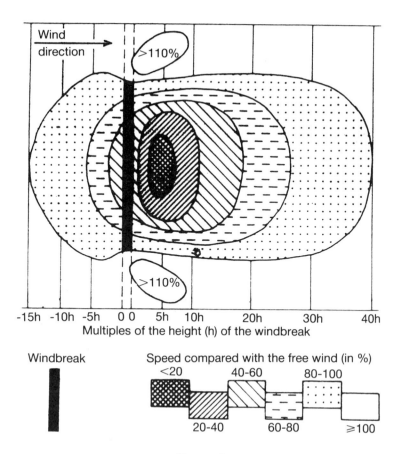

FIGURE 6
Reduction of windspeed around a windbreak of moderate permeability (after
GLOYNE, 1955)

In Senegal, the fixing of the coastal dunes along the 'Grande Côte' has
been combined with a vast coastal curtain shelter of Casuarinas. The first
introductions of Casuarina in the Cap Vert peninsula were made between
1905 and 1914 to fix the sands. They have been poorly respected by the
population. In a communication to the Paris Academy of Sciences in 1950,
Auguste CHEVALIER deplored the reduction and poor state of these pioneer
plantations. Planting on maritime dunes to control sand encroachment
began in 1950 but was stopped in 1960; it was resumed in 1975 as part of a
UNDP/FAO Project based near Kebemer which developed planting techniques and reduced the cost of planting so much that two sponsors, the
IDRC and USAID, agreed to extend the established coastal windbreak, to
the north and south respectively, so that today almost all the Grande Côte
dunes are fixed, and at the same time crops in the vicinity of the curtain

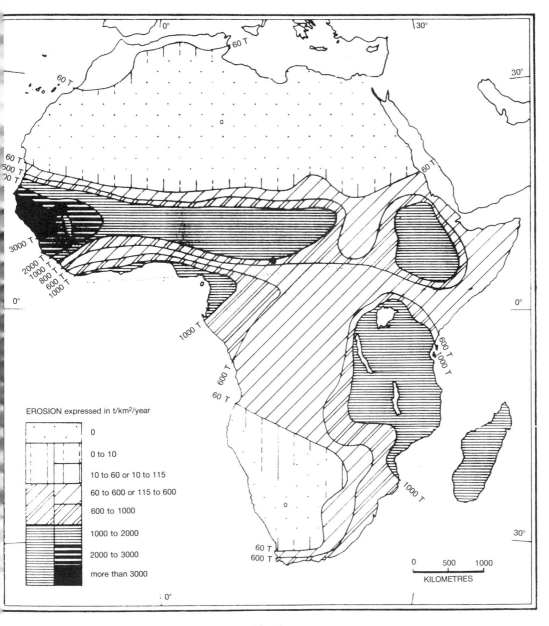

EROSION expressed in t/km²/year

. .	0
I I	0 to 10
	10 to 60 or 10 to 115
▨	60 to 600 or 115 to 600
☰	600 to 1000
≡	1000 to 2000
▤	2000 to 3000
■	more than 3000

Map 1.
'Normal' erosion for Africa (after Fournier, 1960)

105

shelter are protected. This success of *Casuarina equisetifolia* on very poor sand is due to nocturnal condensation of humidity off the sea and the presence on the roots of nitrogen-fixing bacteria, identified by DOM-MERGUES as belonging to the genus *Frankia*.

In the same way, in Sine Saloum, Senegal (rainfall 900-1,000 mm) windbreaks of cashew trees have been developed on sandy soils. The cashew tree is fairly drought resistant and its very low, dense crown makes a good windbreak.

However, *Anacardium occidentale* needs to be planted very close to make an effective windbreak and, in those conditions, yields of cashew nuts are small.

The windbreaks in the Maggia Valley, Niger, were planted between 1975 and 1983. They are in a drier area than those already mentioned, with a mean annual rainfall of around 400-500 mm. Composed entirely of neem trees at the start of the planting campaign, they proved to be only partially effective because eddies were created by the wind passing over their tops. They have been improved by interplanting *Prosopis juliflora,* and then *Acacia nilotica*. The wind speed is reported to have been reduced by between 65 and 80% and the smallholder farmers have seen an increase in yield of around 15 to 25% in the sheltered cereal crops, taking into account the surface area occupied by the windbreaks.

Hedges – whether or not they form part of an alley cropping system – can also act as windbreaks, provided they are placed at the appropriate angle to the wind. Even simple barriers of dead thorny branches often cause sand heaps to form at their foot, proving that they do actually reduce windspeed.

5.2 QUANTITATIVE SOIL LOSS

Africa is unfortunate in having the area in the world with the highest normal water erosion rate. Around the Fouta Djalon massif and throughout Guinea Bissau and Sierra Leone, the amount of earth displaced each year by water erosion is put at more than 3 000 t/km². Surrounding this centre of erosion is a sort of halo covering a good part of Senegal, Western Mali, and parts of the Ivory Coast and Liberia, where normal erosion each year removes 2 000-3 000 t/km². Each year, between 1 000 and 2 000 t/km² are lost in Madagascar, Burundi, Rwanda, a large part of Ethiopia and Mozambique, Tanzania, Malawi, a large part of Zambia, Zimbabwe and Kenya, and a vast territory to the west of Jebel Marra (Sudan) reaching to the Atlantic, approximately between lat. 10° N and 15° N, taking in Sudan, Chad, Cameroon, Niger, Nigeria, Benin, Togo, Ghana, Burkina Faso,

106

Mali and Senegal. Territories forming an arc around the Gulf of Guinea also lose 1 000-2 000 t/km^2. Map 1 (after FOURNIER, 1960) shows the 'normal' erosion for Africa.

The other ACP countries of the Caribbean and the Pacific have equally high normal erosion, estimated at between 1 000 and 2 000 t/km^2/year and slightly less for the south of Guyana.

The data given above refer only to water erosion. To these soil losses, already considerable, must be added losses caused by wind erosion.

If Africa loses immense quantities of soil, it is a fact that less than 18% of those theoretically cultivable (but at great cost) soils are actually cultivated, whereas the proportion is 42% in Central and South-East Asia, and 32% in Central America. Africa feeds fewer than three people per cultivated hectare, whereas Central Asia feeds more than eight. The percentage of land affected by water erosion in Africa is, however, only 11.6% and the total of degraded land is only 35.4% compared with 50% in India and more than 60% in the Middle East. The FAO, jointly with UNFPA and IIASA, has evaluated the present and future human carrying capacity of the land in developing countries. Map 2 (FAO, 1984) shows that between now and the year 2000 some countries will no longer be able to meet the needs of their population out of their own resources, unless a very strict policy is implemented to restrict the birth rate, a very intensive agricultural technology with mixed cropping adopted and massive soil conservation undertaken.

Agroforestry can play a part, but it alone cannot solve all the existing problems. The sorts of measures where the agroforestry approach can help to check quantitative soil loss are listed below (the letters AF have been used to indicate measures where an agroforestry approach can improve the results).

1. Reforestation of land, especially the upper slopes of catchment basins and steep hillsides. AF: correct choice of multi-purpose species, with controlled exploitation.

2. Reforestation and grassing of ravines and building of small dams. AF: correct choice of multi-purpose species, as in (1).

3. Construction of banks, terraces and steps. AF:reinforcement of these structures with rows of woody perennials benefiting production.

4. Planting along contour lines. AF: as in (3), with low hedges rather than trees which would compete with crops; for example, hedges of nectar plants in sunflower crops to encourage bees, which will increase sunflower

seed production and their oil content.

5. Construction of banks to stop surface runoff. AF: accentuate these banks by rows of trees with functions adapted or complementary to the main use (e.g. forage trees with grazing land, or fruit trees with cereal crops).

6. Bank protection. AF: planting along banks of rivers, lakes, reservoirs and canals, to build up as much as possible the mesh of a windbreak network.

7. Reinforcement of banksides of communication routes. AF: well-chosen low woody perennials are often more productive than the grasses generally used for this purpose.

None of these measures is exclusively the province of agroforestry. It must always be remembered that agroforestry is not an isolated technology but one of the many integrated approaches to rural development problems.

A number of agroforestry practices – but not exclusive to agroforestry – are effective against soil losses. Such practices will be used in combination to manage a catchment basin. For this, the principles to be followed will be:

   – to locate all earth works, lay-outs and construction according to contour lines: these will be strictly followed in any ploughing, banking, terracing, soil digging and planting; they will almost be followed for drainage channels, ditches and flood diversion canals; paths and roads will be placed obliquely to them:

   – 'to reinforce', physically and morally, the idea of the horizontality of contour lines by planting woody perennials along them; these plants will have a triple role: they can directly make or reinforce break lines against erosion (for example, fig trees or vines planted at the base of 'fanya juu' banks in Kenya, or hedges along a micro-bank): they make up elements in the permanent landscape structure which oppose any form of shifting cultivation or nomadic husbandry, forming corridors along which it is easier to control the gradual advance of the herds; lastly, if the woody perennials are wisely chosen for their positive ecological and/or economic interaction with other soil uses – thereby constituting an agroforestry system – they have an impact both direct and indirect on production, contributing their fruits, leaves, wood, etc. to the total crops and benefiting other crops by their presence.

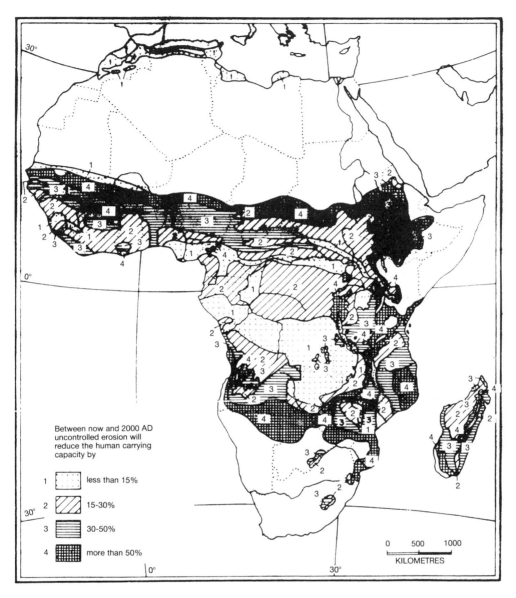

Between now and 2000 AD uncontrolled erosion will reduce the human carrying capacity by

1	less than 15%
2	15-30%
3	30-50%
4	more than 50%

0   500   1000
KILOMETRES

Map 2.
Predicted reduction of human carrying capacity (after FAO, 1984).

109

In using woody perennials to control losses from the soil it is not enough to plant them, even along contour lines. They also need to be managed appropriately. For instance, not all the woody perennials along a single contour line should be filled at the same time. A contoured wooded strip may be completely cut down or, if it is a mixed species strip, it can be cut selectively, avoiding cutting adjacent stands so as not to create a hole in the line of defence. It must be remembered that woody plants, while holding the soil in place with their root systems, also combat erosion by retaining rain on their leaves, so reducing the impact of raindrops on the earth. However, too much shade is often harmful to associated crops and that is why, in the final analysis, the role of the roots is taken into consideration far more often in practice than the role of the foliage.

5.3 Soil fertility

In Africa 'the whole colonization venture was largely inspired by the notion that there were vast stretches of good land available in the tropics' (GIRI, 1985). We know better today; it is now known that the majority of tropical soils, particularly those in arid and semi-arid zones, are poor and fragile. 'The majority of African soils are delicate, deficient in organic matter and generally no more than moderately fertile' (WORLD BANK, 1981). In Burkina Faso, for instance, more than half the soils are very low in organic matter, 85% are low in phosphorus and 61% are nitrogen impoverished. In almost all areas affected by or threatened with desertification, agricultural yields are mediocre because of impoverished, and often eroded, soil. What is more, those yields are falling in many countries, because the land is being continuously exploited without the long fallow periods of the past; the population increase makes it impossible to rest the land for the same length of time as formerly. To add to this, the acidity of the soils and the high temperature do not encourage bacterial activity nor, generally speaking, that of the microfauna and microflora so necessary to the soil. As we have already seen, these soils are also threatened by wind and water erosion. It is reasonable to believe, therefore, that the poverty of the soils is the main reason behind the poverty of the people, and if the only means of arriving at a balance between supply and demand (such as existed when a small population made it possible to practise a shifting cultivation and long fallow periods) were to return to long fallow periods, it would only be to witness an acceleration of soil degradation and general impoverishment.

There is certainly, in theory, one solution: widespread use of fertilizers. But their impact is fairly minimal in the prevailing ecological conditions, and anyway neither the peasant farmer nor the State have the means to pay for the considerable quantities of chemical fertilizers that would be needed. Maybe it is better for them to be dependent on foreign aid for cereals rather than on foreign aid for artificial fertilizers. As we shall see (sections 6.3 and 6.4), agroforestry can help to improve soil fertility to some extent.

The main obstacle to improvement of agricultural output in these countries could be the failure of production systems to adapt:

- the failure of traditional systems to adapt. These were perfectly logical and balanced so long as the population density was low, making it possible to cultivate none but the best land and to have long fallow periods, but this is no longer possible today; one should not underestimate the loss of nutrients that the soil suffers because sometimes a very large part of animal dung production is burned for fuel (BENE *et al.*, 1977). In fact, the fertilizer value of the dung of undernourished animals is low.

- lack of adaptation of imported systems that do not fit in with local customs and traditions. These systems involve costly technological input which neither the peasant farmers nor the State can take advantage of without increasing their dependence, which remain heavily oriented towards export crops and encourage urban areas to economically exploit the rural areas.

Could there not be some adaptation of systems of production which would allow endogenous development? Will not a reaction to the pressing constraints that he is experiencing lead the African peasant to devise a new system, which the history of the peasantry in Europe and other parts of the world shows can be done? In Africa there are examples of ethnic groups who, because they have been hounded out of their lands, subjugated by invaders and forced to take refuge in areas little suited to agriculture, have succeeded in inventing a workable system of production. The examples of the Dogon and of the Mandara Mountains are presented in Appendix 3. The case of the Nubas in Sudan is also interesting: forced off the plains by invading Arabs, they took refuge on the piled granite or sandstone blocks which are the Nuba Mountains and on other scattered heights. There they built low stone walls, brought earth from the plains up on their heads to make micro-terraces that they could cultivate, and on the mountain tops dammed up fissures in the rocks to create water tanks, and there they managed to survive, to retain – at least until the Islamization campaigns of recent years – their cultural identity and to live a life which was no poorer, whichever way one looked at it, than the life of their neighbours.

In a single territory, contrasting methods of exploitation, each one different for each ethnic group, give weight to the theory that improvement

111

of systems of production is indeed possible. The Lela of Togo, studied by RARRAL (1968), obtain derisory yields and only just manage to survive on their 3 or 3.5 ha per active (!) head of population with long fallow periods of 15 to 20 years, while a few kilometres away, on the same soils, some Mossi, 5 to 8 times more numerous per unit of land, produce far more on only 1 ha per active person, because they manure their fields. At the beginning of the century, the Serer of Senegal were feeding 50 people to the km² while the neighbouring land supported no more than 10. At that time, the Serer were already going in for permanent cultivation of their fields, but they made intensive use of animal manure and 'sas' (the Serer name for *Faidherbia albida*). The 'Le Monde' newspaper of 27 September, 1981 reported the successes of a small farmer from Piedmont, settled, since 1973, some 80 km from Ouagadougou, who recounted: 'With my system, although this year's rainfall has only been 480 mm instead of the normal 750 mm, I have achieved a (cereal) yield of almost 2 t/ha instead of the 400 to 500 kilos usually achieved by peasant farmers here', and an Italian Catholic priest near Kedougou, in Burkina Faso, was having success around 1973 in growing and producing fruit from vines so that he did not need to import wine for celebrating Mass . . . I tasted his wine and it was very good. Some regions of India as arid as the Sahel support 200 people per km², to a standard of living hardly different from that of Sahelians.

These examples seem to indicate that the poverty of African soils is not perhaps the major obstacle to improving the situation, and that it is rather that the majority of peasant farmers have not yet discovered for themselves how to obtain the best from their land. CHATEAUBRIAND was over-generaliz- ing when he wrote 'The forest precedes people, the desert follows them', but it is true to say that soils are partly what men make of them, and SCHUMACHER (1978) was moved to write: 'Study what sort of treatment a society subjects its land to and you will come to quite reliable conclusions as to the future it is storing up for itself'.

In only the last few years in Africa, south of the Sahara, longer in the Caribbean and Pacific states where extreme population pressure have forced innovations to take place, there has been a noticeably more pro- nounced trend among farmers to accept innovations and experiment them- selves. It is the most hopeful indication that there may be a resolution to the agonizing problems of malnutrition and starvation. Agroforestry experi- ments play a leading role in this new approach. Remarkable results are being obtained. Here is one example from near Mombasa (MACHEMBE *et al.*, 1983):

Young *Prosopis juliflora* (6 years old) produced 209 m³ of stems and 75 m³ of thick branches per hectare, and a total biomass of 216 t. The leaves

112

TABLE XII

Characteristics of certain legumes commonly used as understorey crops in agroforestry

| | Period | | Habit Variations | | | | cycles (days) | Ecology | | | | soil pH |
	annual	perennial	erect	climbing	trailing	bush		alti-tude (m)	temper-ature (°C)	sensi-tivity to frost	rainfall (mm)	
Vigna unguiculata (L.) Walp. = V. sinensis black-eyed pea, cowpea	+		+	+	+	+	60-240 or more	< 1500	20-32	+ +	500-1500	various if well-drained and not flooded, ideal pH 5.5-6.5: poor drainage on heavy fertile soil
Vigna radiata (L.) Wilczek = Phaseolus radiatus L. = P. aureus Roxb. mung bean	+		+		+		80-120 or more	<1800	30-35	+ +	750-1000 inc. 400 during growing period	very varied, even clayey, but well-drained and not flooded
Cajanus Cajan (L.) Hillsp. = C. indicus Spreng. cajan pea		+	+				130-220	<2000	18-30	+	500	very varied, but neither too poor in calcium nor flooded; prefers deep loams with pH 5-7

and branches of small individuals representing 22.6% of the biomass contained more than half of the nutrients: 60% of the nitrogen, 57% of the phosphorus, 63% of the potassium, 31% of the calcium and 63% of the magnesium. In the larger individuals, the relative proportions were, 50%, 46%, 52%, 24% and 58%. If only the stems are gathered for firewood and the rest of the plant left on the ground, a high percentage of the nutrients in the biomass can be returned to the soil; 70% nitrogen, 67% phosphorus, 77% potassium, 50% calcium and 73% magnesium, However, the removal of firewood represents per hectare:

    1.7 t of nitrogen
    0.12 t of phosphorus
    1.2 t of potassium
    1.4 t of calcium and
    0.1 t of magnesium,

and in order to maintain productivity at the same level, the same amounts of each would have to be put back into the ground in the form of fertilizer or compost.

Table XII gives an example of the chief properties of certain legumes, which have nitrogen-fixing properties, much used as understorey crops in agroforestry.

Trials and studies abound, and there should soon be twice as much data available on the role of agroforestry in maintaining fertility when, for example, the results of more than 20 projects with a high-profile agroforestry content, currently being carried out by the FAO, have been analysed.

5.4 INCREASING SCARCITY OF FUELWOOD

About one-third of the world's population uses wood and charcoal to produce at least 90% of the energy it consumes. Half a billion human beings are without the means to heat food more than once a day. It has been suggested and rightly, notably at various meetings organized by UNEP and the FAO, that for a vast section of the human race the energy crisis is not so much do to with adjustment in oil prices as with lack of firewood. Experts disagree over the definition of man's energy needs. These depend very much on the way of life among different populations.

However, this dendro-energy crisis is nothing new, as RITTER (1983) recalls. Through the ages, there have been other dendro-energy crises. Like every crisis situation, a dendro-energy crisis arises when there is an imbalance between supply and demand, but the supply varies in the different ecological zones and the demand varies according to the way of life. WINDHORST (1979) has evaluated the average production of woody matter per hectare in the major vegetation formations as follows:

wet rain forests	6 t/ha
temperate forests	4
equatorial plain forests	3.5
wet savannas	2
subtropical sclerophyllous forest	1.3
dry savannas	1
pseudosteppes, more or less wooded	0.05-1

But neither population density nor way of life (which determines level of wood consumption) are distributed according to major vegetation formations. Ways of life have a considerable bearing on wood consumption. It has been estimated (MANSHARD, 1982) that the average wood consumption as a function of stage of development, taking the energy in dry wood to be 3600 Kcal/t/year, is:

food gatherers	0.2 m³
hunters	0.5 (more than double!)
traditional farmers	1.5 (three times as much!)
modern farmers	2.6
men of the industrial age	7.7
men with advanced technology	23.3

Man at the most advanced stage of development uses very little wood as a source of energy. The G/Wi San hunter-gatherers of the central Kalahari used less than 0.1 m³/person/year. By contrast, until the beginning of the industrial age at least, by far the greatest proportion of energy was provided by wood, and there must certainly have been dendro-energy crises when population increases reached a certain level at which energy requirements became greater than the immediate environment could produce. The curves in Fig. 7 show the population densities that can be supported by a vegetation type as a function of the way of life.

For the Sahel, GORSE (1984) has made a conceptual model (Fig. 8) showing that where the upward-trending consumption curve cuts the downward-trending production curve at point 1, shortage begins and energy needs then have to be met from sources other than wood (dried animal excreta . . . or solar energy) and/or by using up the ligneous capital until there is none left: then the reproduction curve cuts the absciss axis at point tz. I have applied this model to the wood requirements of the Sahel. As Fig. 8 shows, the rate at which the fire wood requirement in the Sahel will increase between 1980 and 2000 is alarming.

In the light of projections he made in April 1983 in his capacity as forester for the World Bank, and of the various publications of the FAO

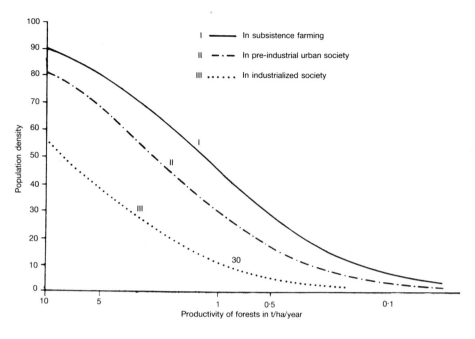

FIGURE 7

Population density and critical point in wood provision (after RITTER, 1983)

(1981 a and b; MONTALEMBERT and CLEMENT, 1983) the situation in the Sahel concerning dendro-energy appears dramatic.

In seven countries (Gambia, Upper Volta, Mali, Mauritania, Niger, Senegal and Chad) covering 5 300 000 km², the population is currently 31 000 000. Of this figure, 4 million live in urban centres. By the year 2000 the population will rise to about 49 000 000, including 9 million town dwellers. Present wood consumption varies according to area, from 0.5 to 1.5 m³ per head/year. It currently stands at 22 000 000 m³ and would normally be expected to rise to 34 000 000 m³ by the year 2000, whereas the theoretical potential for total production would fall in the same period by some 42 000 000 m³ to around 27 000 000 m³. The curves indicating this development intersect towards 1995, which would therefore be the time when demand could no longer be met without destroying the producing capital. In reality, the situation is even more serious, as Fig. 8 shows, since accessible production is hardly more than 17×10^6 m³ (and not 22×10^6) and would drop to 15×10^6 m³ by the year 2000. There is therefore a deficit of the order of $(22 - 17)10^6 = 5 \times 106$ m³ at the present time, which will reach $(34 - 15)10^6 = 19 \times 10^6$ m³ by 2000 AD.

116

What means are available in the seven countries in question to face this situation?

– Bush fallowing will probably diminish but agroforestry measures will probably be developed; so it is accepted that the two agricultural methods together (A on the graph) will continue to produce approximately 12% of maximum consumption by the year 2000, or 4 000 000 m^3, the same as at present: however, if fallow forest land continues to cover some 13 000 000 ha giving on average 0.2 m^3/ha/ year, agroforestry should be able to increase from 12 to 19 million hectares, with production reaching only 2 850 000 m^3/year by 2000 AD, because of low productivity, estimated at 0.15 m^3/ha/year. This estimate ignores the significant increase in firewood production that could be obtained by replacing bare fallow with fallow plus the woody perennial *Leucaena leucocephala,* still at the experimental stage, in particular at the Institute for Savannas in Bouaké (Ivory Coast), the IITA in Ibadan and the Kenya Arid Lands Research Institute (KARI) near Nairobi (Kenya); however, if these experiments are successful, they would not only lead to an appreciable quantity of firewood, but also to good forage (to be used prudently) and an increase in the soil nitrogen.

A look at the curve will explain that in Western Europe the population density never exceeded the critical limit until the advent of the industrial age, whereas in the Fertile Crescent the shortage of firewood must have been felt very early on: in fact, we know that it started to arise 8000 years ago.

– It would be advisable to declare that the remaining forests are a real power reservoir and to strengthen their protection and control by the State, but with the prime aim of producing energy – which is incompatible with the preceding suggestion.

Agroforestry is potentially an important contribution to solving the problem of dendro-energy. During the FAO consultation on dendro-energy held in Addis Ababa on 26-30 November 1984, it was even suggested that agroforestry might well be the last hope of resolving the problem. In fact, agroforestry uses a great number of techniques, each of which, by definition, makes use of woody perennial plants. The cumulative amount of firewood produced by agroforestry is potentially great. The principal agroforestry techniques able to encourage wood production are hedging, windbreaks, fallow land under woody perennials and marginal planting. There are certainly many ACP countries where dendro-energy production is greater in the fields than in the forests. Senegal's Master Plan for forest development indicates that between half and three-quarters or more of rural fuel for burning in the Peanut Basin comes from sources other than forest areas, basically the remaining trees in the surrounding countryside, those left intentionally in the middle of fields like kadd, bushes cleared from fallow ground where that is the current practice, such as *Guiera senegalensis,* but also harvest residue and dung. The history of peanut plantations on Ivory Coast savannas is also revealing. In the North, peanut plantations 6 or 7 years old yielded up to 2,500 kg of fruit on very good soils but only 150 to

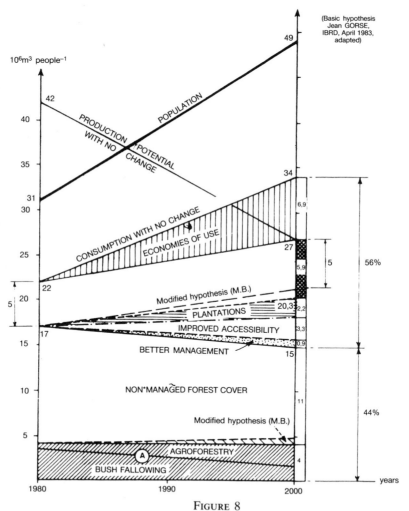

FIGURE 8

Progressive firewood deficit in the Sahel between 1980 and 2000 (after GORSE, 1984, adapted)

118

200 kg on the poor soils that the farmers were prepared to release for planting firewood. But peanut wood is considered poor firewood, making a lot of sparks, few embers and much ash, and interest in it has faded as the problem of firewood supply has increased. It was only in the 1980's that Ivory Coast forestry research in the north began to consider seriously the problem of firewood, and one of the first discoveries made was that little attention had been paid to the acceptability as firewood of the most widely planted species and that many of these such as *Gmelina arborea,* were not popular as firewood with the villagers, or were not very popular, like the eucalyptus or *Cassia Siamea.* Gmelina is said to 'burn round'; the whole piece of wood ignites at once, instead of only one end which can then be pushed gradually into the fire, so controlling the heat. On the other hand, the most popular species for firewood (*Dalbergia Sissoo, Afzelia africana, Ficus Thoningii, F. Roxburghii, Daniellia Oliveri, Anogeissus leiocarpus,* . . .) are hardly used in plantations because their requirements are not well known and because they have the reputation of being very slow growers. However, their yield is not bad and one could quite easily hope for 20 t/ha of firewood in 7 years with a mix of indigenous species, neem and *Cassia Siamea,* as has been demonstrated by the CTFT trials at Dinderesso in Burkino Faso.

But it is becoming increasingly difficult to find plots of land large enough to plant firewood. This is yet another reason to hope that agroforestry can safeguard firewood production: with sixty or so hedges or 100 m long planted rows one can expect to produce as much firewood as on a hectare in the open, planted for this purpose.

For some years efforts have been made to find other ways of obtaining fuel than from the biomass. Figure 9 after LIPINSKY (1978) plots these different ways.

Chemical extraction procedures enable plants to be used as an energy source which would not *a priori* be thought of as such. For example, hexane is extracted from *Calotropis procera.* ARONSON *et al.* (1984) report that from a square metre of plantation, on a single cutting per year, 1 kg of dry matter and 191 g of extractable hexane are obtained, the equivalent of 1.9 t/ha/year of fuel.

This average of 5% extractable hexane is lower than that obtained from other species, like *Asclepias subulatus, Euphorbia mauritanica, E. obtusifolia, E. regis-Jubae, E. Tirucalli* or *Thevetia peruviana,* but if Calotropis gives less in the way of hydrocarbons, it produces more biomass than the euphorbias.

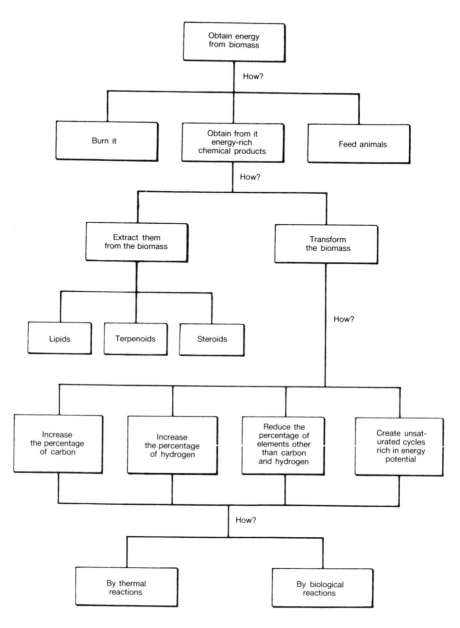

FIGURE 9
Ways of producing energy from biomass (after LIPINSKY, 1978)

Still other species can be grown for hydrocarbon production, such as *Calotropis grandis, Asclepias fruticosa, A. rotundifolia, A. speciosa, Amsonia* spp., *Cryptostegia grandiflora,* and species of the genus *Apocynum, Landolphia, Mascarenhasia* and *Thevetia* and euphorbias like *E. abyssinica, E. balsamifera, E. trigona, E. resinifera.* From this latter, STEINHEIL (1941) obtained 3 t of oil per ha per year. One should be wary, however, of declaring that growing these types of plants can solve the energy problem. As BENEMAN (1979) wrote concerning CALVIN who had predicted (1978) 44 t/ha/year of dry matter from *Euphorbia Lathyrus,* which would exceed the world record for all chlorophyll-assimilating plants for C^3, 'the predicted potential (in dendro-energy) is often inversely proportional to the available information'. In addition, chemical extraction often requires sophisticated technology which may not be within the reach of all developing countries, so that, although the 'Euphorbia' Project in Kenya has given encouraging results as regards biomass production in arid zones, notably with *Euphorbia Tirucalli,* the project has not been extended beyond its initial three-year period because it is evident that in the present state of the Kenyan economy, it is not economic to produce ethanol from biomass. But technically the method has been developed and could be used in other circumstances, for instance if the oil supply were at risk or oil prices rose dramatically. However, there are encouraging results in this field. For example, WEISZ and his co-researchers (1979) have shown that in the laboratory castor oil can give 70% petrol but only 5% gas and 20% oil, whereas jujube oil gives 40% oil and 50% petrol. The range of products obtainable from a single plant by chemical processing is sometimes impressive and perhaps ought to be taken into consideration in the choice of species for agroforestry systems. The following different uses for *Asclepias syriaca,* a woody liana from the arid zones of the Middle East, were studied by BUCHMANN and DOUKE and listed by ARONSON (1984):

Product	% of dry weight	Possible utilization
latex	1.6	rubber
whole plant oil	4.1	chemical intermediaries
polyphenol fraction	7.2	chemical intermediaries
triglyceride oil from the seed	7.2	human food
residue from leaf extraction	16.0	animal food (20% proteins)
fibre ('floss')	11.1	insulating material
'bast fibre'	11.0	rope and paper making
woody parts of pods	12.3	} paper, fuel, furfurol
woody parts of stems	27.6	} compressed panels
	100.0%	

The yield for certain selected elements can also be improved by genetic and/or agronomic treatment. 33% leaf extraction residues can be obtained from a treated species instead of 16% as in the above case from a wild plant, and the amount of latex can increase from 1.6 to 4%.

Genetic engineering opens up new perspectives for plant improvement. CALVIN (1983) and also ARONSON (1984), underline the possibility of borrowing genes from *Copaifera Langsdorfii,* a tropical tree legume, or from Euphorbiaceae of the Croton genus, to boost the potential energy production of *Euphorbia Lathyrus.*

In a few years' time, it is possible that agroforestry systems for arid and semi-arid zones will be devised, in which woody perennials will be used as protection and to assist the growth of new industrial plants at present being researched. Table XIII gives some of these plants that provide oils which could replace oils currently sold on the market.

TABLE XIII

Some plants with oil-bearing seeds currently being researched in the United States (after PRINCEN 1979, 1982, 1983)

Common name of plant	Scientific name and identity	Major uses	Substitutes
crambe	*Crambe abyssinica* (crucifera mediterr.)	lubricants, plastic coatings, foam-inhibitor	rape seed oil
cuphea	*Cuphea* sp.pl.	soap, detergents, special lubricants	coconut oil
lesquerella	*Lesquerella Fendleri* Crucifera of SW USA and N Mexico	lubricant, softener, brake fluid, paint, plastics	castor oil
ironweed	*Vernonia anthelmintica*	coatings, adhesives	epoxydized linseed oil
Stoke's aster	*Stokesia laevis*	coatings, adhesives	epoxydized linseed oil
jojoba	*Simmondsia chinensis*	special ultra-high performance lubricants, cosmetics	whale sperm oil
Chinese tallow tree	*Sapium sebiferum* fast-growing, drought-resistant tree from Asia	liquid fuel	oil

6 SOME AGROFORESTRY PRINCIPLES FOR USE IN COMBATING DESERTIFICATION

A number of the tools and principles of agroforestry are particularly important to bear in mind in combating desertification.

6.1 ROLE OF AGROFORESTRY WOODY PERENNIALS IN CONTROLLING DESERTIFICATION

Woody perennials play a multi-purpose role in agroforestry. They contribute to combating desertification by:

providing a variety of products
organizing the landscape
modifying the climate
bringing about changes in the soil.

Foresters divide woody perennial plants into four categories:

1. *trees*, which are single-stemmed plants more than 7 m tall;

2. *bushes*, which are single-stemmed plants less than 7 m tall;

3. *shrubs*, which are multi-stemmed plants, normally less than 7 m tall; (the underbrush is of low shrubs, less than 1 m in height):

4. Non-grass *lianas* with woody characteristics, which may be several or dozens of metres long and generally require support.

As mentioned before, bamboos and palms, even banana palms (which often have a comparable effect on associated crops to that of woody perennials) and opuntia cacti are often included with woody perennials in agroforestry.

6.1.1 *Role as producer*

Agroforestry systems make every attempt to use multi-purpose woody perennials, i.e. plants that have several uses or products.

The number of uses to be had from a single species is sometimes considerable. Table XIV gives a brief survey of some examples of multiple use for the date palm, tamarind, African locust and the gum tree.

124

6.1.2 *Role in the landscape*

Woody perennials, especially in considerable numbers, play a significant role in ordering the landscape: they break the monotony of arid landscapes and provide landmarks, which is important both practically and psychologically; it is good, when you are journeying on camelback through vast empty spaces, to come across a landmark in the shape of a tree to mark your progress and to provide shade, however sparse, where you can experience a moment of needed rest and relative cool.

Trees *sensu lato* also have an important role to play in the organization of space because they contribute to the establishment of farming rights: traditionally, whoever plants a tree generally has the right to benefit from its products, and, by extension, the planting of trees on a plot of land usually bestows the right to cultivate that land. This is not the case everywhere, however. It is because these rights had been left unclarified that some reforestation operations failed (ARGOULLON *et al.*, 1981): when planters receive no formal assurance that the trees they plant and the products of those trees will be their property, they are not very inclined to plant, only plant if they receive a fee or food in return, and do not maintain the plantations.

So when woody perennials are planted in groups and particularly in rows, they can contribute to management of the territory. Blocks formed by lines of windbreaks in a network can make permanent boundaries which will encourage one farming family to continue cultivating the same block with clearly visible boundaries, rather than to practise shifting cultivation. If the block is large enough, it can then be divided up into plots to allow rotation. This is a kind of shifting cultivation in itself. The difficulty arises because on cultivated land the planting of windbreak networks is usually neglected – as, too, are anti-erosion systems to conserve soils on sloping ground – until after crops have been sown by the farmers and there is recourse to redefining the field boundaries with rows or strips of woody perennials – or by bench terracing or other forms of correction – which farmers do not like. On grazing land, where no rights are established, or no longer so, it is usually easier as far as planting rights go (but more difficult technically because the land is usually more arid than the cultivated land) to use row planting to organize the space. In this way access routes can be marked (to water sources, markets, etc), also cattle grazing routes and blocks of grazing land to be used in rotation, etc.

Table XIV (after VON MAYDELL, 1983 and BAUMER, 1983 b) gives examples of the main uses of four dry zone agroforestry trees.

TABLE XIV

Some uses of four agroforestry trees in dry zones
(after BAUMER, 1983 b and von MAYDELL, 1983)

Name	Trunk or stem	Leaves	Fruits	Bark or fibres	Seeds	Branches and terminal bud	Others
Gum tree (*Acacia Senegal*)	Excellent fire-wood, excellent charcoal	Forage 6.8-7.5 DM/kg of DM with 10-13% DP and 0.12-0.15% P	Forage 4-5 MK/kg of DM, 20% CP and 15% DP and 0.12-0.14% P	Decoctions for gastric infections		Forage	Gum arabic (food, agrofeeding, pharmacy, cosmetics, chemistry, textile & met-allurgy indus-tries, photographic paper), nectar plant. Improves and fixes soil
African locust (*Parkia biglobosa*)	Not very hard or durable but easy to work Bad as fuel	For burns and haemorrhoids	Edible pulp Refreshing fer-mented drink Flour	For colic, vomit-ing, diarrhoea, sterility, bron-chitis, leprosy, venereal disease, pneumonia, caries, filariasis, Guinea worm, oedema, rickets	Vegetable cheese, Seasoning for sauces		Shade Soil improve-ment by the leaves

Species							
Date Palm (*Phoenix dactylifera*)	Very durable, resistant: columns, rafters, water conduits, bridges, fuel	Plaited into mats, baskets, fences, ropes	Delicious long-lasting food of great value, 100 kg/tree/year date syrup	Brushes, brooms	Softened or crushed give: 1. an oil 2. fodder	Palm cabbage, palm wine	Essential shade for oasis crops ornamental
Tamarind (*Tamarindus indica*)	Hardy, hard, durable, coloured: wheels, hubs, tools, gears, mortars, boat planking, toys, furniture, panels Good fuel, excellent charcoal ash for hair removal and tanning	Valuable but undervalued fodder Eaten in soups & sauces Red dye Infusion for asthma, gingivitis & eye inflammations Juice against haemorrhoids and liver complaints	Excellent nutritional value, preservative in various foods (Worcester sauce) Refreshing drink Laxative (Intestinal infections, biliary infections). Poison antidote. Antiscorbutic. Heart toner Gargle. Anti-diarrhoeal ash.	Lotions & compresses for open wounds & skin eruptions	Eaten grilled or fried in flour Eaten by cattle Dressing for wool, jute, paper, printing, glue Oil	Branches favourite food of elephants	Pharmaceutical industry (fruit leaves, bark) Infusion of roots for respiratory ailments and leprosy Nectar plant Ornamental

6.1.3 *Climatic role*

Generally speaking, trees mitigate the effects of climate. This is particularly noticeable in dry zones. The trees have an effect on the air and the wind, on the humidity of the air and the soil, on light and temperature.

On the margins of the Negev desert, ZOHAR (1966) reported by TAPP (1984) showed that an impermeable windbreak increased peanut production by 42%, and this to a distance up to 18 times the height of the windbreak. In the Nile Delta, HUSSEIN (1969) quoted by TAPP (1984) found a 35% increase in the cotton crop, 38% for wheat, 47% for maize and 10% for rice, behind a permeable windbreak up to a distance of 20 times its height.

The FAO report (1976) that in Somalia a 1 km long windbreak made up of two irrigated rows of *Conocarpus lancifolius* produces 350 m^3 of firewood every twenty years, recouping in eight years the cost of planting.

The following make good windbreaks in semi-arid and even arid zones: *Balanites aegyptiaca, Acacia tortilis, Conocarpus lancifolius, Zizyphus spina Christi, A. arabica, A. mollissima, A. nilotica, A. Senegal, Azadirachta indica, Tamarix* sp.pl., *Casuarina* sp.pl., *Eucalyptus camaldulensis, E. microtheca, Parkinsona aculeata, Prosopis* sp.pl., *Terminalia Catapa, Oxytenanthera abyssinica, Dalbergia Sissoo, Leucaena leucocephala, Hyphaene thebaica.*

The qualities of a woody perennial used in this way are:

– adaptability to the local soil
– drought resistance
– tolerance of salinity
– resistance to wind, browsing, pests and diseases
– ease of planting
– regular habit
– rapid growth
– leaf retention for maximum period
– little development of creeping roots
– production: wood, forage, fruits, etc.

Each of these species is best used in the ecological conditions to which it is suited: for example, *Acacia nilotica* will do better than *A. Seyal* on clay; on sand *Conocarpus lancifolius* should a better choice than *Balanites aegyptica*. One should also try to make windbreaks in several storeys with different species: a good combination for an irrigated windbreak in semi-arid zones is an overstorey of *Eucalyptus microtheca*, an intermediate storey of *Leucaena leucocephala* planted on the same line as the eucalyptus and a windward outer row of *Conocarpus lancifolius* cut low to form an understorey.

Even in isolation, a tree has an effect on the wind, by at least altering its course and reducing its force locally. This effect is utilized in windbreaks, aligned perpendicular to the wind, which can be made of dead material (planks, metal sheeting . . .) or of living plants: when these rows are made of bushes and/or shrubs, they are called hedges. This term is also used for alignments of trees.

To be effective and to give the best results, hedges must:

– be filters, that is 40-50% permeable, in order to slow the wind down; an impermeable, or non-filtering, hedge creates air currents that can be more harmful than the wind itself; in the regions where frost is a hazard, permeability reduces frost risk at the foot of the hedge; permeability should increase from the base towards the top;

– be perpendicular to the prevailing wind; if there are several prevailing winds, networks facing several directions are constructed, with the principal lines perpendicular to the most harmful wind (which is not always the strongest if the strongest blows at a season when there is nothing to protect), and the secondary lines perpendicular to other directions;

– be sufficiently long, so that the wind cannot get round them;

– be high, since their effect is felt over a distance proportional to their height;

– not compete with the protected crops, particularly with their roots (this can be reduced by digging trenches to sever surface roots) or overshadow the crops to excess (little risk of this in the tropics where the sun is never low on the horizon);

– be well filled-out below so that the wind does not blow between the trunks beneath the crowns, sometimes with a greater velocity than when there is no hedge at all;

– be as far as possible productive, i.e. not only do service as a windbreak, but provide other usable products: wood, fruits, forage, etc.

129

– be made up of plants of different ages so that they do not all reach the
age for felling at the same time, which would destroy the hedge.

A good hedge, in sum, will be planted in several rows, it will be made
up of trees, bushes and shrubs, not too closely planted and giving a variety
of products, and well filled-in at the base: it will have to be maintained and
rejuvenated by replacing dead plants. Hedges can sometimes be so well
planned that they can make a significant contribution to food production.
In Cameroon, for example, the live hedges of the Bamileke country form a
wood, making an important firewood and timber reserve (*Croton mac-
rostachyus, Ficus* sp. *Markhamia lutea, Albizzia* sp. . . .) and provide
numerous and varied medicinal or edible products (edible leaves of *Ver-
nonia amygdalina*, fruits of *Lannea Afzelii*, avocados, mangoes, kola nuts,
guavas, etc), *Rauwolfia vomitoria* and *Harungana madagascariens* is widely
used in traditional and folk medicine, (rope from the bark of *Peddiea
Fischeri* or *Cordia platythyrsa*, woven baskets and pots for nursery plants
out of the leaves of *Dracaena arborea* . . .). The Bamileke 'bocage' also
acts as a legal boundary to the micro-plot complex which has arisen out of
the relative scarcity of land or high population density (more than 100
people/km^2). Finally, live hedges play a definite role in preventing erosion
and provide the fields with some protection against cattle (DEPOMMIER,
1983).

Given their aim and composition, windbreak hedges have to be considered as part of an agroforestry land use system (DARNHOFER, 1983). For this
reason it seems logical to DARNHOFER 'to apply the principles and methods
of agroforestry to all questions relating to artificial wind protection. Consequently, any demand for a wind protection study should arise from a
diagnostic centred round this problem within the framework of a given land
use system. Because of the complexity of the subject, such an approach
logically requires at each phase, from preliminary diagnostic through to
evaluation of the system adopted, the intervention of a multi-discipline
team of experts'. GUISCAFRE (1961) has given a good description of a
windbreak network to combat desertification in North Cameroon.

Woody perennials, without which agroforestry systems cannot exist,
reduce soil insolation by the shade which they create: this results in a drop
in soil temperature and reduced evapotranspiration, allowing greater biological activity. In arid and semi-arid zones, therefore, there is often more
green matter beneath trees than in the full sun. In the Koutiala region of
Mali, I heard an agronomist reproaching a peasant farmer for having left
too many trees in a field of groundnuts since pod production is less in the
shade than in full sun: the farmer rightly explained that he did not grow
peanuts every year and that two out of four or five years that field was left

fallow, grazed by his animals, and that there was more grass in the shade of the trees than in the full sun; and he added with a twinkle in his eye that even in the years when he did grow peanuts he was not sorry to have a few extra haulms for his cows, which brought him in more than what buyers paid him for his peanuts.

Woody perennials are of special value on grazing land because they are often rich in proteins and provide forage in the dry seasons when there is no more grass, because they allow better grass development in their shade.

6.1.4 *Impact on the soil*

The foliage of woody perennials protects the soil from the pounding of raindrops and in this way helps to reduce erosion. Woody perennials also break down the soil with their root meshes and facilitate water penetration of the soil. They exploit the deep soil with their roots and draw nutrients up into their leaves which, when they rot down on the soil surface, make those nutrients available to more shallow rooting grass or crops.

Some woody plants, such as the legumes, can fix nitrogen from the air and in this way improve soil fertility. Trees traditionally left by Sahelian peasant farmers in their fields include legumes like kadd (*Faidherbia albida*), African locust *Parkia biglobosa*, African rosewood (*Pterocarpus erinaceus*) and bala *P. lucens*, the coral tree (*Erythrina senegalensis*), tamarind (*Tamarindus indica*). Other woody legumes have been introduced, especially for their nitrogen-fixing ability, such as *Leucaena leucocephala* or *Calliandra calothyrsa*.

Dune fixing with woody perennials is not in itself an agroforestry exercise, but it becomes one if the woody perennials not only stabilize the sand but can be made to work for a desired effect on other plants and animals. Behind Merka in Somalia, the scheme for stabilizing the Shalambod dunes could become an agroforestry system: the coastal dunes have been fixed with *Acacia cyanophylla* and *Eucalyptus camaldulensis* and a little humus has started to form on the dunes which have been fixed longest. It would be possible to introduce forage Acacias with a dual purpose, to allow the already present fauna (dik-dik, warthog) to develop, and to exploit the area rationally for the benefit of the local people by cutting branches and transporting them outside the protected dunes area for cattle forage. Since the dunes cover other soils, they make an excellent biome for forestation, particularly if:

- the submerged soil is rich and with no hard crust
- the dune is not too deep

131

so that the roots of subjects planted can take advantage of the subsoil nutrient and water from the sand mass.

The species most used for fixing and rehabilitating dunes in *sensu lato* arid zones include: *Prosopis Tamarugo*, whose salt and drought tolerance is exceptional, but which may require inoculation before planting; *Acacia tortilis*, A. *auriculata*, A. *Senegal*, A. *holosericea*, A. *nubica*, *Prosopis chilense*, P. *cineraria*, P. *juliflora*, *Parkinsonia aculeata*, *Tamarix* sp.pl.; if atmospheric humidity is not too low, bordering the sea for example, the Casuarinas and Opuntias give good results, and can shade cashew, *Leptadenia Spartium* and even Eucalyptus. Finally, several species of Atriplex but especially *Atriplex nummularia* and A. *Halimus*, also *Cassia Sturtii*, make excellent forage underbrush for fixing dunes.

6.2 USE OF MULTI-PURPOSE WOODY PERENNIALS

Agroforestry always tries to use multi-purpose woody plants rather than plants with only one function. One of the reasons is technological efficiency. Another is that this is far closer to the African mentality: just as the peasant farmer sees his physical environment as a whole, with no distinction drawn between *ager, saltus* and *sylva*, so he sees in the tree an indivisible source of services and multiple products. ICRAF has launched an investigation of multi-purpose trees, bushes and shrubs, and a databank is currently being compiled. It is already possible to identify numbers of uses only known to certain groups of people or in certain areas. For example, the possibility of making edible oil from the fruit of *Balanites aegyptiaca*, well known for centuries in the Sudan, by the Kababish, for example, was not known in Kenya, although a neighbouring country, and has just been 'discovered' by UNIDO (1985) along with other properties of this tree. Another example: human consumption of the young leaves of *Moringa oleifera* seems to be known and practised by only about half the areas where this Indian bush has been introduced in Africa and Latin America. The most important use of a species for a given population is not always what the forester thinks.

The major use of a species can anyway vary with time. At Maroua (Cameroon) a stand of bastard mahogany had been planted for timber: when the trees reached a sufficient size for exploitation, it had not yet been possible to supply the local sawmill with a large enough band to saw up the trunks, so that it was decided to retain the stand to serve as a recreation area on the edge of town . . . but when a malaria epidemic broke out with a massive arrival of refugees from Chad, the bark of the trees was gathered for an anti-malarial medicine . . . and the trees died, used for an entirely different purpose from the original intention in planting them. Another

132

example: in the arid zones of Israel, 'limans' are micro-forestations artificially planted on a deposit of alluvium behind an earth bank or small dam across a drainage channel. They act as shelter for the herdsmen's sheep from wind and sun, but on the day of rest they are reserved for picknickers. Neem is very often valued for its shade more than for its wood but if firewood becomes scarce the neem will very soon be cut back drastically to obtain fuel and the shade will be lost. Neem is sometimes valued for its anti-malarial properties or (Haryana State, India) for the insect repellant power of a decoction of its fruit. In the Rif foothills I have seen villagers quite happy for 'calitousses' (eucalyptus) to be planted, not because of the wood but because the leaves make good infusions for coughs.

Foresters are not accustomed to evaluating production of woody perennials in anything but m^3/ha/year, and one international organization has spoken of 'useless scrub' to describe vast woody perennial formations common to the Sahel. Yet people live off that 'useless' scrub and from those woody perennials obtain far more products than just wood: fruit, edible leaves, forage, fibres and cordage, medicines, gums, resins, etc. This tended to be lost sight of in the 1960s: then the wood tended to obscure the trees, but now there is renewed awareness of the fundamental and highly complex role of trees and, what is extremely important, the awareness that has always existed among peasant farmers and village communities is beginning to dawn on the decision-makers and aid-donors and already be seen in some practical ways.

Great efforts have been made to improve and expand many fruit-bearing woody perennials: mangoes, apples, oranges, etc., but many species, although carefully preserved by populations alongside their crops because they produce food, have not enjoyed the same amount of research either in selection or planting. I could mention here for *sensu lato* arid zones: the shea butter tree, *Butyrospermus paradoxum*, so common in Mali, where in certain regions (Kayes, Koutiala, . . .) the peasants sow the nuts directly into the ground that they are leaving fallow, to increase the number of shea butter trees (but little attention is paid to the young saplings thereafter and many are lost); the fruit of the shea butter tree has an edible pulp and a nut from which 'butter' is extracted and is highly prized in many places as a cooking fat; the inferior qualities are used industrially (soap, chocolate, lipstick, etc.): the African locust, *Parkia clappertonia*, whose pulp is edible and is made into sauces, flour and a beverage, but it belongs to regions where taboos forbid artificial propagation (by direct sowing, for example). I could also mention *Cordyla bipinnata* which is sometimes found in the fields – for instance, between Birkelane and Kaffrine in Senegal – in as great numbers as 'kadd' is Serer country. There is also *Icacinia senegalensis*, which is so widespread in the peanut basin of Senegal and used for its fruits and as fire kindling, the baobab, the date palm, *Borassus aethiopum*, the Doum palm, the tamarind, etc.

6.3 Use of nitrogen-fixing woody perennials

Among the woody perennials used in agroforestry, the nitrogen fixers are particularly important for increasing soil fertility without having recourse to chemical fertilizers, which are becoming increasingly beyond the means of the peasant farmer. It was in Senegal several decades ago that the nitrogen-fixing ability of *Faidherbia albida* (Del.) A. Chev., the 'kadd' of the Ouoloffs, known in Niger as 'gao', in Mali as 'balanzan' and in Arabic-speaking countries as 'haraz' was demonstrated. In India, this role is played by *Prosopis cineraria*, although it does not have the same property of losing its leaves in wet seasons (MANN and SAXENA, 1981). But just as traditional edible species are being rediscovered after misguided and unbridled modernization had relegated them to the shadows (OKIGBO and GREENLAND, 1977), in the same way other species of woody perennials are gradually being shown to have the ability to fix nitrogen from the air (*Sesbania* sp.pl., *Aeschynomene* sp.pl. . . .).

ICRAF is willing to undertake research on this theme. Encouraging results have already been obtained, thanks to research contracts associated mainly with Costa Rica (with *Alnus acuminata*) which produces wood and a little shade while improving pasture land, and with *Erythrina peoppigiana* as an understorey to form hedges in semi-arid zones, in Kenya and the Philippines (with *Leucaena leucocephala*). However, it should be emphasized here that there is a crying need for funding of research and that extreme caution should be exercised, as in all fields of biology; the excessive enthusiasm of the inexperienced for species sometimes labelled under-utilized or miraculous in arid zones and widely-distributed publications on subjects still largely unknown can lead to serious disappointments, particularly in arid zones, where the ecology is fragile.

6.4 Increasing soil fertility

Agroforestry can therefore contribute to conservation of soil fertility by using nitrogen-fixing woody perennials but also by increasing litter and helping organic matter to penetrate the soil, and also, where possible, by planting along contour lines. Finally, trying to organize multi-layer vegetation helps to curb wind speeds, retain soils and promote their in-depth exploitation. When dry dung is used as a fuel, depriving the soil of fertilizing agents, the development of woody perennial plantations among crops can contribute to better retention of fertilizers in the soil.

One of the most promising agroforestry techniques for this purpose is alley cropping, which consists of inserting a row of woody perennials, preferably nitrogen fixers, between a few rows of food crops. The art is firstly to make the correct combination of woody plant with one or more crops, so that the mutual benefits will be as great as possible. Then spacing between rows (of crops and woody plants) and along those rows must be carefully planned. Excellent results have been obtained with maize and Leucaena in semi-humid and humid zones (KANG et al., 1981 and 1984), which it is hoped to transfer to sorghum and Leucaena. Blueprints for trials have been prepared (HUXLEY, 1983 a), but the environment is fragile and variable in the dry areas and the utmost care should be taken in carrying them out; ICRAF is ready to collaborate with researchers in adapting blueprints to particular conditions.

6.5 MEASURES WITHIN THE SCOPE OF PEASANT FARMERS

There is a tremendous need for wood in populated arid zones and even more so in semi-arid zones, but state-run plantations are costly. Village plantations and community reforestation are far from being technically efficient. They are rarely maintained, their cost price is variable and somewhat nebulous, but high, and their contribution (in successfully planted hectares) to the solution of the deforestation problem is still a modest one; questions of finance and ownership of products often remain difficult: however, these collective efforts give rise to hope as, too, does the planting of woody perennials for firewood which is beginning now with one farmer here and there, and which has been made the subject of a joint preliminary study by CILSS and IRCAF with the financial backing of the Sahel Club (BAUMER, 1984). There is need for research into how these collective or isolated activities can be made more effective and methods improved. In this context I would like to mention work being carried out currently on bush fallowing, particularly in the semi-arid regions of India and Kenya. This complements the work being done by IITA in Nigeria and by the Savannas Institute and GERDAT in the Ivory Coast, which aims in semi-humid zones to replace two- or three-year fallowing (which produces only a small amount of indifferent forage and is liable to promote erosion) by fallow planting with nitrogen-fixing, fast-growing woody perennials like *Leucaena leucocephala*, which will be capable of:

- enriching the soil with nitrogen,

- contributing organic leaf litter,

- providing forage,

– producing kindling wood.

In this way agroforestry can make a wide-ranging contribution to resolving the energy problem in *sensu lato* arid zones.

In semi-arid zones, associating trees and crops is a way of reducing shifting cultivation, because the farmer does not want to lose the products of the tree he has planted for its foliage, fruits and bark. The tree will also give him wood, especially at the end of its cycle but also from repeat pruning per number of stands and this will reduce pressure on 'forests'.

Associating woody perennials, especially multi-purpose, nitrogen-fixing shrubs and trees, with other crops is often widely beneficial to the latter in semi-arid zones, mainly because it reduces evapotranspiration and improves the soil. Yet almost everywhere where such association is possible it is not used as widely as would be expected, even when it is well-known to the peasant farmers, and the density of woody perennials is often far above the optimum for the best agricultural production.

For it is not enough that the peasant farmer knows exactly which woody species he can associate to advantage with his other crops: he also needs a strong reason to start or continue such a measure and he finds little encouragement to do so. A good incentive to plant would be to offer fruit trees as a reward to farmers who have successfully planted a certain number of other trees. There is a well-known story of the Sultans of Zinder at the end of the 19th century, who punished with death anyone who had cut down a 'gao' . . . which explains the density of *Faidherbia albida* parks in the Matamaya-Myrria-Magaria region. This emphasizes the importance of local authority, civil or religious, involvement in these matters. Among the Dogon, even today, nobody may cut down a tree without the consent of the Council of Elders. In the Peanut Basin and the New Lands of Senegal, the tree cover of cultivated parks is 2/3 on average of what it ought to be, making a theoretical minimum loss to be recouped of 75 000 m^3 per year (when the trees are mature) assuming that 150 000 ha could take an extra 15 large trees per ha with an average production of 0.15 m^3/ha/year. The semi-arid arable zones in the Haryana and Rajasthan states of India are approaching the same kind of size. In other regions, like the central part of Kordofan in the Sudan, or in some semi-arid regions of Tanzania, the increase in wood production on arable land could be still greater, seeing that on average the woody perennial cover is not more than half or even a third of what would be compatible with good agricultural production. So there is an enormous potential for wood production, especially firewood, through extension and intensification of agroforestry practices, and I would repeat that the increase in tree density would in itself reduce the albedo,

136

which could well have a positive effect on desertification.

6.6 CONTRIBUTION TO FORAGE

In arid zones, where extensive animal production is the activity best suited to the environment – with the exception of some favoured spots, like oases – the role of woody perennials is crucial; during the driest time of the year they are often the only source of protein for countless animals. But not all livestock make equal use of woody plants, and in north Kenya LUSIGI (1981) obtained the following usage percentages from more than 10,000 observations:

	camels	cattle	goats	sheep
trees, bushes and shrubs	30	0	30	9
underbrush	48	2	23	24
non-gramineous herbs	11	11	22	30
grasses	11	87	25	37

Unfortunately, little attention has been paid to this question so far and it is often not known even vaguely how to propagate these plants. Who knows how to plant and foster stands of *Boscia, Cadaba, Capparis, Crataeva, Maerua, Ritcheia*, etc? And yet 80% of the proteins consumed by cattle in *sensu stricto* Sahelo-saharian and Sahelian zones comes from acacias and these genera of the Capparaceae family. Almost nothing is known about the ideal density as a function of ecological conditions, but there is some awareness – rarely documented with any precision – of the positive role played by woody plants in the grass cover in reducing evapo-transpiration. This is an important area for research and one which is essential for the survival of pastoralism. On this point, it will be noticed that earlier I talked about extensive animal production and not extensive animal rearing, since I consider it essential that the role of wild fauna in arid zones should no longer be ignored.

The question of animal forage is one of the most difficult in *sensu lato* arid zones and zones threatened with desertification, and ancestral rivalries between agriculturalists and husbandmen are still frequent, like the animosities existing between foresters and stock rearers. It is as we have already seen, foresters shutting themselves in their ivory towers and tending to regard the forests in emerging countries as the 'sylva' of Roman law, separate by definition from the 'ager' (agriculture) and the 'saltus' (pasture).

Agroforestry is trying to find a solution to this serious conflict:

– by research aimed at associating forage crops with the planting of woody perennials, and even eucalyptus, beneath which foresters repeatedly insist that nothing will grow, a claim invalidated by millet crops beneath eucalyptus grown for example in the excellent Project for the Community Reforestation of the Senegalese Peanut Basin (PRECOBA), supported by the FAO with Finnish financial backing, and by the crops of sorghum grown under eucalyptus by the village community of Bamba Thialene in Senegal;

– by the introduction of woody forage plants on pasture land, carefully chosen and distributed to encourage the grass cover;

– by the organization of cutting, gathering, haymaking and even silage-making of the grass cover and the leaves and branches of woody forage plants taken from inside the forest to be stored and consumed outside it, so reducing the fire hazard, and using a technique which can be classified as agroforestry since woody perennial, herb and even indirectly animal production benefit mutually from it;

– by the introduction of forage or multi-purpose species into forest populations; as LE HOUEROU was one of the first to write (1980 a), it seems possible for the future to produce enough permanent forage with browse trees and shrubs to transform pastoral systems into sedentary agro-silvi-pastoral or silvi-pastoral systems; a report on this was published by TORRES (1983), who gives the following as some examples:

* For several browse species of the Sahel BILLE (1980) established a correlation between stem circumference and the leaf and fruit biomass in rainfall of 250 to 600 mm; this relationship can be expressed as:

$$(\log \text{biomass} = a \times \log \text{diameter} + c)$$

where a = 2 and c = 1. That means that for 'trub' (tree and shrub) stems of 5, 10 and 15 cm diameter the biomass will be 0.25, 2.2 and 6.2 kg respectively. An average Sahel tree would therefore produce 1 kg of leaves, 0.250 kg of fruit and 4.5 kg of branches, or a production of 1 t/ha; but this productivity may vary according to the browse regime and local conditions.

* PENNING DE VRIES and DJITEYE (1982) estimated that the annual mean leaf production of woody perennials of the Sahel varies between 50 kg/ha with rainfall of 500 mm and 1 t/ha with rainfall of 1000 mm, with the scrub cover changing from 5% to 100% respectively.

* In northern Chile, 100 *Prosopis Tamarugo* per hectare yield 20 to 70
  kg of pods per tree according to age, between 14 and 22 years
  (ELGUETA and CALDERON, 1971); but generally speaking, there is
  very little statistical data on forage fruit production.

Present knowledge of the forage capacity of trees, bushes and shrubs is
still incomplete, but the following points can be made:

– an increase in production per individual seems unlikely;

– on the other hand, an increase in the density of fodder shrubs by an
  average of 5-15% seems feasible in zones where annual rainfall is
  between 100 and 500 mm and by 10-20% in zones with an annual
  rainfall of 500-750 mm. But this remains to be proved and there will
  be considerable variations according to soil types. Very little is in
  fact known about the root systems of woody perennials in arid zones
  or the maximum number of individuals that can be supported on a
  hectare. Improved knowledge of symbiotes could open up new
  possibilities for planting woody perennials in arid regions and improving their performance. The interplay between woody plants and
  the vegetation beneath them (FOLLIOTT and CLARY, 1972; SHANKAR,
  1981) still needs more investigation.

6.7 CONTRIBUTION TO THE FUELWOOD SUPPLY

According to the FAO map of firewood availability in developing
countries (1981a) six cases may arise in the ACP countries, as shown in
Table XV, which summarizes how the ACP countries of Africa are affected
by the firewood shortfall.

The ACP countries of the Caribbean and Pacific, although showing
differences among themselves, are also all in a crisis situation.

It is known that 80% of energy consumed in Africa comes from wood,
that alarmingly growing numbers of Africans no longer have enough fuel to
cook more than one hot meal a day and that the real energy crisis is the
dendro-energy crisis affecting developing countries, where it is one of the
signs of desertification.

The average sale price structure for wood is also known. In the Sahel, it
is as follows (COULIBALY, 1983):

retail merchant's profit	37%
price to the producer	30%

transport	24%
labour	7%
exploitation tax	2%

Accepted forestry procedures in firewood production have not in general given very good results in the regions affected or threatened by desertification (CATTERSON, 1984).

Block plantations have a poor cost/benefit ratio, because the price of firewood is still low and firewood is still very largely gathered free. These plantations come up against many obstacles:

lack of available land
conflicts over usage rights
low growth rate (FUGALLI line of the 800 mm isohyet)
exacerbation of conflict of interest between foresters and agronomists
lack of technical expertise (FAO, 1974 a; DELWAULLE, 1978)
administrative red tape
high cost (1,000 US$/ha).

Village plantations on the principle 'Shared work for shared gain' remain an almost Utopian dream, since neither the problem of forester/ population relations nor the problem of profit distribution have been resolved.

Management of natural woody perennial formations is still a hopeful area. According to GORSE (1984) management of these formations in the Sahel would mean an increase in firewood production of 900,000 m^3/year by the year 2000. Initially, the listing of forests envisaged their management for multi-purpose ends but, in practice, such management has only rarely been implemented and listed forests have for the most part been forests on the defensive, with the gathering of dead wood and grazing being tolerated. These vegetations must be brought under management; this would cost four or five times less than establishing block plantations and could even be done with management participation by local people, at least where stable and reliable village communities have been set up, as at Bamba-Thialene in Senegal.

Peasant forestry, on the principle 'produce on the family lands the wood the family needs' may be the best chance of solving the dendro-energy problem. This entails an enormous effort of adaptation on the part of the extension services and will have even more chance of succeeding if production is not limited merely to wood but is extended to all tree products in association with other crops: this is the *agroforestry solution*.

Planting trees in the farmers' fields using the agroforestry approach or in small enclosed units around dwellings or anywhere where it is feasible, as well as conserving and managing forests and wooded areas for multi-purpose and permanent ends, may be the key to the environmental stability of the Sahel and other regions affected or threatened by desertification. It could therefore be, as some far-seeing minds had already announced four or five decades ago, the most efficient means of combating desertification while at the same time meeting the needs of the local people. But if there is here a hope of halting the greatest ecological disaster yet faced by man, there needs to be full realization that all the work and all the technology will be in vain if demand and population pressures continue to increase. Our times may be handicapped by a demographic explosion without precedent in the poorer countries and the 'H bomb' (EHRLICH, 1971), but they have one advantage over preceding eras, as Alexis CARREL has pointed out: 'For the first time in the history of the world a civilisation, having arrived on the threshold of its decline, can discern the cause of its ills. It may be that it will be able to use that knowledge to avoid, with the help of the wonderful powers of Science, the common destiny of all peoples in the past'. This was written half a century ago and one must regretfully accept that a widespread and profound awareness has not yet materialized. By profound awareness we mean awareness 'which results in some appropriate action'. The United Nations Conference on Desertification held in Nairobi in 1977 was very positive in the sense that it made people aware of the serious nature of the desertification phenomenon, and yet that awareness did not go very deep; the rich countries refused to recognize that they were concerned and declined to give the financial support asked of them. As for the countries already affected or most directly threatened by desertification, not one of them has given absolute priority to combating desertification in its development plan.

The example of the Senegalese Peanut Basin is a good illustration of a situation which concerns practically all the semi-arid regions threatened by desertification. This region is one where *Faidherbia albida* has traditionally been associated with agricultural crops because of its fertilizing role and for the forage and wood that it yields (cf. section 7.2.1). As a windbreak, it created a 10 m wide strip with increased fertility (DANCETTE, 1968). However, despite its remarkable properties, well known to farmers, kadd is not as abundant as it should be, and over the last thirty years there has been a drop in numbers and little regeneration. On Sob territory (LERICOLLAIS, 1972) no more than a dozen cultivated trees per hectare were being counted ten or so years ago, 66% of which were kadd, it is true, and 7% baobab, 5% *Cordyla pinnata*, 4% *Celtis integrifolia*, 4% *Anogeissus leiocarpus* and 3% *Diospyros melanoxylon,* with some cashew, tamarind, mango, palmyra palm, Parkia, Parinari and, very near the villages, bombax and kapok trees

141

and, on the periphery of the cultivated area, acacias (*Acacia ataxantha, A. nilotica, A. Seyal*), *Combretum* and *Guiera senegalensis*, each of these woody perennials playing a part in the village economy. If this same land could be revisited and a new study made with the same meticulous care as the study made in 1972, it would provide a very valuable document for measuring changes in the landscape and evaluating the evolution of the environment in West Africa. If the same could be done for the pasture lands of Kordofan, which were the subject of a detailed study between 1957 and 1962 (BAUMER, 1968), one would have a yardstick to measure desertification in the eastern Sahelo-saharan zone and would know more exactly how the environment is evolving.

If one bears in mind that:

the number of kadd is lower everywhere than the thirty to forty mature trees to the hectare it ought to be in order to have the maximum beneficial effect on growth of cereal crops:

there are generally very few young kadd, even of kadd with a diameter of less than 15 cm at the height of a man;

the population is increasing rapidly and firewood supply for the present numbers of people is only just sufficient in the Peanut Basin,

it seems absolutely desirable that agroforestry should be developed in this region and that the necessary research/demonstrations should be undertaken as quickly as possible. Special attention would need to be paid to:

– more woody perennial hedges to mark field boundaries,

– more windbreaks,

– more fruit trees in household gardens,

– much more active regeneration and protection of kadd in the field.

In vast areas where crop farming is intensive, for example in the Senegalese Peanut Basin, there is very little natural closely wooded area left and almost all the trees one sees are in the middle of fields, where they are planted and maintained intentionally, often because the leaves will be a final recourse in case of famine, as with Cordyla. These trees provide the population with the bulk of their fuel; since drought has killed quite a number there has not been much difficulty in recent years in finding dead wood and since 1973 the people have been happy to gather the fallen wood,

142

then to chop down with great difficulty the dead trunks that remained standing. Today one sees a distinctly less wooded landscape than in 1973 and in the last two or three years it has become necessary to cut down large live branches for drying and using as firewood. Since desertification has not slowed down the population growth, it becomes more difficult each day to find the some 700 g of dry wood per head burnt every day in the rural areas. Two responses to this situation are already emerging:

1) farmers who have carts make journeys, sometimes of several days, to look for firewood where it can be found in natural forests, usually towards the eastern side of the Peanut Basin or the already much depleted mangrove swamps to the south;

2) some buy wood or even charcoal, usually from truck drivers who bring their load from Tambacounda or Koupentoum in the direction of Dakar; this monetarization tends to take wood fuel out of the hands of the men and into the women's domain.

There is one speedy remedy for this disastrous situation. Each village, each community, each house should quickly plant trees specially to produce firewood; and *Eucalyptus camaldulensis* should not be forgotten in this context for its rapid growth, despite the poor results generally recorded by state plantations in zones too marginal for this species. Without wishing to push it too far out of its territory (it should no longer be planted industrially where rainfall averages less than 800 m if one is planting for profit), it is reasonable to suppose that it will grow better in small community woodlands than in industrial plantations, because the community will take better care of the trees; but this is not always the case, and tree planting should in the first instance be carried out where the people ask for it.

The Serer or Ouoloff peasant farmer often intercrops stands of eucalyptus with rows of millet or sorghum during the early years of the tree's life when not too much shade is produced. In the first and even second years, he even intercrops with peanuts. He has discovered for himself a kind of taungya system.

Plots of firewood or field boundaries can be planted with species such as eucalyptus, to obtain kindling quickly. At 3-4 years a first cut can be made to obtain some small wood, so that it is an advantage to plant close and only to cut every other tree at three-year intervals with, if possible, 3 plots per community, to try to ensure some regular provision. However, at the same time care must be taken to build the cultivated plot up again and replant the fields with the traditional species always grown there by the farmer and which have been so neglected by foresters.

TABLE XV

Firewood shortfall in Africa

	A	B	C	D	E	F
Angola	50			50		
Benin			50	50		
Botswana	60					40
Burkina Faso			50	20	30	
Burundi					100	
Cameroon		50		50		
Cape Verde				100		
Central African Republic	100					
Chad			65			35
Comoros				100		
Congo	100					
Côte d'Ivoire		50	50			
Djibouti						100
Gabon	100					
Gambia				100		
Ghana		40	45		5	
Guinea				100		
Guinea Bissau	100					
Kenya				60		40
Lesotho					100	
Liberia	100					
Madagascar		25		75		
Malawi			100			
Mali			55			45
Mauritania						100
Mauritius				100		
Mozambique			65	35		
Niger			20	42	3	35
Nigeria		30		65	5	
Uganda				100		
Rwanda				30	70	
Senegal	50			30		20
Seychelles				100		
Sierra Leone			100			
Somalia						100
Sudan	30		25			45
Swaziland					100	
Tanzania			60	40		
Togo			50	50		
Zaire	60			40		
Zambia	45			55		
Zimbabwe			100			

A. Satisfactory situation: resources far exceed actual and predicted needs.
B. Satisfactory situation: but decreasing resources could prove insufficient, at least locally, to meet needs in the forseeable future.
C. Critical situation: present firewood resources exceed need but moving towards a crisis situation by 2000 AD.
D. Crisis situation: present firewood resources below requirement levels, forcing populations to over-exploit.
E. Shortfall situation: firewood resources depleted to the point where populations can no longer provide the minimum need.
F. Desert and subdesert zones in a shortfall situation, with very scarce resources and a low population.

(The numbers represent the estimated percentage of each country in each category A to F).
Sources: FAO, 1981a; Moutalembert and Clément, 1983.

In this way, *Faidherbia albida* or kadd, *Cordyla pinnata* or 'Cayor pear' and *Parkia biglobosa* or African locust should be reintroduced into fields wherever they have disappeared beneath the double pressure of mechanization and drought – and planted more densely where they still survive, to achieve the optimum number of trees per hectare. Whereas it is well known that forty or so large mature kadd trees to the hectare produce the best effect on yield from associated crops, less information is available on the impact made by other woody species. These do not have the same role. Whereas kadd is essentially a fertilizer and producer of dry season forage, other species are retained for their important role in providing food for human consumption. But they do have an effect on the production of associated crops, so that beneath Cordyla, for example, it is common to observe:

– a slight reduction in the height of associated crops,

– in dry periods, associated crops are more turgescent and therefore assimilate better than the crops not covered by the trees.

Peasant farmers whom I have questioned have said either that there were no significant differences between yields under cover or outside any cover, or that reduced production under cover was largely compensated for by the usefulness of Cordyla. If it has not already been done, this could be the subject for some very useful research, comparing the under cover and uncovered production of various crops (especially millet, sorghum, peanut, even maize, cotton . . .) associated with various woody perennials, and trying to determine the best number of woody plants to retain per hectare depending on their age or dimensions.

It would also be appropriate to research how retention of a minimum of trees in parklands can contribute to a reduced albedo in the dry season and in this way maybe help to curb desertification.

7. AGROFORESTRY MEASURES TO COUNTER DESERTIFICATION

7.1 AGROFORESTRY PRACTICES

An agroforestry practice is a specific land management operation of an agroforestry nature on a unit of production or management. 'Of an agroforestry nature', means that at least one species of woody perennial is involved and interacts ecologically and/or economically with other elements (animal and/or vegetable) in the system. Several of these practices can be used simultaneously or consecutively in a single system, either to inaugurate it or to maintain it. These practices include the arrangement of the components in the system in time and space in relation to the principal functions of the woody plant component.

ICRAF is currently making an inventory of agroforestry systems. So far, the following agroforestry practices have been identified (YOUNG, verb. com.):

- Improved shifting cultivation

- Bush fallowing

- 'Taungya'

- Alley cropping (or hedgerow intercropping)

- Fringe planting

- Green fences
  - with main function as a barrier
  - multi-purpose

- Multi-purpose woody perennials
  - on arable land
  - on pasture land or improved pasturage

- Afforestation blocks (with multiple use management)

- Protein banks

- Woody perennials as shelter:
  - for crops (windbreaks, screen shelters)

　　　　– for animals
　　　　– for dwellings

　　– Woody perennials in soil conservation
　　　　– on earth banks and terraces
　　　　– along contour lines
　　　　– in hedges

　　– Woody perennials as regulators of the water regime
　　　　– bordering rivers or sheets of water
　　　　– elsewhere

　　– Household gardens

　　– Woody perennials in combination with planted crops
　　　　– with an understorey of cultivated trees, bushes or shrubs
　　　　– with herbage crops
　　　　– with a tree overstorey (for shade or multiple use)
　　　　– with grazing land and cattle

　　– Cattle under woody perennials

　　– Dune fixing

　　– Aqua-silviculture (mangrove for example)

　　– Apiculture using woody perennials (the term 'api-silviculture' is proposed)

　　– Woody perennials in the improvement of living conditions

Many of these forestry practices overlap and, as with any listing, it is not final but is merely a convenient way of grouping practices in agroforestry.

Improved shifting cultivation

The main problem in shifting cultivation is soil degradation and the drop in productivity, particularly through soil erosion. Improvements can include mixed cropping, row planting, windbreaks and fences to protect growing crops.

147

Bush fallowing

Whether in shifting cultivation or in the fallow phases of sedentary farming, periods of rest are necessary for the soil to recover its fertility. If woody perennials are planted on these fallows this helps to improve the soil, while at the same time producing wood, forage or food or a combination of these products. Since the primary role of the woody plants in this case is to improve fertility, nitrogen-fixing species and species producing plenty of easily rotted organic material are used. If the climate is suitable, Leucaena is good for this, although it can be somewhat difficult to control because of its invasive habit. The fallow time is customarily much shorter than the lifespan of the woody perennials planted there, which means that it is not possible to extract the full potential of their products from these bushes; however, it is their influence on soil improvement that is the primary concern and they entirely fulfil this role while still young and before reaching maturity.

Taungya

This is a very ancient agroforestry system, which has been widely adopted, not only in South-East Asia but also in East Africa (Kenya, Malawi, Tanzania . . .), especially in the last 50 years, in establishing industrial plantations (notably *Cupressus* in 35 year rotation) for the production of soft wood timber. In these plantations, maize, potatoes or beans are intercropped between the young plants for the first three or four years, to avoid competition from weeds. The taungya system can also be applied to growing forage crops; for example, as is done in Sudan, using *Acacia Senegal* and *Andropogon gayanus*. The chief problem with this system is the need to plan a planting programme for long-cycle trees with three or four years of crops; the system has proved effective in providing food for forest workers and forage for cutting by cattle rearers.

In Kenya, where agriculture and forestry cohabit harmoniously, as highlighted by SPEARS (1980), 160 000 ha have been planted in the high altitude zones on the 'shamba' system, a Kiswahili word to describe the taungya system. In this system, peasant farmers duly authorized by the Forestry Service grow maize, potatoes and various kinds of beans for 3 to 5 years among the forest trees, mostly cypress and eucalyptus. As WOOD observed (1984), the taungya system has been imposed on poor farmers who lacked land of their own, and was not thought up by the farmers themselves. The social implications of this have been criticized by several authors. It happens more and more frequently, in fact, that young farmers reject the constraints of the taungya system accepted by their fathers, by for example refusing to release the land they have been cultivating and taking

148

the risk of cutting down the young forest trees which they are supposed to be protecting. Because agroforestry assumes the voluntary participation of farmers, foresters cannot accept the taungya system unreservedly, but they can apply it if farmers, driven by need, request it.

Trees planted in the taungya system must have the following characteristics: rapid growth, moderate requirements, modest consumption, no competing roots, tolerance of competition. Associated crops must be shade-tolerant, not be a climbing liana, not be too demanding or invasive, have a short cycle and improve the soil.

Alley cropping

The practice of alternate alley cropping, in which crops are grown between lines of hedges, is applicable in humid rather than dry zones, except where irrigation is possible. The woody perennials used can provide wood, forage or food, as well as shelter to the crops and can improve the soil (the latter especially if nitrogen-fixing woody species are used).

Fringe planting

One of the simplest methods of incorporating woody perennials into an agricultural production system is to plant round fields. This is also a way of reducing the problem of competition between trees and crops, providing there is not another field on the other side of the stand of trees. All the products that a woody perennial is capable of producing can be obtained from properly planted fringe trees. These trees are usually cut back by pruning, trimming or pollarding, depending on the products desired.

Green hedges and fences

Green fences are fences in which posts are replaced by living trees, preferably termite-resistant; either the trees are sufficiently closely planted to form a barrier, or barbed wire is stretched between them. They can be cut above barrier height for wood or green branches. In arid zones, existing trees are often used to form the fence, even though the alignment is not perfect.

Hedges are lines of woody plants one or more rows deep, forming a continuous barrier and cut regularly so that the barrier formed by the mass of stems and branches remains dense.

The problems created by these practices are basically the reaction of the woody plants to repeated cutting, competition between woody plants

149

and crops, relative effects of one range of products (e.g. firewood) on another (e.g. forage). In arid zones, competition between plants in the same hedge generally hinders the progress of this practice.

Multi-purpose trees

Scattered over grazing land or in fields, trees can have a variety of uses, including improving soil fertility, producing firewood, forage, food, textile fibres and medicines. Trees that are deliberately used for several purposes simultaneously are called multi-purpose trees. Problems created by this practice are basically related to the management of the tree and the effects of competition (spacing, size, shade, etc.). On grazing land there is, too, of course, the question of palatability of the forage produced and its nutrient value; here, shade is of particular importance.

Multi-purpose plantations

Multi-purpose wood plantations have been used for centuries as an integral part of farming practice. However, for this to be considered as agroforestry, the species chosen and the management strategy must deliberately aim at meeting the farmer's objectives.

Protein bank

In production systems that include animals, it is difficult to rely solely on annual plants to supply forage during dry seasons or years of low rainfall. Woody perennial vegetation, judiciously used, helps to meet this difficulty; not only does it provide green forage when the grass cover has withered, but it can also supply more protein than grass. The advantage of woody plants in dry seasons is therefore both qualitative and quantitative.

Trees as shelter

In their capacity as shelter, trees can provide shade, protection against wind, forage, wood and food. Windbreaks and screen shelters often increase crop yield, thanks to their beneficial effects on soil and microclimate. The effect on animals is to reduce stress from heat and wind. Around houses, shade and wind protection are often combined with production of fruit, edible leaves for humans and animals, and even firewood. The main points to be considered are the placing of the trees in relation to each other and to the houses and crops, and ways of managing them in order to have sustained production of the desired benefits.

Trees in soil conservation

Woody perennials can greatly assist infiltration and reduce surface water runoff, although a wrong choice of species or poor planting technique can have the opposite effect. Woody plants, whether in hedges or not, can stabilize the soil on terrace edges and other conservation works, and contribute leaf and/or wood products. Particular care should be taken in these systems, regarding planting method and long-term management.

Trees in water conservation

Woody perennials can be used to create favourable conditions for agriculture; for example, to dry out swamps (*Sesbania Sesban* planted on ridges in marshy depressions in Rwanda, enabling sweet potato to be grown) or to protect banks.

Home gardens

The most well-known home gardens are found in high rainfall areas. Made up of numerous plants, both woody and herbaceous, carefully mixed and forming several vegetation storeys, they are in essence multi-purpose. Less complex forms of these gardens also exist in dry zones.

Combinations with commercial crops

When woody perennials are grown for commercial purposes (coffee, cacao, tea, gum arabic), the choice of other components in the system is very important: grass cover, overstorey of shade trees, animal access to the plot, mixed intercropping, etc.

Animals under trees

In the shelter of trees, animals can benefit from the forage production and also the protection afforded. Judicious choice of species is important, so that the necessary quality and quantity of forage are always available, depending as they do on the type, age and physiological condition of the animals.

Dune fixing

The use of woody perennial vegetation to fix dunes has a dual purpose: to stop sand movement but also to create a favourable environment for the production of wood, forage, even food, for animal production (wild game, apiculture) or for recreational purposes.

Aquaforestry

Aquaforestry is the considered use of woody perennials in contact with water to encourage animal or plant production; for example, the use of red mangrove roots as niches for rearing crabs and prawns. Even in arid zones, such applications are possible where sheets of water exist; for example, *Mytragine inermis* or *Sesbania* spp. grown round the edges of semi-permanent pools.

Apiculture and agroforestry (api-silviculture)

Carefully chosen woody species grown for their nectar-producing flowers and pollen valued by bees can boost wax and honey production, particularly if flowering is staggered, allowing the bees to work as long as there are flowers instead of only working for a few months in the year. This is probably the production with the highest ratio of value of products harvested to plant biomass consumed.

7.2 PROPOSALS FOR AGROFORESTRY ZONING

No formulas in forestry technology are universally applicable. The extreme variability of edaphic and climatic conditions, of habits and customs, of political, economic and social systems and of perceived needs, makes it impossible to give an all-purpose formula. In fact, if one wants to apply a range of techniques, this must be done in homogeneous units on the wider environmental level. Rwanda is starting to do this with a view to identifying zones of equal potential for agroforestry, where the same techniques could be applied. What is more, the list of possibilities will also take into account the cost of any operations; in other words, the cost variations of operations geared towards a single overall desired result will be mapped.

In the following sections a very rough attempt has been made to list the chief potentials of agroforestry according to methods of soil use, which themselves largely depend on ecological conditions. Three cases have been considered: pluvial cultivation (7.2.1), stock-raising zones (7.2.2) and irrigated zones (7.2.3). The benefits of inter-zone exchanges are shown in a final section (7.2.4).

7.2.1 *Rain-fed cultivation zones*

Agroforestry was initially developed in rain-fed cultivation zones, both in Africa and in other continents. The most important practices for these zones include alley cropping, taungya, multi-purpose trees scattered through cultivated fields, and hedging.

The almost ideal type of multi-purpose trees scattered among crops is given by the agro-silvipastoral system created around *Faidherbia albida*, which has already been described many times. (See Appendix 2.)

Some observations on the Community Reforestation Project in the Peanut Basin of Senegal, a project in which this tree has again proved its worth, are given below. This is an example of a project making the transition between accepted reforestation schemes and agroforestry, some of whose practices it is already developing; it is noteworthy for the research into participation by the populations involved, for the considered associations of woody perennials with crops and for the use of multi-purpose woody species. Its technical achievements compare favourably with those of conventional projects. Its results in human terms are superior and it seems possible that the measures set in motion by the Project will not cease with foreign aid.

Development of the Community Reforestation Project in the Peanut Basin

The Peanut Basin of Senegal suffers from a serious shortage of firewood. The equilibrium between supply and demand has been upset by the population increase and a passion for mechanization which has led to many field trees being cut down to allow the machines to move more freely. Aware of the people's difficulties, the Government of Senegal launched the community reforestation project in the Peanut Basin (PRECOBA) aimed at helping the populations to supply their own wood requirements and, more particularly, their firewood needs. The Project has a particularly interesting approach, very similar to the 'D and D' method of ICRAF (see 8.3), and its results are so encouraging that it seems useful to point out some of its main aspects here.

The Project began with a sociological survey that looked at the actions and motivations of the population in relation to trees (DENEVE-STE-VERLYNCK *et al.*, 1982). Already by the way in which it was conducted, the survey had caught the imagination and gained the interest of the people, and in fact all the Project personnel, including the shorthand typists and drivers, took part in the survey alongside rural development agents already at the site, so that there was no need for interviewers from outside. Subsequently, the interviewers were pleasantly surprised to find that they were being consulted before any type or method of action was decided upon, and this created a climate of trust. It is true that the human milieu was already very well known, and without some outstanding previous studies (PELISSIER, 1966; LERICOLLAIS, 1972; DELPECH, 1974 a and b; GASTELLU,

1974 and 1981) the enquiry could not have had the success it did. The enquiry discovered first of all that agricultural and ecological knowledge is often sound and that the peasant farmer's breadth of knowledge is greater than previously believed. From the very interesting data collected and summarized in table form (ALEXANDER *et al.*, 1982) it is clear that:

- the family performs many actions that benefit trees: planting, protecting young or mature trees, 'yaram sas' or collective pruning of kadds to assist their growth and to stop cattle browsing them, etc.

- family consumption, and that of the family herd, are by far the most dominant concern, way ahead of commercial considerations,

- caring for trees is a concern in direct proportion to the amount of responsibility the respondent has in the management of land,

- the demand for products from the tree, particularly for firewood, but also for fruits and honey, exceeds availability,

- the needs expressed by the women centre around fruit trees and wood for fuel,

- it is not customary to plant trees primarily for fuel (hence the Project's trend towards encouraging local species rather than eucalyptus, and fruit trees with wood that will burn,

- the prohibition on pruning certain species (kadd, dimh) is seen as an additional difficulty in building up reserves of wood for burning during the rainy season,

- the most sought-after species are kadd for its well-known fertilizing properties, then mango, baobab, neem and all multi-purpose trees included in various agroforestry systems,

- whenever the peasant farmer plants trees, the crucial prerequisite for him is always knowing for certain that he will benefit from the operation; 'it has to be admitted that tree regulation does not encourage tree development, for example, the 'endemic' uncertainty as to who will benefit in future from massive planting schemes constitutes a considerable obstacle to village reforestation' (DE-NEVE-STEVERLYNCK *et al.*, 1982).

DENEVE-STEVERLYNCK and his colleagues concluded their analysis of reforestation measures taken or supported by the rural training services

154

and/or external financing sources with the following remarks:

'The National Forestry Commission basically launches schemes that are 'diffuse' or of general benefit: replanting of listed forests, creation of public parklands, creation of a vigilante brigade to preserve the forest capital, etc. In the Fatick department these schemes are essentially state run, but proposals are submitted for the approval of rural Councils to ensure the co-operation of local authorities. These are supposed to collaborate in designating land for planting, recruiting a labour force and deciding on methods of payment. There is not yet any 'popular participation' as regards choice and method of operations, nor concerning the future beneficiaries of the plantation. Village woods are becoming involved in moves towards participation and operations on a smaller scale, but first attempts have not achieved the expected results. Under cover of community reforestation, these operations have to be seen as a 'present' from the administration, in the hope that populations will gradually become interested in this kind of scheme.

'The Human Promotion campaigns ('one woman, one tree; one worker, one tree' . . .) launched on the occasion of visits to the departments by official delegations and followed up by rural counsellors and Technical Representatives of the National Forestry Commission at Rural Centres level, are having varied success. They are often regarded as a 'nine-day wonder': the upkeep and watering of these plantations, undertaken in a moment of enthusiasm and goodwill by the people, is often subsequently relinquished entirely to the Forestry Commission.

'The Society for the Development and Improvement of Agriculture (SODEVA) works in the extension service tradition and through its thorough training techniques targets the peasant producer, singly or in groups. Local initiative is given the maximum stimulus ('the more the peasant farmer can do for himself, the better') and the notions of profitability and return are driven home to planters and nurserymen. In this way there is an increased chance of launching operations in line with the people's needs. Nevertheless, the success of these schemes is often compromised by the technical and organizational problems (late planting supervision . . .) which can have something to do with the personality and commitment of the agent.

'In assessing reforestation schemes, a distinction needs to be drawn between nurseries and plantations.

'Nurseries require regular and sustained work for 3 to 18 months, but have the advantage of being a short-term operation and have much in common with market gardening. The heavy work is done in the dry season, investment is minimal and delivery of plants is an instant source of revenue.

'A nurseryman who sells 3 000 eucalyptus plants at 30 CFA francs per plant, for which he has invested between 5 and 10 F in equipment (grow-bags, tools, . . .) earns 60 000 to 75 000 CFA francs net after 4 months. The objectives are clear, risks limited and production and marketing decisions are taken by a 'decision centre' which is easily identifiable (one person or a small group of people).

'The same is not true of plantations: in certain cases planters buy their plants (sometimes even before they have been produced in the nursery), they put in much work at a time when farm crops are requiring all their resources (if they are compensated, they sometimes have to wait for their money or supplies), and they will not reap the benefit inside 10 to 15 years. It is a long-term project, with production and marketing decisions not always coming from the same decision centre. In the case of community plantations, the objectives are often fixed by an 'outside' body (administration, project) which provides finance and materials, while the labour is supplied by the local community, which runs the risk of possible failure without any assurances as to the future benefits of the operation. As has already been said, having the responsibilities for decisions, investments, risks and benefits in the hands of different people reduces the motivation of those who are supposed to be the village wood producers.

'Protection of naturally occurring field trees is primarily a matter of supervision, and this can be promoted by securing the awareness of all concerned or, in some cases, by installing gabion fencing. This latter solution has the disadvantage of being onerous without being infallible'.

PRECOBA is an important contribution to the practical search for a solution to the firewood problem, by its work in popularizing economical wood-burning clay ovens and, in particular, its successful attempts to create awareness, enlist co-operation, and then total responsibility from the populations concerned, as regards their own reforestation problem and especially the planting of woody perennials like kadd, jujube, guava and mango among their crops. It is one of the most successful and promising integrated rural development programmes, basically because of the agroforestry spirit in which it has been approached. It is entirely due to that spirit that the Project has a chance of becoming sustainable and repeatable. The Co-Director of the Project has done his best, and this is not very usual, to see to it that his presence becomes unnecessary at the earliest possible moment – 'doing away with his own job category' to paraphrase Amilcar CABRAL – so that the Project can be run entirely by nationals once the conceptual, training and trial planting phases have been completed.

Results are many and varied, but the most important – and the most difficult to quantify – is the creation of a new approach to reforestation, in which the peasant farmer decides and acts and where the forester becomes no more than an adviser.

A second training and implementation phase, run entirely by Senegalese nationals is continuing on into 1986, which should ensure the consolidation of results and their extension into the districts of Ouadiour, Colobane and Ndofane, or 4, 4 and 3 new rural communities respectively, where only 8 were involved in the initial phase. A third phase, of implementation only, is due to be completed in the Fatick department in 1988.

To sum up, the results of the project include:

– individual replanting of trees on small plots;

– community reforestation, with a success rate of over 80%; for the most part this was basically using *Eucalyptus camaldulensis*, but other species are being used with increasing frequency and for some reforestations (already covering more than half the area): kadd, cashew, *Acacia tortilis* var. *Adansonii*, jujube, casuarina, *Parkinsonia aculeata*;

– a successful experiment to regenerate *Acacia Seyal* from shoots and seedlings with a 3-year prohibition on their use in order to obtain a really productive silvo-pastoral system.

– assisted regeneration of kadd by stump thinning and pruning of thousands of individuals, mostly in the middle of cultivated fields; this operation is being widely adopted as peasant farmers become increasingly aware of its value; it illustrates well the move away from a community reforestation project towards an increasingly agroforestry project:

– 280 ha of Palmyra palm planted with 5×5m or 10×10m spacings on agricultural land;

– an ongoing experiment in the management of 16 000 ha of natural forest aimed at creating a silvo-pastoral system controlled by the peasants themselves;

- experiments in planting palm with 12 × 12 m spacing over 1 ha in each plantation of eucalyptus, to bring variety of species and result in a agro-silvicultural system: vegetables, cereals and fruit under palm trees;

- a list of strike rate of species according to the soil: (cf. Table XVI) the 'dior' soils are leached or unleached tropical ferruginous soils, sandy, either of homogeneous structure to more than 1 m in depth, or with a little more clay and especially non-indurated iron oxides at 50-60 cm; the 'dek' soils are sandy loam, slightly more clayey than 'dior' soils, generally hydromorphic and often calcareous deep down; 'ban' soils are silt and clay.

- experiments on deep collar planting, which show that compared with normal planting, *Eucalyptus camaldulensis* thrives on dek soil but not on dior, while *Faidherbia albida* does better on dior than on dek soil. For *Zizyphus mauritiana*, however, greater height is attained by deep planting without affecting strike rate (100%), while on dior soil normal planting seems to give greater height for *Acacia tortilis* var. *Adansonii*;

- a better success rate on community reforestation than individual plantings, because the community foremen, appointed by the community chairmen, have received some systematic training.

TABLE XVI

Strike rate of species on different soils at PRECOBA, Senegal
(after DIALLO and JENSEN, 1983 and DIALLO, pers. comm.)

| | Soil Type | | |
	'dior'	'dek'	'ban'
Faidhebia albida	78	88	89
Acacia tortilis var. *Adansonii*			98
Eucalyptus camaldulensis			96
Anacardium occidentale			85
Zizyphus mauritiana			98

Instruction is progressively reduced in order to test the validity of the training given. The first 4 training nurseries were dismantled in 1983 and the newly-trained nurserymen made available to rural communities. Twelve of these have set up their own nursery, for which the project provides the materials, continues the instruction (a weekly visit) and orders seedlings for field replanting and experimental plantations. The community supplies land and water and each has approved a 300 000 CFA F loan for the purchase of seedlings for large-scale planting. In the extension zone, 6 training nurseries have been set up and these are visited three times each week. In 2 of these nurseries, 4 women (2 × 2) are receiving training as nursery women. One state nursery at Fimla continues its production of seedlings to cover possible failures in the community nurseries; in 1983 it produced approximately 30 000 *Eucalyptus camaldulensis* and 3 000 *Anacardium occidentale,* while the 18 community nurseries produced:

139 500	*Eucalyptus camaldulensis* (but this number will drop each year until 1986)
39 500	jujube (1986 target: 70 000)
35 500	kadd (1986 target: 70 000)
11 500	cashew
7 250	*Acacia sieberiana*
6 000	*A. tortilis* var. *Adansonii*
6 000	*Prosopis cineraria* (1986 target: 30 000)
5 900	*Albizzia Lebbeck*
5 000	neem
2 000	*E. microtheca*
200	*Cordyla africana*
3 475	various local species (mango, guava, etc.)

It should be said that all the kadd, almost all the Prosopis, more than half the Albizzia and *Acacia tortilis* are planted in fields, that is in agroforestry systems. The remaining Prosopis, Albizzia and Acacia and almost all the Cordyla are planted on grazing land, in silvi-pastoral systems. Almost all the fruit trees and neems are used in household gardens – agroforestry yet again.

One locally trained nurseryman has discovered how to achieve 100% germination with *Acacia sieberiana*; he leaves the seeds 3 to 4 minutes in the boiling water during scarification instead of taking the pot off the fire as soon as the water boils.

Large-scale reforestation extends over uninterrupted stretches of 10 to 15 ha per community. In 1983, 210 ha of trees were planted. The areas are chosen by the community. The foremen receive a week's training, learning about land clearing, staking, hole digging, the assisted regeneration of kadd, running a work site, paying the work force and task distribution. A point to note is that the sense of community is so widespread among the

Serers that they often reject payment per hole and prefer to share out equally among themselves the total lump sum awarded for number of holes dug. This ties in with an observation made by GASTELLU (1974), that when the members of a community decide to undertake a common task over the year, they all devote exactly the same number of hours to it, without any need for control.

Field restocking is carried out at the request of a farmer: it will be over a continuous stretch of 50 ha of land, sometimes with several owners involved, and the land will be arable. This is true agroforestry. The project proposes a foreman to receive training, a hole-digging, planting and protection subsidy, and which trees to plant. Direct costs amount to 30 000 CFA F per hectare, inclusive of the foreman's wage.

The project is also collaborating with the Centre for Study and Research into Renewable Energy (CERER) in a campaign to popularize improved wood-saving cooking hearths and is organizing training sessions on their construction, upkeep and use.

Lastly, I have observed the following points:

– in the community nurseries, the cost price of tree saplings is 24.8 CFA francs and the cost of fruit trees 83.4 CFA francs. These same products sell for 30 and 150 CFA francs respectively in the SODEVA nurseries;

– a man can dig 4.5 holes/day in dek soil and 9 holes/day in dior soil;

– generally speaking, for block reforestations one can reckon on a direct expenditure within the project of 150 000 CFA francs/ha, 85% of which is labour costs, to which must be added 50 000 CFA francs of World Food Programme (WFP) supplies and 100 000 CFA francs contributed by the community (labour, land clearing, hole-making).

Table XVII details the 1982-1983 costs for 10 ha of single block community reforestation. It shows that the price of community reforestation is no lower than state reforestation, but the enormous advantage of the approach of community reforestation as conceived by PRECOBA is that it encourages communities to participate and that the local population benefits from considerable sums in remuneration. It has been such a great success that village nurseryman will now earn a good living without any further subsidy, so keen are the peasant farmers to buy trees (50% of them fruit trees) for planting.

TABLE XVII

Cost of PRECOBA reforestation in 1982-1983
(Diallo and Jensen, 1983)

	Price of 10 ha in CFA francs	CFA F/ha
Labour		
Land preparation		
Foreman January-June		
6 × 25 320 F/month	151 920	
Clearing 20 m/d/ha		
remuneration with products obtained or with MAP supplies	(for the record)	
Hole-digging 90m/d/ha		
remuneration with MAP supplies	(for the record)	
Total land preparation	151 920	15 200
Planting and upkeep		
Foreman July-September		
3 × 25 320 F/month	75 960	
Planting 65 m/d/ha		
650 × 972 F/day	631 800	
Upkeep 15 m/d/ha		
150 × 972 F/day	145 800	
Total planting and upkeep	853 560	85 400
Security		
One guard October-July		
10 × 25 320 F/month	253 200	25 300
Total Labour	1 258 680	125 900
Seedlings: 25*F + 5 F transport		
6 250 × 30 F/seedling	187 500	18 800
Materials	40 000	4 000
Equipment: 98 000 F		
paid back over 2 years	50 000	5 000
Total direct expenditure	1 536 180	153 700

* Labour represents 52% of this amount.

7.2.2 Stock-rearing zones

What Zaroug (1984) writes concerning the arid and semi-arid regions of the Near East is unfortunately true of the same regions over the whole of our area of study: there has been some awareness here and there of the importance of indigenous forage trees, bushes and shrubs, but nothing like the necessary practical effort has been made to improve and use these to increase the supply of forage.

The advantages of browse plants over grasses for forage can be summarized as follows:

– because of their generally deeper and more spreading root systems, woody perennial plants are better able than grasses to exploit the poor water resources in the soil and to withstand one or more droughts;

– a good number of woody plants form their leaves before the rainy season and if they are palatable help bridge the lean time at the end of the dry season, when the grass cover has disappeared or has very little nutritional value;

– certain parts of woody plants are significantly richer in proteins than are grasses, especially in dry seasons, to such an extent that without woody plants it is likely that many animals would not survive;

– they create protected microclimates in which evapotranspiration is reduced, enabling grass to grow around them.

In addition to these forage advantages, woody perennials have other remarkable qualities: they help to reduce wind speeds, they break the monotony of the landscape and create landmarks, and they protect soil against erosion.

It must also be said that woody perennials are sometimes the only plants capable of tolerating high salt levels; for this reason, they are essential elements in agroforestry systems of the silvo-pastoral type peculiar to saline soils, where they provide both the bulk of the forage and the bulk of the fuel. On desert margins and in arid zones there are vast tracts of salt lands which can be productive if correctly managed. Numerous studies, notably Australian (MALCOLM, 1982), Israeli (FORTI, 1971) and by UNESCO have shown that woody bushes of the right kind have enabled yields of sheep meat almost as high as those of the neighbouring, non-saline land. This salt meadow sheep meat is often much prized for its special flavour.

In order to give maximum production, to regenerate and even to survive, woody perennials need a maximum of attention and protection. They need management. If an imbalance is created between what the tree has to offer and what is demanded of it, the system breaks down rapidly. This is what often happens in many regions under threat of desertification. For example, in the Wadi Azum valley at Darfur (Sudan), the admirable equilibrium created over generations between nomadic and sedentary populations is being destroyed under the combined assault of persistent

162

drought and the population increase. The river bed is bordered by 'haraz', *Faidherbia albida*, which is a great nitrogen-fixing tree and so encourages crops grown beneath it, and the pods of which drop to the ground when ripe in the second half of the dry season, enabling the nomadic herds, which in this season do not find any crops to raid, to survive. The sedentary populations used to benefit from the trees that fertilized their fields and the nomad populations also benefited in their turn, after the crops had been harvested. As much as twenty years ago, conflict flared up between the two populations: the nomads cut down more branches of 'haraz' than was good for the health of the trees and wanted to leave their animals longer under the stands of 'haraz', coming into conflict with the farmers who wanted to start cultivation. Today, the situation has considerably worsened, because the population is continuing to increase and because of the persistent drought which has lasted nearly twenty years in that area (cf. Fig. 3): the only 'haraz' left is very old, often with hollow trunks and in poor condition, there are no young trees and no regeneration. The trees cannot regenerate because more and more animals are being kept on the land for longer periods, and young plants are browsed and die; previously, any offence involving browsing of crops or young trees (young seedlings grow naturally in fields where the soil is broken down and they were protected there by the farmers) was punished by the village chiefs or group leaders, but with independence everyone felt free to do anything and sanctions were no longer imposed. The nomads now keep their animals longer under the 'haraz' and the farmers, in urgent need of land, have given up protecting the trees. This has created a dramatic situation where the absence of natural regeneration, if it is not rapidly compensated by:

planting young 'haraz' raised in the nursery,
protecting these young seedlings for several years,
protecting any suckers appearing on their stocks and roots,
management of the 'haraz' plantations,

will sooner or later result in:

a drop in soil fertility,
loss of an important forage resource,
the river banks becoming uninhabitable,
impoverishment and migration of the people.

Examples of this kind of grazing land degradation are not infrequent. I have compiled the following list:

Burkina Faso, in 1973, absence of regeneration of acacias for at least the previous 5 years between Ouahigouya and Dori, attributable more to overgrazing by herdsmen from Mali and Volta than to the onset of drought;

Cameroon, in 1981, absence of young woody saplings other than those being introduced by the 'Green Sahel' Project on deep sand in the extreme north east of Margui-Wandala, between Mora, Ganse and Kossa where there are normally abundant seedlings of *Guiera senegalensis, Boscia senegalensis, Acacia Senegal, Combretum aculeatum, Zizyphus mauritiana, Dichrostachys glomerata, A. stenocarpa, Anogeissus leiocarpus,* and even *Faidherbia albida*: the only seedlings found were *Calotropis procera*, a plant which usually indicates over-exploitation and is generally not eaten, or only very little, by cattle; the absence of young plants was due basically to unauthorized burning in an attempt to obtain a new grass cover, and to overgrazing, itself due to an overload of animals on the pastures caused by reduced grazing land through agricultural expansion north of Maroua;

Chad, where since 1957 the very small amount of woody plant regeneration was noted on grazing routes and around settlement areas like Moussoro and Massakory, through overgrazing by a sharply increased number of animals benefiting at that time from particularly abundant rainfall.

Ethiopia, in 1984, total absence of young regeneration on the perimeter and even within the forest reserves to the northwest of Addis Ababa;

Ivory Coast in 1983, scarcity of scrub regeneration between Bouake and Ferkessedougou, and the shrinking pasture due to agricultural expansion;

Kenya, in 1984, the almost total absence of acacias under 5 years old in the Tugen foothills overlooking Lake Baringo;

Madagascar, in 1979, eradication of almost all young seedlings through uncontrolled grazing between Ambatondrazaka and Antananarivo;

Mali, in 1984, absence of regeneration because of overgrazing and repeated fires in the bush savannas of Natie, Mpedougou and Bougouni, etc.;

Mauritania, in 1980, the total absence of regeneration of woody perennials, both of *Acacia Senegal* in the Boutilimit region and of *A. nilotica* in the Senegal valley, and even of *Commiphora africana* between Nema and Oualata;

Mauritius, in 1975, the disappearance of some endemic species despite heroic efforts to protect them by the Director of the Forestry Service, who also runs the Pamplemousse Botanic Gardens and the Royal Society of Arts and Sciences;

Niger, in 1968, between Tanout and Zinder, where the announcement of the opening of new water boreholes had brought an uncontrolled influx of herds, extreme scarcity of very young woody plants;

Nigeria, in 1971, total eradication of young trees by farmers extending their fields between Kano and Katsina, where formerly some trees were always left in the fields for forage and/or fruit, sometimes even simply for their pleasant shade;

Senegal, in 1980, almost total absence of regeneration of *Faidherbia albida* because farmers had abandoned the custom of protecting the young plants; thanks to major efforts by the Forestry Service and in particular the community reforestation project in the Peanut Basin, the situation has improved, and in some areas farmers not only protect young seedlings but raise them during their early years;

Somalia, in 1985, where outside reserves no woody plant of less than 5 years other than what has been planted was seen on the grazing land between Mogadishu and Bulo Berti;

lastly in Uganda, in 1969, near Kabale, the systematic destruction of the shrub vegetation on a pretext of eliminating the tsetse fly, and between Nimule and Gulu, scarcity of young woody plants due to bush fires and over-grazing.

Overgrazing not only destroys plants which are eaten by the animals, it also prevents them from becoming established because the ground is heavily trampled and becomes hardened, and this hampers germination, particularly at the start of the rains. Overgrazing is often the consequence of uneven distibution of rainfall, which creates local concentrations of herds. But rainfall that is too scattered can negatively affect the fodder supply because it has a depressive effect on pasture, according to the studies of Toutain and de Wispelaere (1977); scattered rainfall, according to them, encourages the rapid emergence of young shoots, it makes forage in the rainy season but 'the ground cover is not guaranteed, particularly on high

165

ground and the common grazing land less protected from the various erosion hazards; it reduces the potential usable forage for the dry season and makes it very difficult to bridge the gap before the following rainy season. Pasturage then tends to contract, with the forage supply concentrated in the lower part of the plant where the water balance is compensated'.

Many countries threatened by desertification often have regulations for the conservation of natural resources, but it is rare for these to be enforced, especially since the 1960s when many States gained their independence.

Even in silvo-pastoral systems it is from the town that desertification emanates. The main cause of environmental degradation is the tendency of traditional nomadic groups to settle. This is the case with the Rendille and the Gabra in North Kenya where LAMPREY (1981) points out that centres of human and animal concentration are forming and expanding rapidly around the scarce wells and water holes, but especially round the deep boreholes which have recently been brought into service. The permanent availability of water is the chief motivation for these concentrations. These foci offer shops, schools, medical centres and famine aid centres, and also protection against inter-tribal raids, mainly by cattle thieves, that have once again become commonplace. The lack of security in vast stretches of territory is a good enough reason not to venture out into them and the cause of the heavy overexploitation of less dangerous regions. Circles of desertification are created around settlement centres, gradually becoming larger, and there is a direct correlation between desertification and sedentarization, which is proof that the mobile herd is better able than the sedentary one to maintain natural resources in good condition. Another disadvantage of sedentarization may become apparent, as in northern Ferlo (Senegal): there the people's staple food is milk, and because the animals now only feed in a restricted area since boreholes have created permanent watering points, and so are eating a smaller variety of plants, trace-element deficiencies can develop in the people's diet: one can see people eating earth to make up the 'salts' they lack.

It is in intervening in silvo-pastoral systems that agroforestry must tread most warily, because these systems are usually found in the most arid areas of a country or on marginal land, also because population density is low and supervision difficult, and finally, because for various reasons, often low or zero profitability, grazing land has always been given less attention (that is to say, in practical terms less money has been invested in it) than arable land: consequently, less is known about the interactions operating between woody perennials and other products of the soil in grazing areas

166

than in other areas subject to, or threatened by, desertification. This does not, however, mean that nothing at all is known or that nothing can be done.

The prime objective of agroforestry in grazing areas is to try to increase the number of browse trees, bushes and shrubs, especially those that can act as protein banks during dry seasons; these woody plants can be introduced in small reserves to be planted near permanent water sources and especially near wells that have a warden. They can also be planted around temporary pools and water sources, but it is also possible to introduce (or re-introduce) them as single specimens on grazing land. However, this is a costly and risky business, because the distances between the nurseries and planting places are enormous and there is a high mortality rate of plants in transit. The unpredictability of rainfall in these areas, which are often arid, is an additional hazard, often making it necessary to replant several years running, until a year with sufficient rainfall allows seedlings to start growing, followed by enough successive years with sufficient rainfall for them to become established and able to withstand drought. Direct planting of pre-treated seeds in a shallow furrow (which, if the soil is not too hard, can be made with a harrow drawn by a dromedary) has been reasonably successful with grasses. The same method could be applied to seeds of woody perennials, particularly Acacias, Prosopis, Parkinsonias and Maeruas. In all cases it is essential that areas planted in this way should be made strictly out of bounds to grazing for several years so that the plants have time to become strong enough to tolerate browsing. This almost always means having alternative forage reserves available for the habitual users of the areas placed out of bounds. These reserves can be other pastures opened up to grazing (for example, by making a watering place), irrigated forage crops, or stocks of hay or silage from other parts of the country, or feed provided by international aid.

However, the most economic method of increasing the numbers of browse shrubs is to protect natural regenerations. Although the exact mechanism of these regenerations is not known, they generally occur after a good rainfall has followed the passage of livestock. Acacias are particularly prone to such regenerations. They make choice eating for cattle, but normally are so intensively browsed that at best only a few individuals survive. If action is taken in time to protect the regeneration process, the protected sector will rapidly develop into aerial grazing of increased value. This method has been practised successfully, notably in Niger, where even in years of indifferent rainfall new browse areas have been created in this way.

Any decision to propagate browse plants must take into account – and this is a fundamental rule of agroforestry – the impact of the grass cover. It is known that the grass cover is greatly affected by the presence of woody perennials: reduced evapotranspiration in their shade, fertilization of the soil around them by deposits of organic matter (and possibly by the bacterial activity of mycorrhiza) improve the quality and quantity of grass. However, if the woody plants are too close together or the shade too dense, this can have a depressive effect on the grass cover, partly because of competition for available water.

The choice of woody species to introduce into a silvo-pastoral production system – as in an agro-silvo-pastoral system – depends on several factors. As ROBINSON (1983) pointed out, the same applies to where they are placed (on community or non-appropriated grazing land, on private pasture, around the edges of fields or in the fields themselves, near water courses, etc.) and to the way they are managed (planting, waterings, irrigation, protection, shaping, training, lopping, trimming, coppicing, distribution in terms of age, frequency, etc.). Heading the list of these factors are the main purposes that woody plants are required to fulfil within the system (fodder supply, shade, firewood); for example, if the main objective is to provide forage, a wide range of species must be looked at in order to avoid the risks of non-palatability or fatigue, even toxicity, that are always a hazard with a single species, and attention must be paid to the times at which the parts of the woody plants consumed as forage (leaves, fruits, branches, . . .) are available and how their nutritional value evolves, in such a way as to establish a forage nutrition calendar that will make it possible to supply suitable forage of the right quantity and quality throughout the greater part of the year. If shade for animals is the main reason for increasing the woody plants, a study must be made of the places where the cattle are during that time of year and at those hours of the day when the heat is at its fiercest, and the needs of each type of animal must be analysed: sheep can find shade under low shrubs, but cattle cannot; also the needs of each category within the same species: lambs are much more sensitive to heat than ewes. The side-effects of the operation also have to be taken into consideration: for example, what will be the effect of tree production on neighbouring crops or grazing? Environmental repercussions also have to be considered: for example, the introduction of woody perennials may create perches or nesting places for grain-eating birds which may ravage neighbouring cereals, especially if there is an oasis or irrigated area in the middle of grazing land; woody subjects can also harbour glossina at a moment when non-tolerant cattle are occupying these areas. To recap, some of the points to be taken into account are:

– labour resources; for example, if zero grazing has to be carried out, cutting and transport require a large labour force; less labour is needed for trimming and none at all if browsing is unrestricted;

– flexibility of pastoral management; for example, are other fodder resources available while the grazing area is being planted and the young woody plants being protected by a prohibition on grazing?

– land availability, avoiding conflicts of interest.

The various *Prosopis* are drought-resistant, nitrogen-fixers and palatable. On the Pacific coast of Latin America the algaroba or fruit of *Prosopis chilensis* was used as food and fodder long before the arrival of Christopher Columbus. The tree is still grown, even on poor soils in areas with a rainfall of between 250 and 12 500 mm/year. According to BENE *et al.*, (1977), pod production can be as much as 4 tonnes or even more per hectare and the pods contain 9% protein, 47% non-nitrogenous extract, 0.6% fat and 25% raw cellulose. Their fodder value compares favourably with barley. The flour obtained from them makes a nourishing food which can be eaten uncooked and keeps well. When one reflects that in some regions a quarter of the family budget can be spent on fuel for a single hot meal per day, it is worth remembering that the edible seeds and pods of these trees need no cooking.

Prosopis have a high calorific coefficient which makes an excellent source of firewood and charcoal. Their powerful root system enables them to produce pods and forage, as well as nectar much sought-after by bees, from their third or fourth year. Their wood is hard and durable and highly prized for posts, stakes, house construction and furniture.

It remains difficult, however, to distinguish between the different species and varieties. Hybrids are capable of back-crossing with parents and sometimes a line obtained in this way can stabilize (CHANDLER, 1979). It has been asserted (POULSEN, 1979 b) that the species and varieties best suited to the Sahelian and Sudanian regions have not yet been identified conclusively. According to BURKART (1976) *Prosopis juliflora* (Swartz) DC. is different from *P. chilensis* (Mol.) Stuntz.; others consider that the *glandulosa* variety of *P. juliflora* common in Texas and California is a true species. This is an illustration of the complexity and confusion of taxonomy. In practice, it is important to know the exact origin of the seeds, because wide variations in cold-resistance etc. have been observed.

Prosopis alba Gris. is used primarily as a windbreak and browse tree. The fruits, when ground, give an edible flour.

P. juliflora is a very good sand stabilizer and can tolerate great heat and poor and saline soils; it can survive on 150 to 700 mm precipitation a year. The fruits are edible. They contain up to 27% glucose and 17% protein. The leaves are eaten by animals, except those varieties with a high tannin content.

The wood is excellent for burning, and because it is so long-lasting, railway sleepers are even made from it. Root competition and an allelopathy would prejudice the growth of grass cover; therefore it should be used with caution in agroforestry.

Two objections are often raised against the use of Prosopis in Africa: 1) it can become invasive; 2) it is an exotic. On the first point, one would be only too happy in certain very degraded, not to say denuded, regions to find an invasive plant with as many qualities as Prosopis; for the rest, if the necessary precautions are taken, especially on irrigated land where there is constant surveillance, it is relatively easy to control an incipient invasion; if invasion has commenced with no control, it can become impossible to halt. This is what happens, for example, with *Acanthospermum hispidum*, a weed imported from the USA through the western and then the eastern ports of Africa, which in the space of about a century has spread through almost all the semi-arid zones of Africa, where its sharp fruits pierce the hides of animals and cause abcesses. Another weed, lantana, has invaded thousands of hectares of pasturage in East Africa. As for the indigenous versus exotic plant question, it is irrelevant. The important point is to use the plants that give the best possible results in a given environment. Of course, care must be taken to conserve the genetic heritage and preserve as many species as possible, but it should be remembered that 6 soya varieties of Asiatic origin account for the total soya production in the USA, more than 50% of the wheat grown in Canada depends on Kenyan germinating plasma, and at least one-third of the leguminous forage cultivars sold by Australia have their origin in the Maghreb.

According to MYERS (1983), 10% of plant species threatened with extinction before the year 2000 could be used to make medicines and pharmaceutical preparations whose worldwide sales could amount to several billions of dollars per year towards the beginning of the 21st century.

Although population density is generally very low in areas of extensive stock rearing, it often exceeds the human carrying capacity of those regions. In Kenya, for example, not only the areas of extensive stock rearing but all categories of land are already supporting a greater human population than their carrying capacity (see Map 3), as Jim CREES (1984) and others have pointed out. Consequently, that population cannot hope to raise its standard or security of living by agriculture or animal husbandry, and since little employment is being created in urban and industrial centres, there must be real concern for the future. Although improvement of living standards must be considered as the top priority in the arid regions where populations are fighting each other in order to survive, it is difficult to see how, in practical terms, this can ever be achieved if population growth is not rapidly curbed.

Organized population migrations to spread demand more evenly have sometimes been tried. They very rarely succeed and, in the context of nomadic or transhumant herdsmen, e.g. the Masai or the Kababish or the Woodabe, who are generally perfectly adapted to their milieu – ecologically, economically and culturally – they are impracticable; the least change in customs and practices creates severe, even lethal, disturbance. This is in line with all the laws of biology and ecology: the better an organism is suited to its milieu, the more difficult it is to change that milieu without serious consequences for the survival of that organism. So, any change of the environment (in the total meaning of that word, namely cultural) should only be contemplated with the most extreme caution. Such changes imposed on traditional milieus usually result in an increase in unemployment, delinquency and prostitution. To a certain extent, moreover, those who wield the power and take the decision to radically alter the way of life of others without their consent are abusing that power and they exert a sort of social imperialism in decreeing for others that one life style is better than another.

In the Sahel, herdsmen have for long been in a confrontation situation with agriculture, and many of the originally nomad populations are involved, directly or indirectly, in agricultural activities (LAMPREY, 1983). Directly, in that either part of the originally nomadic population devotes itself to agriculture, or the population goes in for growing crops for part of the year and for nomadism the rest of the time. Indirectly sometimes, when nomadic groups used sedentary slaves to cultivate the land and grow the cereals they needed. But it is not always like this: in East Africa, stock-rearing populations do not have any agricultural tradition. They depend almost entirely on livestock products: milk, blood, meat, and are only just beginning to learn to complement their diet with other foods that they obtain by barter or by selling their animals or, more rarely, milk, meat, hair or hides, or from a distribution of food aid. Basically, therefore, all their needs are met by their herds and flocks. Before the colonial period, each ethnic group had a strict internal discipline, even a legal system, which ensured the controlled use of natural resources, primarily water and fodder resources, so that everyone had a fair share of those resources and so that there would be sufficient resources held in reserve for the hard times. Epidemics periodically decimated men and beasts. A kind of family plan-

171

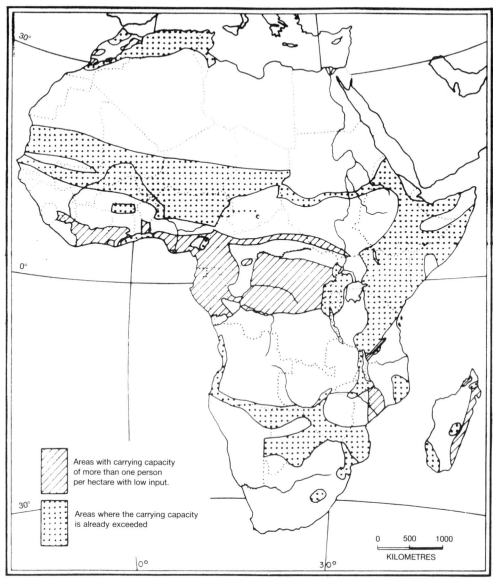

Areas with carrying capacity
of more than one person
per hectare with low input.

Areas where the carrying capacity
is already exceeded

MAP 3
Human carrying capacity and population density in Africa (adapted from FAO, 1984a)

ning existed, aimed at maintaining the strength of the group; in some cultures, the family was limited by the requirements of the dowry, which was calculated so that no new family could be set up unless it possessed the requisite number of animals to be self-sufficient; in others, it is the initiation ceremonies giving access to distinct clans, like that of the 'ilmoran' or warriors among the Masai, that curb and regulate marriage and procreation possibilities, so allowing the elders to adjust to some extent the fertility of the group to the available food resources. The suppression of these practices, which show a remarkable adaption of man to his environment, could result in dramatic upheavals, leading populations into all kinds of unfortunate aberrations.

In periods of exceptional drought in pre-colonial times in Africa famine, disease and conflicts over the use of the meagre existing resources guaranteed an adjustment between human and animal populations and the carrying capacity. From the beginning of the colonial period, efforts were made to prevent tribal wars and to fix boundaries between different groups. It was already estimated that resources were being over-exploited and, while recognizing that the usages laid down by the councils of elders were well founded, the colonizing governments wished to take progressively more control of the way natural resources were used, to such an extent that they were soon seen by the people as oppressors, and all the more so in that the combined efforts of the Health and Veterinary Services rapidly exacerbated the human and animal pressure on the land. In many cases, a situation was reached where councils of elders no longer wanted to have anything to do with pastoral control, preferring to leave that responsibility – at least officially – to the occupying powers.

Then in the 1960s, when many African countries achieved independence, the new governments no longer concerned themselves with these controls, which seemed to them so many useless constraints, while at best the old discipline persisted as a mere shadow. In practical terms, every animal owner became free to graze and browse his herds and flocks wherever and whenever he wanted; sometimes laws were even promulgated declaring that grazing land belonged to everyone. An inevitable irresponsibility and rapid over-utilization of natural resources ensued, with every individual following his own instinct to maxmize his herd, at the expense of others if need be, without any regard to the maintenance of forage reserves in case of famine. Furthermore, the food handouts given by international aid in times of famine only served to aggravate the lack of concern among both stockmen and governments alike.

Consequently, today the situation in grazing areas in zones of extensive cattle rearing is grave. Nomadism is a thing of the past, now that the doctor and the veterinary officer have appeared on the scene. Yet one would not wish to see the most characteristic features of nomadic cultures disappear, namely their contribution in nobility of mind, hospitality and conviviality, robustness and rigour, sense of adventure and responsibility. Perhaps agroforestry could help to preserve a little of these qualities, notably in silvo-pastoral systems where wildlife would have a place.

Silvo-pastoral systems and wildlife

In arid and hyper-arid conditions, wild animals are often better than domestic animals at using the meagre water and forage resources, which they convert more efficiently into proteins. There are also, and have been since prehistoric times, human populations whose principal means of existence is the harvesting, processing and utilization of wild life and its products. In addition, many herdsmen on desert margins and in arid zones and even marginal crop growers find in wild game a far from negligible food resource, valued both as a complement to the diet and indeed an emergency source of food in times of drought, but also sometimes as a delicacy. Unfortunately this resource is under threat both from man and from exceptional droughts. Many wild animals adapt well to drought, sometimes in quite original ways: the gerenuk or Waller's gazelle meets all its water needs by eating only browse plants and the Grant's gazelle and eland can cool their blood by several degrees before it reaches the brain, thanks to a mechanism which pumps blood from the carotid via the nose where it is cooled before flowing into the brain, essential since the brains of animals only function at a temperature of about 37°C; a temperature rise of 5°C has been recorded in the body of the eland without any change in the temperature of the blood flowing to the brain. However, by destroying the small amount of vegetation (even woody perennials) that wild animals use for food, exceptional droughts, can result in wholesale slaughter of species in some areas. But man remains the greatest predator for wildlife; 'Technological Man', equipped with motor vehicles and firearms (often automatic) far more so than 'Traditional Man' who was better adapted to the environment and had less deadly weapons.

Table XVIII (from ANDERSON and HERLOCKER, 1973) shows the seasonal changes in the use game animals make of natural vegetation in the Ngorongoro crater in Tanzania. It shows that associations including a large number of woody plants (asterisked) are used for a much longer time and therefore more efficiently than associations where herbs predominate. There are apparent differences, but at no point is only one type of vegetation used by a single animal species, although sometimes one species of vegetation is used more than the others.

174

TABLE XVIII

Seasonal changes in the use of vegetation types by the wild fauna in the Ngorongoro crater
(after ANDERSON and HERLOCKER, 1973)
An asterisk (*) denotes types with a high woody content

Vegetation type	Jan	Feb	Mar	Apr	May	Jun	Jul	Aug	Sep	Oct	Nov	Dec
Cyperus/Aeschynomena A marsh complex									rhinoceros, reedbuck, brindled gnu, hippopotamus, zebra, elephant			
Chloris/Cynodon herbage									zebra, gnu, mainly greater ungulates			
*Acacia xanthophloea/Achyranthes forest						mainly rhinoceros, elephant, hippopotamus, zebra, gnu, waterbuck						
Low pseudo-steppe with scanty Sporobolus/Odyssea							mainly Thomson's gazelle					
Low pseudo-steppe with Sporobolus/Cynodon												
Low grazing with Cynodon/Digitaria			mainly gnu, zebra, Thomson's gazelle									
Low savanna with Cynodon/Digitaria			mainly gnu, zebra, Thomson's gazelle, hartebeeste									
Savanna with Pennisetum/Cynodon/Andropogon					mainly gnu, zebra, eland, Thomson's gazelle							
Savanna with Cynodon/Andropogon/Digitaria						zebra, gnu and gazelle						
Savanna with Andropogon/Digitaria/Themeda						zebra, hartebeest, eland, gnu, gazelle						
High savanna with Themeda/Setaria & Lippia						gazelle, zebra, gnu, buffalo, hartebeest / mainly Grant's gazelle, zebra, buffalo, elephant, eland, hartebeest						
*Forestation/forest/brush complex			mainly zebra, buffalo, eland, Grant's gazelle, klippspringer, elephant, hartebeest									

Variations in palatability and digestibility of different vegetation types are an important factor in the local migration of fanua. The crude protein content and digestibility coefficients of the leaves of certain browse plants in the dry savannas of Rhodesia are listed below:

	Crude Proteins as % of the DM		% Coefficient of digestibility for the leaves	
	Leaves	Branches	Crude Proteins	DM
Melhania acuminata	15.9	6.9	71.1	48.6
Grewia flavescens	15.1	6.9	70.1	53.5
Grewia spp. (*)	14.4	7.4	69.2	35.3
Combretum apiculatum	12.8	6.5	66.6	47.4
Colophospermum Mopane	12.3	5.0	65.6	41.3
Commiphora mollis	10.9	5.1	62.4	46.1

(*) hybrid crosses between G. bicolor, G. monticola and G. subspathulata

Table XIX shows preferences of some wild animals in their utilization of low savanna or forest grazing.

TABLE XIX

Ecological dispersal or superposition in the use of various habitats by wild animals. Top portion after LAMPREY (1963 and 1964); bottom portion after FERRAR and WALKER (1974).

Domestic animals, too, have their feeding preferences, usually even more pronounced than those of wild animals; since domestic animals have more choice over the plants they eat, the result is a selection in reverse order of quality of grazing, more pronounced than with wild animals. The most common way of measuring fodder preferences is to compare the total time an animal spends browsing or grazing a single species. The findings

176

show that goats and dromedaries browse much more than they graze, whereas zebras and cattle graze 99% of the time they are feeding. In a bush savanna in East Africa, goats prefer Combretaceae and *Colophospermum Mopane* if present; they can devote up to 200% of their browsing time (which in itself represents a little over 50% of feeding time) eating one species, whereas one often finds more than 50 woody species in their gut. In Sahelo-Saharan bush savanna, goats prefer the Mimosas, which may make up as much as 75% of the plants they browse.

It is possible to increase production of wild game products in silvo-pastoral systems by appropriate management measures to control desertification. The aim is to provide species of wildlife that need to be encouraged with the browse plants that they need. The needs and preferences of wild animals vary, and it is not only important that the browse be available for the longest possible period: for migratory animals it must be available during the most suitable period. Animal proteins for human consumption can be obtained from the game, primarily for the local populations and then, if there is a surplus, for consumption outside the production zone, (but that presents problems of conservation and transport). Other products can be very important. For example, hides and ostrich feathers have a high commercial value; skins and trophies do, too, but there need to be very strict controls on obtaining, marketing and exporting these; and lastly, tourist safaris can be of great educational and economic value. Alongside natural production of wild animals, there will probably in future be more and more controlled production, or 'game ranching', and of ungulates in particular. This method is justified for the following reasons:

- Domestic cattle are ill-suited to arid and semi-arid regions in which their productivity remains low. With goats they are responsible for the desertification of vast tracts of land in *sensu lato* arid zones, especially in Asia and Africa.

- The wild ungulates have become adapted to arid surroundings, especially in their resistance to drought, high temperatures and disease.

- They often live in mixed species groups which exploit the plant species more diversely and they cause less damage to the vegetation than do domestic animals.

- Game ranching is better able than domestic livestock rearing to yield a good income, more protein and a production less subject to climatic variation. But this formula is not possible unless it is officially and legally recognized as a method of land use.

Exploitation of wildlife is normally only considered administratively for its touristic or hunting aspects and not as a more general source of goods and services. But it is precisely because the management of wildlife can be the most appropriate use of areas of land while respecting the environment that a silvo-pastoral system based on the wildlife can often be recommended. There are areas (e.g. many of the hyper-arid regions) where it is probably the best possible use of the very meagre resources. The Saharan regions, for instance, where they are not being exploited for oil or other mineral resources, appear capable of producing nothing better than the addax or the oryx. But these highly threatened species will disappear completely if serious management measures are not taken. The example of the reconstitution of the beisa oryx herd in the Sultanate of Oman shows that it can be done. For management of the fauna to be a profitable proposition, the habitat must be adequately diversified, isolated and re-siliant to biotic and abiotic variations. There also needs to be very clear definition of user categories and of the methods of utilization and control.

In general, controlled exploitation of the fauna is not compatible with agriculture, except perhaps for birds like the bustard, the guinea-fowl and the francolin, but these are not browsers and so hardly concern agroforest-ry, even though they need wooded cover. But in certain situations this exploitation can be combined with livestock and forestry, and particularly with forms of silvo-pastoralism paractised by nomadic or transhumant populations on the margins of hyper-arid regions.

If consideration has to be given to the sociological, cultural, economic and environmental dimensions of wildlife use in silvo-pastoral systems, there is also a need, as pointed out by Gilbert CHILD (1985), to develop better management techniques and production systems that will make best use of the biological and ecological advantages of wildlife management. It is not sufficient to apply management methods adopted in very different circumstances. Management methods must be developed specially for this new approach. There is a particular need to develop usable woody vegeta-tion more widely utilized by wild than by domestic animals. KING and HEATH (1975) showed, for example, that the oryx did not yield well if it was penned in a corral at night like domestic cattle, because it could not use the night-time dew, a habit which is natural to it and which enables it to get by with very little surface water.

It would be possible to develop the following ungulates in desert and semi-desert regions within the context of combating desertification through silvo-pastoral systems:

	Western Africa	Eastern Africa	Southern Africa
The North African oryx			
Oryx dammah	+		
The addax			
Addax nasomaculatus	+		
The Dorcas gazelle			
Gazella dorcas	+		
The Dama gazelle			
Gazella dama	+		
The rhim or Loder's gazelle			
Gazella leptoceros	+		
The gemsbok			
Oryx gazella		+	+
Grant's gazelle			
Gazella granti		+	
Soemmering's Gazelle			
Gazella soemmeringi		+	
The springbok			
Antidorcas marsupialis			+

7.2.3 *Irrigated zones*

In irrigated zones, the presence of trees – in the widest sense – is often a cause of conflict; many farmers claim that trees attract birds, particularly the red-tailed quelea which eat cereal crops. It is true that many birds congregate in trees as well as nest there – and one bird species may markedly prefer a particular tree species (which is an incentive not to plant those trees where a harmful bird species likes to nest; since this choice is variable and depends on several factors, an ornithologist should be consulted about which tree species to avoid). But it is evident, as emphasized by quelea experts at an FAO meeting in the Tsavo Park (Kenya) in January 1985, that the number of predatory birds is more or less the same in any field, whether or not it has trees in it or round its perimeter. Besides, there is a method, all too little used, for controlling the quelea, and that is the use of birds of prey. It is known that a pair of birds of prey are enough to scare away birds which are their habitual prey from an area of approximately 500 to 2,500 ha according to the species present. It is therefore possible to calculate the number of pairs of birds of prey that theoretically need to be kept in a crop-growing area to scare away birds which would otherwise eat the crops. In fact, there is another, more constructive, attitude that can be taken towards these bird pests, a kind of 'Chinese style' attitude (the Chinese do not have a word for 'weed', since every plant has a potential positive use): crop-eating birds should be looked on not as a nuisance but as, for instance, a source of protein (BAUMER, 1985). Birds can be eaten direct or turned into dog and cat food.

In conclusion, I believe that the advantages to be drawn from the presence of trees in irrigated crops outweigh any disadvantages, especially if adequate measures have been taken in time to limit the number of harmful birds (there are also many useful birds, one must remember, particularly insectivores) and to turn them to good account.

The main agroforestry practice in irrigated arable zones is the use of woody perennials to provide shelter for crops. In the form of windbreaks, for instance, woody plants can reduce the mechanical and dessicating action of wind; reduced evapotranspiration allows a yield increase of up to 25%. But woody plants also consume water and an exact balance sheet of their advantages and drawbacks needs to be made before deciding to use them.

Main advantages	Main disadvantages

They reduce evapotranspiration
Mechanical protection (sand)
Wood production
Forage production
 	
Food production
Shade
They have a fertilizing action
  (leaves, nitrogen-fixing bacteria) etc.
	They consume water
	Root competition
	Shelter for seed-eating birds
	Risk of raising temperatures
	  (if too dense)
	They take up land
	Shade

Root competition also has to be taken into consideration. The best way to offset this is only to use woody perennials with poorly-developed lateral root systems. Another way is to dig a trench between trees and crops, but it is very difficult in irrigated crops to prevent the trench becoming a gutter. Lateral roots can also be severed with a long narrow iron spade.

In irrigated systems, hedges can also play an important part in reducing wind speeds and evapotranspiration, as well as providing products (fruits, forage, firewood, etc), to complement the crops they protect. One of the woody plants currently being used for this purpose, particularly in the Sudanese Gezira and the vegetable gardens on the Gambian frontier near Tambacounda (Senegal), is *Leucaena leucocephala*; planted along irrigation channels with narrow spacings (10 to 20 cm), Leucaena grows very rapidly and is capable of providing a considerable amount of forage. It can be cut several times a year, up to once every two months; one solution frequently adopted is to let a main stem grow and to lop it to the same height each time. This way a trunk several centimetres in diameter is obtained quite quickly. As the saplings have been planted very close to each other, the stems form a sort of transparent barrier which acts as a brake on the wind, marks plot boundaries clearly and stops straying animals. The forage can also be exploited without letting a thick woody trunk form, by cutting

180

much lower, between 5 and 30 cm, as is the practice in humid zones, notably in Australia (FERRARIS, 1979), in Hawaii (BREWBAKER *et al*. 1972), in Fiji (PARTRIDGE and RANACOU, 1973), etc.

The amount of fodder produced from an irrigated hedge of Leucaena is quantitatively and qualitatively superior to the yield from the same irrigated surface area of lucerne. Naturally, it depends on the height and frequency of the cutting: with the Peru variety and a distance of 90 cm between rows, the yield is more than two and a half times higher than with a 30 cm row spacing, with the same 5 cm spacing between plants (FERRARIS, 1979) But with 20 cm spacing along rows 244 cm apart, and cutting twice as frequently, i.e. every four weeks, foliage production per stand is greater still (for fodder and mulching). These findings are interesting but, in practice, crops (particularly cereal crops) only benefit from being inter-cropped with hedges of Leucanea if nitrogen availability is the major pedological constraint and if cereal production levels are low (e.g. of the order of 10t/ha for maize). In soils that are richer, particularly in nitrogen, there is less active fixing of nitrogen in the air by the root nodules and the advantage of using nitrogen-fixing woody plants is obvious. On the other hand, on depleted soils, Leucaena – bearing natural or inoculation-induced nodules – can be a great help in increasing production, particularly of cereals, and in conserving soil fertility. This can be maintained either by mulching with the leaves and branches of Leucaena or, indirectly, by animal droppings if Leucaena is used as forage. Other nitrogen-fixing legumes can be used in a similar way, notably *Calliandra macrothyrsa, Gliricidia Sepium, Cassia Siamea* and *C. spectabilis, Erythrina* sp.pl., *Sesbania* spp. One of the advantages of Leucaena and Calliandra is their great flexibility of use: they can be treated according to need; for example, planning a programme of enrichment by direct mulching, but deciding to use the leaves and young branches as irrigated forage if a drought deprives cattle of other fodder resources. The stems can also be cut down and allowed to dry for firewood. In every case, an agroforestry system is characterized by the biological and economic interaction of woody perennials and the crops they are protecting and enhancing.

Oases constitute a special case of an ecotope where irrigated crops are usually grown. They are often under threat or in the process of disappearing through encroachment by the desert. Agroforestry can make an effective contribution to rescuing oases. Various types of oases:

– along intermittent water courses like the In Gall Wadi in Niger;

– below foothills around the fringes of arid basins like those around Agades;

– in the middle of deserts and sometimes at the foot of more or less
sandy escarpments like Bilma or Fachi, again in Niger,

are seriously affected by desertification and are disappearing. As MAIN-
GUET (1982) has written, the causes are deterioration of the climate, a
depletion of water sources, aggravation of aeolian geomorphological mechanisms (increase in sand deposits and removal of the topsoil), textural
changes of sandy soils and accelerated salination processes. To these must
be added the socio-economic human causes:

– variation in the composition and numbers of herds and flocks: for
example at Bilma caravans of camels are not so frequent now and
some families have to store a whole year's collected salt,

– changes at a technological level in every sphere (crop growing,
irrigation, transport, etc.),

– fall-off in productivity of some crops,

– aggravated state of human malnutrition,

– increase in the rural exodus, altering the distribution of age groups,
with a lack of the middle age group (especially men),

– transition from a barter economy to a semi- or total money economy,

– change in needs, and social and political situations (new regimes,
new frontiers, State interference).

Agroforestry's potential contribution to this is obvious. Many oasis
dwellers have unknowingly been practising agroforestry for centuries. The
appropriate techniques are:

– using trees which go deeper down to find water and can tolerate
having part of their trunk buried in sand: the date palm is the best
example here;

– planting a filter hedge on the edge of the oasis to keep back wind and
sand; a multi-storey hedge, for example chaste tree/pomegra-
nate/*Acacia Cyclops* or *A. holosericea* (which are tending to replace
A. tortilis and *A. Seyal* . . .which indicate deep clay);

– within the oasis, more planting of multi-purpose hedges: henna,

182

Opuntia Ficus indica smooth or prickly, fig trees;

- planting fruit trees and bushes in among the crops: apricot, pomegranate, fig;

- planting micro-windbreaks of cereals in irrigated crops, to protect lower-growing crops;

- sand fixing around the oasis with *Euphorbia balsamifera, Panicum turgidum, Leptadenia pyrotechnica,* etc.

An attempt could be made to introduce *Faidherbia albida.*

But the oases, which owed their existence in the past to their role as a staging post for caravans and as a granary for nomads engaged on rezzous, can only survive if a new economic role is found for them, such as tourism might give (though this has the attendant risk of loss of cultural identity). At least one of the great historic oases of the Southern Sahara like Chingueti, Tichit or Oualata could be saved by the setting up of an International Institute for the Dromedary, a measure which is long overdue.

7.2.4 *Intercontinental transfer of agroforestry concepts*

The potential of agroforestry in controlling aridization is obviously not confined to Africa alone. It is just as great for Latin America. Incidentally it is in that part of the world that some of the most important work on nitrogen fixing with Prosopis has been done (FRANCO, 1982). One of the commonest factors in desertification in Latin American countries is erosion caused by the violence of rainfall on soils with very little plant cover. Forestation of those soils would considerably, if not totally, halt erosion, but the great need of the ever-growing population for arable land would rapidly cancel out any such solution: even if the necessary effort could be devoted to establishing a tree cover in a few years, the pressure of surrounding populations would soon make itself so strongly felt that it would be impossible to prevent the clearing of the newly planted forests before they even became fully productive. One agroforestry solution, at least in certain cases, might work: it consists of authorizing new land for arable use but with the proviso that woody perennials be planted and proper agronomic practices applied. As far as possible the woody plants should be multi-purpose species, fast growers and nitrogen fixers, so that it quickly becomes clear to the peasant that it is to his advantage to plant them. Numbers, arrangement in time and space and above all the distribution of their root system in the ground must be determined to achieve an anti-erosion effect that mimics as closely as possible the effect of a total forest cover. But a good herbaceous cover of perennial grasses with deep roots is as effective against erosion as wooded cover. Therefore, as part of the anti-erosion measures, strips of grasses should be liberally planted along contour lines. Among the woody species lending themselves to agroforestry use in the notorious hunger zone of North-East Brazil, VASCONCELOS (1985) mentions exotics like leucenas and prosopis, but also woody forage legumes like the 'juca' *Caesalpinia ferrea*, the 'sabia' *Mimosa caesalpiniaefolia* and the 'mororos' Bauhinia sp.pl.

Since the ecology of North-East Brazil resembles that of the Sahelo-Sudanian zone, some indications are given below which might stimulate interest in making transpositions to the African continent. North-East Brazil is closer to the equator than the Sahel, but the predominant climatic features are the same as in the Sahelo-Sudanian zone: semi-arid with hot winters and very hot summers (C1a), sub-humid with hot winters and very hot (D1a) or hot (D1b) summers. Among the most promising xerophilous plants for North-East Brazil VASCONCELOS mentions the following indigenous woody perennials:

i) for wood production:

   Schinus terebinthifolius or 'aroeria'
   Astronium urundeuva
   Schinopsis brasiliensis or 'barauna'
   Tabebuia caraiba or 'craibeira'
   Erythrina velutina or 'mulungu'
   Tecoma chrysostricha or 'pau-d'arco-amarelo'
   Tecoma ipe or 'pau-d'arco-roxo'
   Dalbergia cearensis or 'pau-violeta'
   Mimosa caesalpiniaefolia or 'sabia'

ii) for forage production:

   Zizyphus Joazeiro or 'juazeiro'
   Caesalpinia ferrea or 'juca'
   Bromelia laciniosa or 'macambira'
   Bauhinia sp.pl. or 'mororo'

iii) for waxes and oils:

   Copernicia cerifera or 'carnauba'
   Onidoscolus phyllacanthus or 'favela'
   Croton sonderianus or 'marmeleiro preto'
   Licania rigida or 'oiticica'
   Jatropha Curcas or 'pinhao'

184

iv) for fibre production:

Neoglaziovia variegata or 'caroa'

v) for starch production:

Manihot Glaziovii or 'manicoba'

vi) for fruit production:

Spondias tuberosa or 'umbu'.

In the very dry parts where humidity is insufficient to allow use of grasses along contour lines, forage cacti are used, notably of the genus *Opuntia*. Although anatomically they do not contain wood, opuntias are classed as woody perennials in agroforestry because of the similar role they can play.

The genus *Opuntia* comprises 258 species, about a hundred of which originate from Mexico. There is a sub-genus *Platyopuntia*, in which the parts forming the stem are flattened in oval or round racket shapes, and the sub-genus *Cylindropuntia*, in which the articulations are cylindrical. Although their root system is quite shallow, it holds the soil well and encourages water infiltration, thanks to the density and interweaving of the root mass. The stems are erect or prostrate, prickly or smooth. It is the articulations of the stem, always green, that ensure photosynthesis, water absorption and transpiration; the cladodes are clad in a thick cuticle which considerably reduces evaporation and allows a long accumulation in the tissues of a great quantity of water (up to 98%); but turgescence varies considerably with changes in the water table and, in periods of severe drought, opuntias can collapse and become extremely emaciated and dehydrated, though they soon regain their turgescence once moisture is again available. The rackets can therefore make a water and forage reserve for a good part of the year. In addition, the fruit, which is ripe about 17 weeks after setting and weighs about 100 grams is edible in most of the species, raw or cooked, and is used in the making of sugars, honey, jellies, liqueurs, wines and spirits; selection work is being carried out, notably in Mexico, to develop characteristics such as: low number of seeds, large size, high sugar content, pleasant flavour, travel-tolerance, etc. In Mexico, a distinction is made between the cultivated and wild or 'forest' 'Barbary figs' ('figueiras-da-India'). Among the cultivated species, some of which are tetraploids or octoploids, *Opuntia amyclaea*, *O. Ficus-indica*, and *O. megacantha* are probably the most important; the second of these species is now distributed worldwide, notably in North Africa. Whereas the fruits of an ordinary

185

cultivar of *O. amyclaea* weight 110 g and yield 17 t/ha, a selected cultivar can yield up to 30 t/ha and individual fruits can weigh as much as 220 g. Of the wild species most researched with a view to systematic utilization, *O. streptacantha* stands out for its height, which may reach 3.5 m and an annual production of green matter of approximately one tonne. Other species, like *O. leucotricha*, *O. robusta* and *O. hyptiacantha* are also being bred for their fruit.

Many, however, are used essentially as forage plants. This is true of *O. Ficus-indica* which was introduced into North Africa in the last century, and its cultivation for forage purposes in association with other plants constitutes a true agroforestry system there, with clearly defined management rules (MONJAUZE and LE HOUEROU, 1965). Also important as forage plants and having their place in silvo-pastoral, agro-silvo-pastoral or agropastoral systems are: *O. robusta*, *O. amyclaea*, *O. streptacantha*, *O. Engelmanii*, *O. Lindheimerii*, *O. phaeacantha*, *O. stenopetala*, *O. leucotricha* and *O. cantobrigiensis*. But it is a Cactaceae of another genus, *Nopalea cochenillifera*, originating in the 'Zona cactologica' of Mexico (situated between 100° and 102° 30'west by 22° north) which appears to give the best forage yields in terms of absolute value, especially in North-East Brazil. Grown with 2 × 1.5 m spacings, it can yield 300 t/ha of rackets after three years. However, this plant is less drought-resistant than the Opuntias.

It should be noted that whereas many Cactaceae are highly drought-resistant, good forage plants and good fruiters, good yields are only obtained using the appropriate methods of cultivation. It is therefore not enough to introduce Cactaceae, they need to be cultivated. The best material yields are obtained on good manured, cultivated and maintained soils, in an alley-cropping system with other crops. This method also gives the best economic yields.

8. PRELIMINARY STEPS TO EFFECTIVE AGROFORESTRY

8.1 POLITICAL WILL AND PLANNING

If one accepts that the agroforestry approach can be a highly effective weapon in the fight against desertification, ways must be found of developing that approach on a wide scale. The normal channel would be a massive concentration and stepping-up of extension work on all aspects of agroforestry, enlisting the participation of populations (cf. section 8.3). Such a decision can only be based on the political will of governments and it can only be implemented within the framework of national planning. As COULIBALY (1983) observed: all development policies must be based on national effort; every nation must move forward by developing its own basic technology so as to extract the maximum profit from its national wealth: a population which is not self-sufficient in the basic needs cannot aspire to real independence.

Planning for national development has only become a tool of the majority of governments in the last few decades, broadly speaking since the second world war, when many nations, much weakened by conflict, sought to accelerate the process of economic development, thereby rejecting the concept of an evolution resulting from the invisible working of market forces. The USSR was the first country to inaugurate, at least officially and under that name, a national plan. By so doing, it rejected the idea that the 'invisible hand' of the market could lead to a general material improvement for the peoples in the Soviet bloc, simply by the free play of indiviuals and enterprises acting in their own interests; it rejected the concept of improvement of social conditions merely by giving free rein to market forces, and installed a 'visible hand' in the process of actively seeking to bring about economic and social improvements. In Africa, the majority of nations have attempted to plan since their independence; generally faced quite suddenly with a new economic context, they saw planning as a way of controlling their future. Rejecting a continuation of a state of affairs which perpetuated or accentuated social inequalities, the majority of countries began to formulate objectives which implied change instead of stability, growth instead of stagnation.

There are degrees of planning, and if planning involves having objectives it also demands that the means should exist to define those objectives and to attain them. This gives rise to two observations:

1) since one never has all the means necessary to achieve all the

desired objectives, a choice has to be made, objectives have to be placed in some order of priority;

2) definition of the objective depends on the information and basic data available, and it is possible to start planning with very few means and with vague objectives which gradually become more precise.

Planning is a repetitive process, and we shall return to this theme: the thinking must move back and forth continuously between

facts of the problem ⟷ means ⟷ objectives

There is complete and permanent interaction between the elements of planning. Planning is a dynamic process, a movement and not a state. The formulation of national objectives is more complex than deciding where to go on holiday, but the procedure followed is similar. National objectives are defined within the framework of a policy. A policy is a coherent body of strategies indicating how the objectives, aims, programmes and projects arising from it can be attained. The objectives are formulated at national level, like the policies; they are indications of intention, direction pointers. The aims are more precise and more detailed objectives; unlike objectives they are quantified.

In order to fulfil these aims, appropriate strategies are needed; these will be expressed in concrete terms by programmes. The programmes are then divided into activities or projects.

There needs to be real understanding that planning, if it is to be successful, cannot simply be imposed from on high. Its success will be proportional to the mutual feedback between the planner and the planned. Such feedback is an essential condition for the reconciliation between agroforestry and planning. In its essence, agroforestry tends to meet the needs of the peasant as he himself perceives and experiences them: it cannot then easily accommodate authoritarian directives from the top without consultation and total agreement from the bottom. I support BETTELHEIM's (1971) contention that the participation of the masses (cf 8.3) is necessary, as is also 'the total dedication of the professional politicians to the national interest'. I agree with him when he writes: '. . . one must guard against a bureaucratic and financial conception of a development plan'. Nothing is more dangerous, in this context, for an under-developed country than to imagine that all that is needed is for a steering group to ask a few experts to prepare a development plan, then to turn to overseas countries to obtain the necessary credit to carry out the plan' and again '. . . a development policy cannot be guaranteed, as some believe, because an 'elite' is called upon, unless that elite is essentially an elite of devotion and self-sacrifice'.

8.2 THE TIME FACTOR

There is great elasticity in biological balances and, however serious the threat of desertification, one might feel tempted to say that the danger was perceived 50 years ago and that life still goes on, notwithstanding, or else to relax with the reassuring idea that the recurrent patterns of climate that over the last few years have accentuated the desertification phenomenon will not continue for ever, and that all will be well when successive years of plentiful rainfall return. Or to take a defeatist attitude along the lines that many a civilization, many a culture, many a people have disappeared and yet the Earth continues to turn.

Another attitude is apparent from the observation made by CARREL, (already mentioned in section 6.7). It consists of the desire to make use of knowledge accumulated as much by traditional man as by the man of science in order to help populations affected by desertification meet the needs they perceive. This attitude is perfectly compatible with the agroforestry approach, which relies on local wisdom while at the same time making use of the most advanced scientific data.

To take the example of the pastoral way of life. Projects have to be planned with the herdsmen and for them; if projects continue to target areas which lie outside the herdsmens' major concern – i.e. survival (for example, increasing meat exports) they will continue to be examples of exploitation of 'peripheral zones' by 'metropolitan nuclei', from both the domestic and international points of view. Management of grazing land in developing countries in particular can and must be aimed at 'B zones' (HENRY, 1975) or traditional economies with low energy consumption, to give these economies the opportunity to free themselves from the invasive economy of high-technology 'A zones'. There is no other way to succeed and that is why it is very important that it should succeed, to prove that a New Economic Order is possible, that different values and cultures can coexist and that the fate of the most disadvantaged is not hopeless. It is not a question of moving back into an old order but of making sure that, without disorder or confrontation or upheaval, a transfer of technology (and, if possible, finance) is instituted on a much more intense level from the rich world to the poor world. 'Protection must be given to the most fragile structures in rural life, which still fulfil an essential function in the balance of society. At the same time, it must be made easier to introduce massive and effective technological solutions which are best adapted to local ecological constraints' (HENRY, 1975).

Unfortunately, the application of these principles and the setting-up of agroforestry projects are a slow business. Yet there are good effective and proven technological solutions available to combat desertification in dry zones, from the hyper-arid to the semi-humid: windbreaks, alley cropping, association of woody perennials with crops, hedges, green fences, micro-windbreaks, etc.

The time has surely come for a massive effort to apply here and now all that agroforestry is known to offer, while at the same time continuing studies and research that will lead to an even better understanding of agroforestry systems and techniques, their dynamics and the optimum conditions for their use. If even half of what is known were applied consistently, there is no doubt that the advance of desertification would be brought up short. If action is delayed it may be too late, because the elasticity of systems has its own limits, and there is a danger that soon, in matters of environmental degradation, a point of no return will be reached, if we have not arrived there already.

Since the political will exists to stop desertification, and since proven technological means are to hand, is it not possible to concentrate efforts and funds into multiplying agroforestry activities to halt the desertification process?

8.3 PARTICIPATION

As BELMONT (1984) says, 'It . . . seems necessary to clarify the highly ambiguous notion of participation. For some, this word merely signifies mutual information passed between inhabitants and decision-makers. For others, it implies consulting the inhabitants. For yet others, it suggests a direct say in the decision-making'.

It is now generally acknowledged that development is not possible without the participation of the populations and sub-populations concerned. The term 'endogenous development' (SACHS, 1980) has been created to designate a method for developing a system that is self-sustaining with the minimum of input from exterior sources, particularly foreign ones. But although there may be agreement on this point, there is less of a consensus on how to elicit that participation of populations. It has to be said that often the 'elicited' participation is no more than the simple desire not to thwart the 'eliciting' authority, for fear of punishment. This is because in many cases civil servants (and foresters in particular) have not departed from their military attitude, and have remained the representatives of authority . . . even of repression, at least in the minds of the peasants, when what is needed is a change of attitude, putting oneself at the service of the people and acting henceforth as behind-the-scenes organizer. This presupposes a different kind of training from that generally followed (which is more often than not in completely different surroundings from those where that knowledge will be put into practice). It will no doubt be more difficult to change attitudes among civil servants, attached as they are to their status and prerogatives, than those of the peasant farmers, who are in more direct touch with the realities.

It was discovered as much as fifteen years ago that sector-based operations, financed by the United Nations principally, had not given good results, and a scheme for integrated rural development projects was launched. These have been no more successful. It is not enough to change a title in the hope that this will change the spirit of a programme. As a hadith of the Prophet reminds us: 'God will change nothing in their life so long as there has been no change in their heart'.

I share the views of SCHOON BROODT and VAN ZIMMEREN (FAO, 1976) on popular participation and projects:

> 'We believe that thinking is on too grand a scale, excluding any useful participation or interest by the populations at whom it is aimed and even the authorities.

> 'The size of projects, the sometimes considerable number of aims to be fulfilled, and the consequent extent of the compensatory obligations, always accepted in theory but rarely applied, dissipates efforts and troubles the people for whom these projects are thought up'.

This participation also implies the development of a sense of solidarity. Just as governments appeal for international aid, arguing the necessity for more even distribution between the rich nations and poor nations, within countries themselves a greater solidarity needs to be shown in better distribution of existing wealth, including natural resources. Participation is a form of sharing. Many palaeontologists, like LEAKEY and LEWIN (1979), maintain that the adoption of the sharing principle by peoples moving from gathering into hunting not only constituted a capital transformation of their way of life, but marked the divide between man's behaviour and that of our nearest animal relative. In sum, sharing made Man. Perhaps it is participation that will enable the human race to continue.

Small-scale projects should not rely on foreign experts, since experience proves that when these people depart they have not usually had time to train local experts capable of replacing them. It is necessary to think in terms of limited participation by foreign experts (regular consultants rather than resident experts) who, in the interests of economy, will preferably be chosen from ongoing projects running in neighbouring countries.

Another feature of small-scale projects will be the modesty of financial means put in at their inception so that they can be replicated by the population itself, with very little external financial aid, if any.

One must strike while the iron is hot. Many governments have made considerable efforts to make the population aware of the need to protect the tree and renewable natural resources in general; these efforts have begun to bear fruit. Action needs to be taken speedily before the population's interest starts to flag.

Incentives will be used to encourage local people: food aid, small competitions between schools, villages and groups of herders, competitions for gathering forage seeds, competition for the finest ram, for the best vegetables, etc. Care must be taken, however, not to create a begging mentality where the peasant no longer does anything except for a reward, payment or compensation, as is too often seen after projects of the 'Food for work' type.

Popular participation must be backed up with greater governmental effort to combat desertification. This should have priority in any government's thinking and, a necessary corollary, should carry budgetary priority.

To foster participation in the populations concerned, as well as to help civil servants and experts to find a new approach, the 'D and D' (Diagnosis and Design) method has been developed: this is a method of identifying and planning small-scale rural development projects, involving total commitment by the population concerned right from the start of the project.

The 'D and D' method (RAINTREE, 1983 a; ICRAF, 1983 a and b) is an interdisciplinary approach aiming to help agroforestry agents identify the priorities for research on techniques, based on outlines of appropriate agroforestry techniques derived from a diagnostic analysis of the needs and potentialities of land use systems. Fig. 10 shows how D + D operates and Fig. 11 shows the iterative process of diagnosis and development within the cycle of a project.

D and D methodology is all to do with participation, associating as it does those who are habitually the 'acted upon' with the definition and choice of action for development, and particularly with improving systems

192

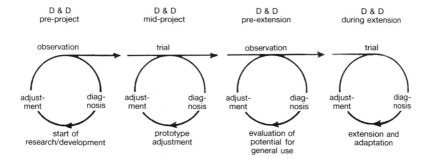

FIGURE 10

The iterative process of the D & D method within the cycle of a programme of development and extension of a technology (after RAINTREE, 1983a)

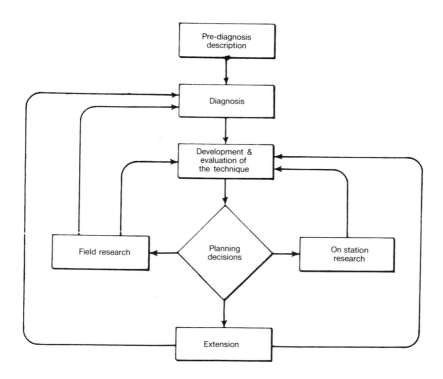

FIGURE 11

Stages in the adjustment of a project incorporating the D & D approach in the project's internal orientation system (after RAINTREE, 1983a).

of production. But whatever the chosen system, it will be useless if it is not accepted by the 'actors' concerned, farmers and herdsmen, but also tradesmen and consumers. And if it is true today that the system of cereal production in Africa has hardly evolved in the past 25 years, it is not only because of the lack of the technical ingredients needed to evolve, or because the peasants were resistant to all progress – on the contrary, all the indications are that they are receptive to innovation – but because the peasants saw no advantage in change. Cotton growing has increased spectacularly in the Sahel whereas cereal growing has continued on traditional lines, the reason being that the peasant found it to be in his interest to modernize the former, whereas government policy for low-priced cereals and the bad organization of cereal markets discouraged innovation in the producers. The growing dependence on food aid in the Sahelian countries is not due to a lack of natural resources, it is not due entirely to the period of drought being experienced, nor to the inadequacy of available techniques – the proof of this is that in 1981-82, after a very good rainy season, food aid remained indispensable – it is also, and perhaps mainly, due to existing policies, to the exploitation of peasant populations by governments in favour of their urban clientele, to a rural world whose place in the Sahelian social order is no longer recognized.

Finally, on participation, it must never be forgotten that the interests of the different protagonists in an agroforestry system are not always the same. The interests of men and women do not always coincide, as FORTMANN and ROCHELEAU (1985) have shown; therefore, all the possible motivations of the different sub-groups making up a population have to be studied carefully, before the system that will give satisfaction can be identified. Among the examples given by these authors, that of the village of Reni, in India, near the Tibetan border, is of special interest: there, 27 village women barred the way into a forest when 50 men from a neighbouring village, some of them armed, came with an entrepreneur to exploit the wood: they maintained that if the forest disappeared they would have to go much too far to find firewood. In the village of Dungari Paitoli (Chaimoli District, Uttar Pradesh), the women successfully opposed the men who wanted to clear the village trees to grow commercial potato crops; they argued that the loss of the trees would mean that they had to walk an extra 5 km a day to gather firewood. In both these examples the need to take the views of women into account in future collective decisions was recognized, and the idea that multi-purpose trees should be planted wherever possible, to meet specific needs, was accepted. However, the women asked for trees producing firewood, forage and food products whereas the men preferred saleable timber or fruit. It was also observed that interest varied according to social class; the well-off and educated women, having more time than the rest, are more willing to become involved and tend to dominate organiza-

194

tions, formal or informal, which may prevent the others from taking part.

But the surest incitement to participation is the personal interest to the peasant himself. In this regard, HOEKSTRA (1985) has clearly shown the importance of the private discount rate that the peasant brings to his choice of an agroforestry technique or system; allowing only for the extreme values of the variables, a table can be drawn up of peasant categories:

Category of peasant	Nutritional Level	Trend of Production and Income	Level of Consumption	Private Discount Rate
1	low	downwards	low	at high risk
2	low	upwards	high	at very high risk
3	high	downwards	low	at very low risk
4	high	upwards	high	at low risk

Group 3 peasants will be most inclined to participate and to adopt new agroforestry techniques, whereas group 2 will be the most reluctant. But agroforestry systems carry less risk than others through being more diversified and less subject to variations caused by physical factors than agricultural systems. Consequently, group 2 peasants may decide to lower their private discount rate when they have seen the results of agroforestry systems (for group 3 peasants) and have had convincing reports on those systems; they will then be more ready to participate in a judiciary system able to enforce them. Such a system can well be very localized, but even at that level it implies that a power of sanction exists, and this entails costs of organization.

For a technique to be readily acceptable and invite participation, it must (ROGERS and SHOEMAKER, 1971) have easily grasped advantages, be compatible with local customs, not be too complicated, be easy to test and easy to observe. Like forestry, agroforestry uses perennial woody plants, and therefore it takes years before the results are visible.

Special efforts have to be made to introduce only those techniques that deviate very little from those already known, so as to meet with the least resistance possible from the peasant farmers. RAINTREE (1983 b) has set out the strategies for encouraging adoption of agroforestry techniques. He devised the D and D approach in order to facilitate that adoption. Agroforestry attempts particularly to develop the unexploited potentials of the previous production system, to correct any weaknesses in that system, and to solve what the farmer sees as the most important real problems, because involvement and participation can only be won if the farmers or husbandmen concerned see something in it for themselves. To paraphrase

195

HOSKINS (1982), one could say that while foresters and agronomists are looking for ways to introduce modern agroforestry, it is the peasants who, in the last analysis, will decide whether the practices being proposed to them really reduce their risks, enable them to manage their resources more effectively or bring them any particular advantages. They will judge the new ideas according to their advantages over the existing systems, in the light of the growing pressure on resources from an expanding population, demographic changes, the increased technology required and their own aspirations.

8.4 LAND TENURE AND OWNERSHIP OF TREES

The problem of land tenure and ownership of trees is a fundamental one. There are numerous examples of tree-planting efforts by populations which have failed through lack of maintenance. Often, work is carried out to prepare the ground and plant the seedlings because of the incentive of cash or free food, as in the 'Food for work' project, and here it is the immediate benefit that persuades the peasant to plant and not a real interest in trees. In addition, ownership of the products (the trees themselves, foliage, fruit, . . .) is not usually clarified. In Cameroon the 'Green Sahel' planting sites have not been kept up and are dying because either the Forestry Service did not make it clear that plantations established within the framework of the operation belonged to them and that the peasants could buy the wood that they had planted, or the villagers feared that the village chief would monopolize the products for his sole use (ARGOULLON et al., 1981 a).

If the trees in a field automatically belong to the owner of that field, there is no problem. But ownership of trees is often complex. Sometimes the planter is the owner, regardless who owns the land on which the tree is planted. Sometimes trees are planted on a borrowed field: in this case custom varies widely in different areas: the planter will be the owner of the tree, for example, if the owner of the land lends it for a certain length of time (which varies in different localities and sometimes with the local spokesmen of the central authority or by tradition). In French-speaking West Africa, strict rules have been devised defining the ownership of a planted tree, but they are little respected, particularly since 1960. These regulations generally forbid the felling of any tree without a permit and although their application leaves much to be desired, few owners of land are inclined to plant trees or even to protect natural regenerations when they know that they will not be free to exploit those trees. Such dispositions are naturally a hindrance to agroforestry extension, and also to all further planting by individuals, villages or communities: those who plant want to know where the fruits of their labours will go, when and in what propor-

196

tions. Such planting operations are therefore only acceptable if all the parties involved, including the forestry services, the political powers and the local administration unanimously pass an agreement clarifying these points.

The political feasibility of many forestry projects founded on the support of the population can be problematic, simply because no appropriate local organizing body exists. It can happen that communities need the decision of an authority concerning resource management practices; for example, if it is a question of no longer treating renewable resources as a mining operation but of adopting sustained exploitation; yet often there is no one of administrative rank to take such decisions.

It is true to say that a participatory agroforestry can help enormously in resolving Africa's serious problems of management of natural resources to combat desertification because the renewable resources on that continent are relatively few and because it is on these meagre resources alone that the majority of the people live. To be acceptable, solutions must improve production and not be costly: these two features of agroforestry differ considerably from purely forestry solutions, which are costly. However, as soon as they become collective, agroforestry solutions are also costly, particularly in management. At individual level hardly any forestry activities cost almost nothing, because they also require some form of support, such as the compilation of a coherent set of ownership rights and a judiciary system able to enforce them. Such a system can well be very localized, but even at that level it implies the existence of a power of sanction, and this entails costs of organization.

Again, there are certain matters requiring co-ordinated measures that go beyond the decision-making powers of an individual or even a small group, even if these are only agroforestry measures. This is what happens, for example, when a catchment basin is to be restored, using agroforestry; it is then not only a question of individual wishes to use agroforestry solutions, there must also be some co-ordination of each individual measure taken.

One of the reason why agroforestry solutions are not costly is that they always try to follow the ways already known to the peasants concerned and to gradually broaden these out, rather than to blaze new trails. In existing systems there is nearly always some element completely accepted by the population that can be used to develop some agroforestry technique. In the dry zones of Africa, customary measures such as:

- the use of *Commiphora* or *Euphorbia balsamifera* or *E. Tirucalli* cuttings to make hedges,

- the conservation of shea butter or African locust trees in cultivated fields,

- the association of *Faidherbia albida* with cereal crops,

are already well integrated into the ecological and socio-cultural environment.

These are the kinds of practices, already well proven by use, that agroforestry systems must build upon.

In the same way, the aim must be small beginnings followed rapidly by good results. It is often a good idea to start with the household garden, where there is no ownership dispute, rather than at field level, for example. The peasant farmer, through poverty and uncertainty about the future, prefers to minimize the risks rather than take the chance to increase his profits. In fact, for a long time, so-called development projects were much more oriented towards cash crops than towards growing food, and when attention began to turn to the latter it was often with the accent on market gardening, for the benefit of the towns rather than to meet the needs of the country-dwellers. This, incidentally, supports my theory that desertification comes not from the North or from the South but from the towns! It is only recently that, thanks in the main to some non-governmental organizations, interest has been focused on the household garden. Very small in area, it still plays a considerable role in family economy and in the social structure. Copiously manured and under constant surveillance, it is a privileged place where technical innovations can be gently introduced. The household garden also shelters some domestic, milking and young animals (usually belonging to the women) and the granaries are sometimes found there when they are not part of the living quarters themselves. The household garden is therefore the nearest place to the house where essential food is grown, but it is also the ultimate resource of the peasant farmer in the event of famine and it is there that he keeps his last source of wealth, to be eaten only as a very last resort, the favourite goat or milch cow. The household garden in fact comes within the woman's domain, giving her one of the keys to power: control of precious food resources and the final source of milk in case of famine. The household garden is therefore an ideal place to introduce or develop woody perennials which can help meet the peasant's needs.

If he needs shade, for example, a neem or a mango can be recom-

198

mended. Naturally, the ecological conditions need to be taken into consideration, and also the individual situation of each farmer. One farmer will prefer neem because he knows that this tree repels insects and that a decoction of the fruit in water makes an insecticide; another will prefer mango because he is more interested in the fruits.

If the farmer wants forage for his domestic animals, he might be encouraged to plant in his household garden, if it is big enough, a *Faidherbia albida* which will give him pods and foliage and will also enrich the soil. Or he could receive help in modifying the hedge customarily grown round his household garden by adding to it an overstorey of some forage species like *Acacia tortilis* or a Prosopis. Around household gardens there is a risk that Prosopis will invade the crops, but it is only a slight risk, because permanent surveillance means that seedlings or suckers can be uprooted as soon as they appear. *Salvadora persica* can also be used to create an overstorey with a double role of producer and protector of the understorey; this species will give forage and at the same time small pieces of wood to rub round teeth and gums.

A major advantage to be gained from applying agroforestry methods to household gardens before introducing them to the fields is that there is no ambiguity about ownership and that supervision is easy. In fact, the major fault of present handling (one dare not talk of management, we are still far from that in many cases) of land threatened by desertification is straying animals. No progress can be made so long as this continues. Let us be quite clear on this point: it is not a question of abolishing herd mobility or nomadism, but of stopping all uncontrolled movement of animals, singly or in groups unsupervised by one or more shepherds. Except in bygone times when there was under-population, no country in the world has managed to meet its food needs and have a stable agriculture (*sensu lato*) with straying animals.

Nowadays, the archaic free wandering of animals is still the general rule in ACP countries affected or threatened by desertification and this imposes a restraint on the development of agroforestry in fields a long distance away from dwellings; the young woody perennials planted there or being assisted to develop need to be protected against foraging cattle. If they are planted far away from dwellings, one must either:

- rely on any surveillance the farmers themselves are able to provide when they are in the fields (but that only covers a small part of the year);

- protect the trees individually, but that is costly and, since the protec-

199

tion is generally made of cut thorny branches, this means drastic and regrettable destruction of wood;

- protect trees collectively by an enclosure, which means making hedges around the fields; but the hedges themselves need protection while still young, requiring surveillance or thorny branches; this question of hedges is often one of the keys to balancing systems of production;

- or organize permanent surveillance, not by satellite but by a mounted (for rapid mobility) and armed (to inspire respect) guard, sufficiently trained and on terms with other people to be able to put over to offenders the reasons for carrying out that protection duty. This kind of surveillance is costly and requires organization; it presupposes the ability to legislate and impose fines. In addition, for the educational effect to play its part fully, it is a good idea for the supervising role to be taken in turn by every member of the group standing to benefit from having a guard: this will avoid the creation of a sort of para-bureaucracy that would almost inevitably end in abuse of power and creation of a privileged caste. Such a develop-ment must be avoided at all costs, because if straying cattle are a plague in Africa, bureaucracy can be another . . .

8.5 TECHNOLOGY AND RESEARCH

There is a close link between the problems connected with develop-ment of agroforestry technology and research. In agroforestry, research is confronted with a situation different from other traditional fields of agron-omic research: there is no considerable corpus of accumulated data for reference, as there is for animal nutrition, crop genetics, plant propagation or many other fields. Agroforestry is confronted by questions that are as yet unanswered. Although many agroforestry practices are very old, a systema-tic inventory of agroforestry systems was only started a few years ago, and only a few systems have been described in detail; perhaps no more than three systems have begun to be described in what might be called a properly scientific way:

- the 'khejri', *Prosopis cineraria*, system in India,

- the 'kadd', *Faidherbia albida*, system in Senegal and in arid areas of Africa,

- the 'dehesa' system, currently being studied in great detail by a Franco-Spanish team from the Casa Velasquez.

200

Even in each of these three systems, large numbers of questions remain to be elucidated. For example, in the case of the *Faidherbia albida* system:

- It is not known what causes leaf-flush in dry seasons and leaf-fall in rainy seasons; this knowledge might make it possible to identify some mechanism that could be manipulated and even transferred to other species;

- little is known about the part played by bacterial nodules in fertilizing the soil and what part is played by animal droppings;

- little is known about the activity of bacterial nodules according to tree age; even less is known on whether stands of equal or mixed ages give the best nitrogen-fixing results;

- it is not always known which is the best way to grow a tree or a stand of trees to obtain the most positive effect on associated crops;

- where forage production is concerned, exact data are lacking on when to cut off branches, how much and how often;

- etc.

One of the difficulties in establishing and evaluating agroforestry techniques is that they are peculiar to one situation and to a given environment and are not universally applicable solutions. No proven methodology is yet available for evaluating the effects of various techniques, and only now is a research methodology being set up for studying agroforestry systems and their potential in all their complexity. The following words appear in the charter of the International Council for Research in Agroforestry (ICRAF): '. . . to encourage and support agroforestry research and training activities, to facilitate the gathering and diffusion of information about agroforestry systems and to help in the international coordination of agroforestry development'.

In consideration of the particular difficulties arising from this, ICRAF has not tackled the development of technologies directly, but has concentrated on the development of methodologies for generating appropriate forestry technologies (STEPPLER and RAINTREE, 1983). Since it is not possible to develop a method for doing something without at the same time doing that thing, the method followed by ICRAF runs in tandem with setting up the appropriate technologies in selected locations, not only in Kenya (Machakos region, because numerous studies have already been conducted there which have produced a wealth of useful data) but also in countries (Costa Rica, India, Peru, Rwanda, Sudan, etc.).

Unlike the traditional agronomic sciences (or at least as they were approached up until twenty or thirty years ago), agroforestry is not concerned with specific products in isolation but in interactions between components of systems, one of which by definition is the woody perennial plant. The 'product' studied by agroforestry is in fact a complete system of land use in which woody perennials interact ecologically and/or economically with other components. Therefore ICRAF has adopted a systems approach to agroforestry. Each system varies according to numerous factors, such as ecological factors, and from region to region, from country to country (because the political objectives or the economic situation will not be the same), from one type of crop to another and from one field to another. This extreme diversity is further accentuated by the personal objectives of the peasant farmer, by the agricultural components of the system (maize or sorghum, sorghum or millet, etc) and even by the objectives of the person analysing the system. This leads to identification of production sub-systems (for example, depending on the products and the needs met: forage, food, shelter, energy, cash, social advantages and integration into the community, etc.). It is a matter of analysing what will be likely to meet particular needs and not measuring some kind of variable: this is the first step in the D and D methodology. The next task is to determine how the analysis shall be carried out, and here too the method is original compared with the classic approach to products analysis, because it takes into account both the production aspect and also the role of conservation. Chosen systems must not only help to boost production above the level of previous systems, but they must be sustainable and capable of being self-perpetuating without exhausting natural resources: these are environmentally sound systems.

Once this diagnosis has been made, it is possible to identify directly the agroforestry technologies already present in the system and to improve them and/or begin a programme of research and development with a view to generating new technologies specially suited to solving problems identified at the diagnostic stage. Both approaches are generally adopted simultaneously. When these technologies have been identified and adjusted, it remains to incorporate them into the framework of local production systems. Finally, the point of departure is reached again, with an analysis of the limitations and potential of the newly created system, which starts up a new cycle of diagnosis and adjustment (Fig. 10). The method, like the development itself, is iterative. Its complexity also requires that it should be operated by multidisciplinary teams of workers.

HUXLEY (1983 a) has produced a report on the question of research in agroforestry. Finally, the objective of forestry research is to find the plants and the best ways of combining them (always with at least one woody species) to best meet the needs of the farmer as he perceives them and of the community to which he belongs, by creating systems of production that are stable, sustainable, multi-purpose and of high productivity.

9. CONCLUSIONS

The scientific approach to agroforestry is new. Agroforestry means much more than interplanting trees among crops or growing tree legumes; agroforestry systems can be complex, involving arrangement of the components in variations of space and time. To succeed, agroforestry requires studies and preparatory work, i.e. research, covering environmental, technical, social and economic aspects. Greater reliance on legumes is not enough. The problems of current land use need to be diagnosed, constraints on solutions studied, available technologies identified and complementary research projects set up.

Because this approach is new, few scientific findings are yet available, but their number is increasing and it can reasonably be expected that the methodologies developed by ICRAF and the body of doctrines at present in preparation will be backed up in a few years' time by a large number of facts and that a much more complete and above all more detailed range of technologies will become available to apply in specific cases. What needs to be recognized here and now is that the agroforestry approach does not claim to solve every problem nor to be appropriate in every case, but that this approach and especially the objective application of the 'D and D' methodology, make it possible to determine when an agroforestry solution is possible or if another solution, for example forestry, or agriculture, is preferable. Where feasible, the agroforestry solution is particularly significant in its anti-desertification effect for numerous reasons, the four most important of which are:

- it tends to meet the needs of the peasant farmer as he perceives them;

- it uses for preference local, low-cost input within the peasant farmer's means;

- it increases total productivity;

- it stabilizes the production unit and makes it less vulnerable to variations in the physical and socio-economic environment.

More precisely, the advantages offered by agroforestry are:

- it promotes or introduces the use of woody perennials capable of maintaining or improving soil fertility, for example:

* by addition of organic matter to the litter,

* by biological nitrogen fixing,

* by solubilization of phosphorus through mycorrhiza or bacterial activity;

– woody perennials improve the physical properties of the soil (water retention capacity, permeability, aggregate stability, regularization of the temperature);

– the deep tree roots reduce the negative effect of nutrient leaching;

– nutrients migrate upwards, via the tree roots from deep soil levels and become available to more shallow rooting crops by way of the forest litter;

– correctly positioned woody perennials minimize erosive action of wind and rain;

– in some cases, when the ground is protected by a sufficiently extensive plant cover, less effort is needed to eliminate weeds;

– agroforestry cultivation practices are among those that aim to maintain the plant cover of the soil, unlike conventional agricultural practices of scrub clearance and soil preparation which often mean erosion of the top soil, compaction, destructuring of the soil or degradation;

– agroforestry practices are sufficiently simple and close to the farmer's own ways to be introduced without clashes or difficulties, and they do not have the high cost of conventional systems;

– lastly, agroforestry systems can prove particularly elastic and flexible in responding to needs that vary in space and time, notably because such systems use multi-purpose trees, bushes, shrubs, underbrush, palms, bamboos and cacti and because they often meet several needs: food, forage, firewood, medicines, fibres, etc. in varying proportions in space and time that can be altered by the user.

All these advantages tend to increase the biological productivity of soils. In this way agroforestry, where applicable, really is an excellent weapon against desertification, which has been defined as the loss of productivity of soils. Where it can be applied – and this is determined by the

'D and D' methodology – agroforestry is a tool for biological redemption.

As BEETS (1985) has written, in the last few years agroforestry has enjoyed ever growing popularity because it was thought that it could solve all or nearly all the problems of environmental degradation and agricultural production. This was an over-simplification and a half-truth. Another error has been to consider agroforestry as a branch of forestry, which it is not. Agroforestry is only one of the possible tools for putting the land to good use, and it is in the hands of the peasant farmer. Its implementation is made difficult by the rigidity of established structures, which are ill-suited to a multi-disciplinary approach such as that needed for agroforestry to function.

The agroforestry approach is well-suited to small farming units and to great silvo-pastoral expanses alike, firstly because it primarily uses local woody perennials, plants and animals that are familiar to the people and very often admirably suited to the conditions. Even the preferred manner in which trees are planted in agroforestry singly or in small groups in suitable micro-climates, as opposed to a large concentration of trees, is more suitable to the environment: no one can reasonably believe that very extensive mass planting could succeed in conditions such as prevail in regions under threat of desertification. But solutions such as those favoured by agroforestry, aimed at making the best possible use of the particular features of the land, adapting plans to the soil potential and at the same time to the needs of the people, do have a chance of succeeding.

Other reasons why agroforestry is well-suited to tackling the problems of desertification and well-received by the populations are that it can be seen to serve people in seeking to respond to their needs and that the techniques it proposes although based on highly complex research, are not all that far removed from those used by the peasant farmer, and certainly less remote than those often proposed in grand projects for modernization, mechanization or any other vogue term. However, the techniques that agroforestry can propose are not easy to apply because they never occur in isolation but are applied collectively and simultaneously. It is a principle of agroforestry not to aim at a single objective, such as increasing food production; but at the same time to meet several needs of the peasant as he himself sees them. The complexity of this task does not deter him since it accords with his own approach to his surroundings: for him, the environment is an indivisible whole, not compartmentalized into field, forest and pasture, and he perceives all the problems of his environment as all one integrated problem. It therefore comes naturally to readily accept that an agroforestry technological package suggested to him is aimed simultaneously at a series of multiple objectives, such as increasing and improving the quality of food production, producing forage and firewood, erecting hedges and creating shade.

Agroforestry is still ill understood and little known. Ill understood, because it often spoken of incorrectly, with no real knowledge of what it is about and giving the word a sense that it does not possess. Little known, because we still do not know all the mechanisms of interaction between woody perennials and other products of the land, plant and/or animal. What we do already know has enabled us to claim that it is perhaps the best means of resolving the problem of dendro-energy and that it should be given priority among the known methods of increasing dendro-energy resources (FAO, 1985 a) and, more generally, that it is one of the most promising weapons with which to fight desertification (FAO, 1985 b). If agroforestry research and development rapidly receives even more attention and yet more effort is put into it, if the development of agroforestry is well co-ordinated between the different institutes, organizations and agencies with an interest in it, and if this is done very quickly, and extensive use made of the little that is already known, then one can reasonably expect agroforestry to be a highly effective brake on desertification.

But desertification will not be stopped by agroforestry alone and it will only be halted if all the nations agree to make a gargantuan concerted effort. Despite the warning given by the United Nations Conference on Desertification, which stressed that it was a question of life or death for a

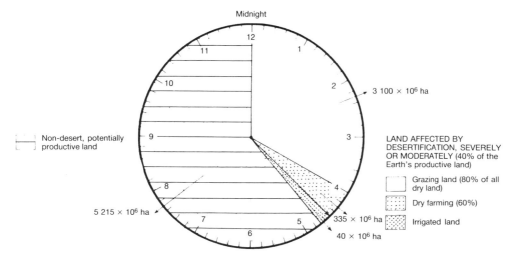

FIG. 12
Desertification: a time bomb (after TOLBA, 1985b)

207

part of the human race and perhaps in the long term for the whole of humanity, that appeal has gone largely ignored.

The last figure in this document, Fig. 12 (after TOLBA, 1985 a) attempts to bring home that the fight against desertification is a race against time, against death. It is still possible to save the Earth, but we must start immediately and use every means: agroforestry can play an effective role in this rescue bid.

10. APPENDICES

In continuation:

Appendix 1 – Scientific names of woody perennials appearing in the text and some of their common names

Appendix 2 – The kadd or *Faidherbia albida* (Del.) A. Chev (= *Acacia albida Del.*)

Appendix 3 – Seven traditional agroforestry production systems from Africa

Appendix 4 – Woody agroforestry species for the dry regions of Africa

APPENDIX 1

Scientific and common names of woody perennials mentioned in the text and some of their common names

In the interest of brevity, authors' names have not been given after Latin names in the text. The following list remedies this and makes clear which Latin names have been accepted. Some synonyms are indicated by an arrow pointing to the Latin name preferred in this text. In some cases, common names have been indicated.

Acacia albida → *Faidherbia albida*
  A. ataxacantha DC. (Mimosaceae)
  A. Caven Hook. et Arn. (Mimosaceae)
  A. Cyclops A. Cunn. ex G. Don (Mimosaceae)
  A. farnesiana (L.) Wild. (Mimosaceae)
  A. horrida (L.) Willd. (Mimosaceae)
  A. mellifera (Vahl) Benth. (Mimosaceae), Acacia mellifera
  A. nilotica var. *Adansonii* (Guillem. et Perrot.) O. Ktze (Mimosaceae), neb neb
  A. nilotica var. *tomentosa* (Benth.) A. F. Hill. (Mimosaceae), gonakié, gommier rouge
  A. nubica Benth. (Mimosaceae)
  A. pennata (L.) Wild.
  A. polyacantha Wild. var. *campylacantha* (Hochst. ex A. Rich.) Brenan (Mimosaceae), thorny acacia
  A. pruinocarpa Tindale (Mimosaceae)
  A. raddiana → *A. tortilis* ssp. *raddiana*
  A. Senegal (L.) Willd. (Mimosaceae), gum tree (white), vérek
  A. Seyal Del. (Mimosaceae), seyal, thorny mimosa, in arabic 'thal'
  A. sieberiana DC. (Mimosaceae), Sieber's acacia
  A. stenocarpa → *A. Seyal*
  A. Tortilis → *A. Tortilis* ssp. *tortilis*
  A. tortilis (Forssk.) Hayne ssp. *raddiana* (Savi) Brenan (Mimosaceae), 'seyal' in arabic

A. tortilis (Forssk.) Hayne ssp. *tortilis* Brenan (Mimosaceae)

A. Victoriae Benth. (Mimosaceae)

Adansonia digitata L. (Bombacaceae), Baobab

Adenium obesum (Forssk.) Roem. and Schult. = *A. Honghel* A. DC. (Apocynaceae), monkey baobab

Aeschynomene elaphroxylon (Guillem. and Perrot.) Taub. (Papilionaceae) aeschynomene with light wood

A. pulchella Planch. (Papilionaceae), elegant aeschynomene

Afzelia africana Sm. (Cesalpiniaceae)

Albizzia Chevalieri Harms (Mimosaceae)

A. Lebbeck (L.) Benth. (Mimosaceae) dark wood, woman's tongue acacia, dark wood acacia

Alnus acuminata O. Ktze (Betulaceae)

Anacardium occidentale L. (Anacardiaceae), cashew gum, cashew tree

Annona senegalensis Pers. (Annonaceae), corossol, custard apple (of Senegal)

Anogeissus leiocarpus (DC.) Guill. and Perrott. (Combretaceae), African birch

Atriplex Halimus L. (Chenopodiaceae)

A. nummularia Lindl. (Chenopodiaceae)

Azadirachta indica A. Juss. (Meliaceae), neem, margosa, Indian lilac

Balanites aegyptica (L.) Del. (Balanitaceae), desert date tree, Egyptian myrobolan

Bauhinia rufescens Lam. (Cesalpiniaceae)

Bombax costatum Pellegr. and Vuillet (Bombacaceae), kapok tree (with red flowers)

Borassus aethiopum Mart. (Palmaceae, Borassoideae), ron palm

Boscia angustifolia A. Rich. (Capparaceae), narrow leaved boscia

B. salicifolia Oliv. (Capparaceae) Willow-leaved boscia

B. senegalensis (Pers.) Lam. ex Poir. (Capparaceae) Senegal boscia

Butyrospermum paradoxum → *B. Parkii*

B. Parkii (G. Don.) Kotschy (Sapotaceae), shea butter tree

Cadaba farinosa Forssk. (Capparaceae)

C. glandulosa Forssk. (Capparaceae)

Caesalpinia ferrea (Cesalpiniaceae)

Cajanus Cajan (L.) Millsp. (Papilionaceae), cajan pea, pigeon pea

Calliandra macrothyrsa (Mimosaceae)

Calotropis procera (Ait.) Ait. f. (Asclepiadaceae) Sodom apple, silk tree (Senegal)

Capparis corymbosa Lam. (Capparaceae)

C. decidua (Forskk.) Edgew. (Capparaceae)

C. tomentosa Lam. (Capparaceae), African caper tree

Caryca Papaya L. (Caricaceae), pawpaw tree

Cassia Siamea Lam. (Cesalpiniaceae), sindian

C. sieberiana DC. (Cesalpiniaceae), ratu

C. Sturtii R. Br. (Cesalpiniaceae)

Casuarina equisetifolia Forssk. (Casuarinaceae) filao

Celtis integrifolia Lam. (Ulmaceae), nettle tree

Ceratonia Siliqua L. (Cesalpiniaceae), carob tree

Combretum aculeatum Vent. (Combretaceae)

C. cordofanum Engl. and Diels (Combretaceae)

C. glutinosum Perrott. ex DC. (Combretaceae)

C. micranthum G. Don (Combretaceae)

C. nigricans Lepr. ex Guill. and Perrot. (Combretaceae)

C. panniculatum Vent. (Combretaceae), paniculate combretum

Commiphora africana (A. Rich.) Engl. (Burseraceae), African myrrh, African
  bdellium

Cordyla africana → *Cordyla pinnata*

  C. pinnata (Lepr.) Miln.-Redh. (Cesalpiniaceae), pennate cordyla

Crateva Adansonii DC. (Capparaceae)

Cupressus lusitanica Mill. (Cupressaceae), Portuguese cypress

Dalbergia melanoxylon Guill. and Perrott. (Papilionaceae), Senegalese ebony

  D. Sissoo Roxb. ex DC. (Papilioneae)

Daniellia Oliveri (Rolfe) Hutch. and Dalz. (Cesalpiniaceae) Oliver's daniella

Derris indica (Lam.) S.S. R. Bennet

Dichrostachys cinerea (L.) Wight and Arn. (Mimosaceae), bell mimosa

Diospyros mespiliformis Hochst. ex. A.D.C. (Ebenaceae) false ebony, West
  African ebony

Entada sudanica Schweinf. (Mimosaceae), Sudanese entanda

Erythrina peoppigiana (Walpers) O.F. Cook, (Pappillionaceae)

  E. senegalensis DC. (Pappillionaceae), erythrine, coral tree

Eucalyptus camaldulensis Dehnhardt (Myrtaceae), camal

  E. microtheca F.v. Muell. (Myrtaceae), small fruit eucalyptus

Euphorbia balsamifera Ait. (Euphorbiaceae)

  E. royleana (DC.) Boiss. (Euphorbiaceae)

  E. Tirucalli L. (Euphorbiaceae)

Faidherbia albida (Del.) A. Chev. (Mimosaceae), kadd, haraz, gao, balanzan

Feretia apodanthera Del. (Rubiaceae)

Ficus capensis Thunb. (Moraceae)

  F. gnaphalocarpa (Mig.) Steud. ex A. Rich. (Moraceae)

  F. ingens (Mig.) Mig. (Moraceae)

  F. iteophylla Mig. (Moraceae)

  F. platyphylla Del. (Moraceae)

  F. Roxburghii Wall. (Moraceae)

  F. Thonningii Blume (Moraceae)

  F. Vogelli (Mig.) Mig. (Moraceae)

Gardenia erubescens Stapf and Hutch. (Rubiaceae)

  G. ternifolia Schum. and Thonn. (Rubiaceae), Jupin's gardenia

Gleditschia triacanthos L. (Cesalpiniaceae), honey-locust tree

Gmelina arborea Roxb. (Verbenaceae)

Grewia bicolor Juss. (Tiliaceae)

  G. flavescens Juss. (Tiliaceae)

  G. mollis Juss. (Tiliaceae)

  G. tenax (Forssk.) Fiori (Tiliaceae)

  G. villosa Willd. (Tiliaceae)

Guiera senegalensis J. F. Gmel. (Combretaceae), n'guere, nger

Hyphaene thebaica Mart. (Palmaceae, Borassoideae), doom, doom palm

Icacina senegalensis A. Juss. (Icacinaceae)

Khaya senegalensis (Desr.) A. Juss. (Meliaceae), Senegalese mahogany, bastard
  mahogany

211

Lannea acida A. Rich. (Anacardiaceae)

   L. microcarpa Engl. and K. Krause (Anacardiaceae)

Leptadenia pyrotechnica (Forssk.) Decne (Asclepiadaceae), desert broom

   L. Spartium → *L. pyrotechnica*

Leucaena leucocephala (Lam.) de Wit. (Mimosaceae), leucaena

Maerua angolensis DC. (Capparaceae)

   M. crassifolia Forssk. (Capparaceae)

Mangifera indica L. (Anacardiaceae), Mango tree

Milosa pennata L. (Mimosaceae)

   M. pigra L. (Mimosaceae), pink mimosa

Mitragyne inermis (Willd) O. Ktze. (Rubiaceae)

Moringa oleifera Lam. (Moringaceae)

Neurada procumbens L. (Rosaceae)

Opuntia Ficus indica L. (Cataceae), Barbary fig, prickly pear

Parkia biglobosa (Jacq.) Benth. (Mimosaceae), African carob tree, purple mimosa

   P. clappertoniana → *P. biglobosa*

Parkinsonia aculeata L. (Cesalpiniaceae), thorny American gorse

Phoenix dactylifera L. (Palmaceae), date palm

Piliostigma reticulatum (DC.) Hochst. (Cesalpiniaceae)

   P. Thonningii (Schum.) Milne-Redh. (Cesalpiniaceae)

Prosopis affinis Spreng. (Mimosaceae)

   P. africana (Guill., Perrott. and Roch.) Taub. (Mimosaceae) African prosopis

   P. alba Gris. (Mimosaceae)

   P. chilensis (Mol.) Stuntz. (Mimosaceae)

   P. chilensis var. *glandulosa* (Torr.) Standl.

   P. cineraria (L.) Druce (Mimosaceae)

   P. juliflora (Sw.) DC. (Mimosaceae)

   P. spicigera L. = *O, cineraria*

   P. Tamarugo F. Phill. (Mimosaceae), tamarugo

Psidium Guajava L. (Myrtaceae), guava tree

Pterocarpus angolensis DC. (Papilionaceae)

   P. erinaceus Poir. (Papilionaceae), vene, Senegal rosewood, Gambian kino

   P. lucens Lepr. ex Guill. and Perrott. (Papilionaceae), bara fi (bambara)

Racosperma aneurum (F. Muell. ex Benth.) Pedley, comb. nov.

   R. cambegei (R. Baker) Pedley, comb. nov.

   R. holosericeum (Cunn. ex. G. Don) Pedley, comb. nov.

   R. victoriae (Benth.) Pedley, comb. nov.

Retama Raetam Webb. and Berth. (Papilionaceae), retam

Salix subserrata Willd. (Salicaceae)

Salvadora oleoides Decne (Salvadoraceae)

   S. persica L. (Salvadoraceae), araka (in arabic)

Sclerocarya Birroea (A. Rich.) Hochst. (Anacardiaceae), plum tree

Securidaca longepeduncalata Fresen. (Polygalaceae), snake tree

Securinega virosa (Roxb. ex Willd.) Baill. (Euphorbiaceae)

Sesbania grandiflora Poir. (Mimosaceae)

   S. Sesban (L.) Merrill (Papilionaceae) sesban

Sterculia setigera Del. (Sterculiaceae), (gum tree) mbep, Sénagalese plane tree

Stereospermum kunthianum Cham. (Bignoniaceae), mozo iri (bambara)

Strychnos innocua Del. (Loganiaceae), inermous strychnos

   S. spinosa Lam. (Loganiaceae), thorny strychnos

Tamarindus indica L. (Cesalpiniaceae), tamarind tree

Tamarix senegalensis DC. (Tamaricaceae), Senegal tamarix

Tecomella undulata (Smith) Seemann (Bignoniaceae)

Terminalia avicennioides (Guill. and Perrot.) (Combretaceae)

   T. Brownii Fresen. (Combretaceae)

   T. macroptera Guill. and Perrott. (Combretaceae), Senegal badamier

Vitellaria paradoxa → *Butyrospermum Parkii*

Vitex chariensis A. Chev. → *V. Doniana*

   V. diversifolia Bak. (Verbenaceae)

   V. Doniana Sweet. (Verbenaceae), black plum tree

Ximenia americana L. (Olacaceae), sea lemon, sea plum

Zizyphus Joazeiro Mart. Reise Bras (Rhamnaceae)

   Z. mauritiana Lam. (Rhamnaceae), jojoba tree

   Z. spina Christi (L.) Desf. (Rhamnaceae), jojoba tree, Christ thorn

The kadd or Faidherbia alba (Del.) A. Chev. (= Acacia albida Del.)

Kadd is the Woloff name for a tall tree called *Faidherbia albida* (Del.) A. Chev., which may attain a height of 20 m, with a root depth of as much as 30 to 40 m. As recalled by LE HOUEROU (1979), 'this species, whose place in the system was uncertain until recent years, is clearly distinguished from the Acacias by a great many morphological, ontological and cytological characteristics which now more logically class it with a monospecific genus of the Ingae group (*Albizzia, Enterlobium, Pithecellobium, . . .*) ensuring transition towards the Acacia group, as predicted by A. CHEVALIER as early as 1934'. The main characteristic of the species is a periodicity in bud activity and dormancy and in leaf-fall that is totally opposite to that of other tree species of tropical savannas (PORTERES, 1957). A few other species have an aberrant cycle of this kind – *Salix subserrata*, for example. One of the consequences of the cross-season rhythm of kadd is that it is in leaf from the start of the dry season, bare during the rainy season and fruiting in mid-dry season. In practical terms this means:

– animals can feed on the leaves throughout the dry season and on the fruits during one of the most difficult periods of the 'bridging time' (from February to May in the Sahel, for example);

– crops, mainly cereals and sorghum, can grow at the foot of the tree without hindrance from shade.

In addition, the crops benefit from the animal dung deposited around the tree and from nitrogen enrichment of the soil by the abundant bacterial nodules on the tree's roots. All these characteristics make this a kind of miracle tree which very significantly increases yield in the fields, where the absence of creeping roots avoids any competition with crops and where it is assiduously maintained by farmers. Much research has been done on the fertilizing role of kadd, notably by CHARREAU and VIDAL (1965); numerous authors have stressed its considerable benefits (DUGAIN, 1959; GIFFARD, 1964, 1972 and 1974; HALEVY, 1971; PELISSIER, 1953; PEYRE DE FABREGUES, 1963, 1967 and 1970; RADWANSKI and WICKENS, 1967; BAUMER, 1980; etc.). Compared with a soil cultivated without kadd, a soil cultivated beneath *Faidherbia albida* shows an average increase of

7% clay	134% assimilable phosphorus
43% equivalent humidity	40% water storage capacity
60% total carbon	160% organic matter
70% exchangeable magnesium	100% base exchange capacity
100% total nitrogen	
100% exchangeable calcium	

In Senegal it has been found that about fifty trees to the hectare give as much as 300 kg organic nitrogen or 50 kg of potassium chloride (24 kg K) or 80 kg of bicalcium phosphate (31 kg of soluble P_2O_5 and 25 kg Ca); or 125 kg of dolomite

(15 kg Mg and 25 kg Ca) or 100 kg of agricultural lime (43 kg Ca).

In Niger, according to DELWAULLE (1977), 50 trees/ha would give the equivalent for the top 20 cm of earth of:

413 kg of CaO or 620 kg of lime/ha
42 kg of K_2O or 70 kg of potassium chloride/ha
60 kg of total P_2O_5 or 50 kg of bicalcium phosphate/ha
30 kg of assimilable P_2O_5 or 225 kg of supertriple/ha.

At the Institute of Agronomic Research at Bambey, in Senegal, it has been calculated that sorghum shows an 85% ear weight increase and a 32% increase in grain weight when crops are grown under kadd: the average production figures were 600 kg some distance away from the Faidherbia, 1 000 kg 5 m away and 1 700 kg 3 m away. By contrast, a depressive effect was observed on peanut – another legume – and only 1 839 kg/ha of pods were obtained from beneath Faidherbia, compared with 2 813 kg/ha away from the tree, with a haulm production of 2 761 and 2 587 kg/ha respectively. Beneath kadd, peanut suffers from excess nitrogen in relation to phosphorus and potassium: if these two elements are added in sufficient quantities, production becomes slightly higher beneath Faidherbia than away from it. This would make it fairly easy and not too costly to introduce peanut into rotation plans for fields where there are Faidherbia growing; however, it is more popular to grow millet in those fields.

The nutrient value of Faidherbia pods and leaves has been the subject of many studies (BOYNES 1940; WEST, 1950: AUDRU et al. 1966; BOUDET, 1972, etc).

The leaves, which contain 7.04% crude proteins in the dry matter and 1.2% fats, produce excellent forage right in the middle of the dry season, but farmers prune the trees badly and to excess, which leads to a drop in production. However, recovery is swifter than with the majority of the other acacias, and Faidherbia can be pruned every year if the pruning is not excessive. Branch lopping is generally controlled; cutting small branches gives better results if it is done between October and January than when done between February and April (HIERNAUX et al., 1978, 1979). The value of the forage produced is such that the normal number of cattle in North Senegal is doubled in areas where *Faidherbia albida* is grown (DANCETTE and NIANG, 1979). The foliage is certainly important as a forage source, but the pods are even more important and have the added advantage that they keep for a long time; it has been estimated (JUNG, 1967 and WICKENS, 1969 quoted by DELWAULLE, 1977) that a mature tree could produce 125 kg of pods with a forage value twice that of good hay or dried peanut or rice haulms. So with 20 mature trees per hectare it is theoretically possible to feed 1.3 head of cattle per ha, which will produce 9.1 l of milk or 910 g of live weight each day. The following values are taken from LE HOUEROU (1979):

	leaves	fruits
net energy (Mj/kg DM)	6.2-6.9	5.5-6.2
nutritional quotient = $\dfrac{\text{digestible proteins}}{\text{forage unit}}$	130-160	90-120

Comparison with a European hay shows that the pods have a poor fat content but an average protein content, whereas the leaves, with a medium fat content, have a protein content which puts them in the ranks of excellent quality forage. The carrying capacity of bush savanna in dry seasons is therefore less than that of fallow land planted with kadd, where there is often a load rate of 400 kg live weight to the hectare. It is estimated that the load on bush savanna could be increased by at least 50% by introducing Faidherbia in places where it can thrive.

In periods of famine, the seeds are boiled and peeled for human consumption (PARDY, 1953). Lastly, kadd, like all trees, produces wood, which makes fuel of medium quality and is used to make small objects, pegs, boxes, hut frames. The branches of *Faidherbia albida,* like those of acacias, are thorny and used to make barriers to exclude cattle; but these thorns, although they are fairly lethal to the tyres of motorized machines, are not sharp enough to prevent browsing, so that young plants need to be protected from cattle for a few years.

The thesis by FELKER lists data acquired on Faidherbia in 1978. Although agro-silvipastoral systems built around Faidherbia throughout its range, from Senegal to Somalia, from Transvaal to Angola, in Pakistan, India and the Arabian peninsula, are everywhere considered to be amongst the most effective, many questions remain, for example:

- How is leaf flushing triggered in the dry season and leaf-fall during the rains? Would it not be possible to identify some mechanism that could be manipulated and even applied to other species?

- What part do bacterial activity and animal droppings play in the fertilizing properties of the species?

- What is the best management system (and the best pruning technique) for the different products yielded by the tree and from the point of view of the impact on associated crops?

Lastly, new lines should be bred for improved performance, particularly for rapid growth and a heavy fruit yield. However, enough is already known about this species to be able to develop agroforestry schemes around it, and in many countries over the last ten years more effort has been made to plant Faidherbia in the fields. There have been failures, particularly where it has been forgotten that the tree requires quite a high water table which the taproot must be able to reach before the tree begins to grow upwards. Methods of raising in nurseries, of planting and of caring for young plants have been perfected, as has the management of shoots; but results from planting in situ still need to be improved. Growth is rapid when the position is right: on average, 50 cm/year for the first three years in the Sahel, but individuals have reached a height of 290 cm after three years and, on the Kenyan coast, 250 cm in 2 years.

APPENDIX 3

Seven traditional agroforestry production systems from Africa

1. The System among the Bougage (Niger)

The system among the Bougage who live in south-east Niger and practise agriculture and husbandry at the same time has been described by SEIF EL DIN (1984). It consists of leaving a small area of cultivated ground fallow each year.

Each family possesses a patch about 100 to 200 metres long and 20-50 metres wide, depending on availability of land. The huts and animal shelters are erected at one end of the patch and moved 20 to 30 metres each year. The ground around last year's buildings is taken out of production and left fallow for a period of five to eight years, depending on available land. In this way the soil's fertility is well maintained, in a rotation of animal fertilization and resting; but the system loses its efficiency when the ratio of population to available land increases, since it is then necessary to reduce the fallow time, which impedes restoration of soil nutrients.

Since the same family is always responsible for one particular strip of land, the farmer readily protects the woody perennials (*Acacia Senegal, A. tortilis, Balanites aegyptica, Celtis integrifolia, Tamarindus indica, . . .*) because he knows that he and his family will profit from their products, especially wood and forage. However, he hesitates to plant trees, because the country's laws governing forestry do not provide for the protection of trees owned by individuals. When the legal protection of natural resources has been revised, as demanded by the Maradi Agreement, conditions will be extremely favourable to the development of a balanced agro-silvi-pastoral system.

2. The System among the Zarma (Niger)

The system practised by the Zarma in Niger has been described by SIDIKOU (1974). It is a good example of traditional strategy for facing problems posed by a hostile environment. The small farmer sows millet thinly so as not to lose too much seed if the rains come late; if these seeds germinate, he sows the rest; if they do not, he begins again. He sows several fields at one- or two-week intervals to spread the chances of germination. Several different varieties of millet are used: m'bouga, which takes between 60 and 70 days to mature, which is sown very early to provide food to bridge the gap, and sometimes very late, in fields that have been cleared during the rains, to benefit from any late rains; darankole, with a medium cycle, for the dunes; hainikirey, also with a medium cycle, for finer soils; and sommo, a late variety with a 120-day cycle, highly tolerant of the drought succeeding the rainy season, and which can be weeded late. A survival of the times when raids by the Tamacheck were feared more than a plague of locusts, though those were devastating enough, the dwellings are closely grouped to facilitate defence, and the land is farmed in such a way that it forms concentric areas around the villages. The first circle or 'hali' is made up of heavily manured gardens where tender crops such as okra are grown and where trees are retained for their special food (*Tamarindus*

217

indica) or forage (*Faidherbia albida*) value. The second circle is made up of fields cultivated for 6 to 7 years, intermixed with fallows left 2 to 3 years. Various useful trees are retained in the second circle or 'koirate', such as *Acacia nilotica* and *Balanites aegyptiaca* for their leaves and fruits much favoured by cattle, *Faidherbia albida* for its fertilizing capacity and for the good fat pods available for cattle towards the mid-point in the dry season, but which are often stored until the end of the dry season to provide bridging fodder and *Sclerocarya Birroea* which is used to make tool handles and all sorts of everyday objects. Beyond is the least well defined of the circles, comprising 'zighi' or distant fields, which were dangerous in uncertain times and which now are difficult to supervise, which explains why a rudimentary hut is often put there to shelter a member of the family who will stand guard during the growing season. The 'zighi' are moved every few years and have tended to become more and more numerous over the past forty years since peace has reigned among tribes. Beyond again was the 'forest', which in times of famine provided a variety of fruits, leaves and edible seeds. But this harmony with the environment which enabled the people to survive famine (1911-1915) and the destruction of harvests by locusts (1913-1914, 1926-1927, 1929-1931, 1944-1955 and 1969-1973) is disappearing under increased human pressure. At the same time, the numbers of livestock have risen considerably, to such a degree that their fodder needs entail more distant forays, a loss of manure, unavoidable herding either by village herdsmen or by Peuhls with, in both cases, a loss for the owner of an appreciable quantity of milk . . . and of an animal from time to time. We are witnessing an appreciable change in farming systems. The 'sons of women', i.e. the descendants of sons of women married to foreigners (which is becoming increasingly frequent), since they do not have the right to settle within the village boundaries, go off to settle beyond the 'zighi' and the forest is disappearing, the same forest which ensures their food supply in times of famine.

There you had, and still have, an agroforestry system where the deliberate interactions of woody perennials with crops and animals were of three types:

agro-silviculture in the 'hali'
agro-silvi-pastoralism in the 'koirate'
silvo-pastoralism in the 'zighi'.

3. The system of the Dogon of the cliffs (Mali)

The description of this system by GALLAIS (1965) is a classic of its kind. I shall attempt a resumé here. The decision of most of the Dogon to settle on steep cliffs after the occupation of the Seno plain by the Mossi and Peulh invaders was a political decision: a large population was squeezed onto stretches of agriculturally poor and harsh, but easily defendable, ground, where they set up acropolis villages on scree-covered slopes or hidden in ravines.

Land distribution follows very strict rules. 'Collective land ownership, periodic redistribution of the most productive ground, a gerontocratic management, all ensure for the dwelling unit an egalitarian cohesion and a religious sense of the ties that unite the whole community with the earth. . . . Any kind of economic domina-

218

tion is done away with, thanks to the periodic redistribution of the means of production. All this greatly attenuates for the individual the constraints of his environment'. (GALLAIS and SIDIKOU, 1978). Furthermore, since the Dogon must live within a spatially very restricted framework, he has been obliged to adopt a strategy for intensive cultivation which enables him to obtain yields superior to those of plains agriculture, and which comprises: arranging terraces to take advantage of slopes, even very steep ones, without risk of erosion, constructing very high ridges – up to 70 cm – to retain rainwater, intensively using manure produced by young cattle penned in the yards of the houses, adding alluvia or more fertile soils to the fields, sometimes gathered from several kilometres away, but of most interest here, creating a plot of useful trees, far more dense than is found on the surrounding plains: kadd, of course, but also net tree, tamarind, false ebony, horseradish tree, Senegal rosewood, etc. These trees are self-seeded or carefully protected sprouts, or young trees dug up from the neighbourhood and transplanted, or they may be the result of artificial sowing, (even, as I have seen done near Sanga, using seeds carefully raised in animal dung). What is more, these trees are grown methodically and not left to themselves: the saplings are protected by stakes that mark their position or individually screened with thorns if they are in a place frequented by cattle; the trees are pruned so that their lower branches do not interfere with crops and, apart from *Faidherbia albida* and the tamarind (the former because it does not provide shade for crops since its foliage appears out of season; the latter because it is valued for its fruits and shade), are severely pruned to reduce canopy shade: the lowest branches are not lopped near the trunk, but nearly all the branches are lopped a certain distance from the trunk, so that they retain some foliage, often used as forage. This is certainly agroforestry, the deliberate interaction between trees, crops and animals.

This portrait of the Dogon system would not be complete without mentioning the highly sophisticated art of storing harvests (notably by the use of foliage, roots and bark as insecticides in the barns, another feature of agroforestry), the art of an irrigated agriculture in water impoverished soils, the use of cattle as draught animals and for manure, and the extreme caution shown in toiling to produce a considerable amount of millet which, although it has low profitability, does mean that there is always food available for basic self-sufficiency. The success of the cliff Dogons' production system means that despite their very hostile environment they are less vulnerable to famine than their neighbours, and that they even manage to sell vegetables (onions, sweet potato, peppers, tomatoes), fruits (guavas, mangoes, pawpaws, jujubes) and tobacco to the people of the plain!

4. The system of the Ouoloff at Guidakar (Senegal)

The production system of the Ouoloff in the village of Guidakar in the lower Senegal valley has been summarized by GALLAIS and SIDIKOU (1978). This village has grown up behind the dyke bordering the river, with a highly multi-clan structure: the Seye, Taye, Nian, Ndiaye, Ouad, Diop and Seck are all represented and each family owns land according to an unequal and irregular distribution. Collective planning is precluded by the fact that there are so many clans and because of family ownership of land. Since the end of the nomad rezzou, towards the beginning of the century, the population has been growing at an ever faster rate, forcing mass permanent or seasonal emigration to St. Louis, Senegal, and especially to Dakar. The major crops (notably rice) are grown in the 'oualo', or flood plains; the 'deri', a type of non-flooding terrace, are used for growing millet. The farmer grows millet to buy rice for his own consumption, because the government have succeeded in making rice-growing the pivot of the local economy and in substituting a market economy for a diversified and largely self-sufficient economy. The strategy of the village was also to extend the community boundary on the other side of the river and to avail themselves of the millet from this reserve space. This came to an abrupt end with the independence of Mauritania: it was no longer permitted to take food crops freely across the frontier. The farmer adapted to the new situation by selling his surplus rice harvest in Mauritania where prices have for long been higher. In addition, the Senegal river is undergoing development and the Diama barrage will be considerably more complicated to cross, by day or night, for the purposes of conducting some transaction. But the most disturbing development as far as the village is concerned is the government's expropriation of 33% of its territory to create a listed forest. These 150 ha of land were used mainly by the flocks and herds, which in future will be breaking the law if they graze there. The silvo-pastoral system, which more or less guaranteed the village's milk provision, no longer exists. It is true that animal protein in the diet was also obtained from the river, but fish cannot wholly replace milk. It ought perhaps to have been possible, rather than to opt for an uncompromising listing of the forest, to collaborate with the villagers to make an enriched environment, aimed at producing forage, firewood, berries and timber for them.

5. Systems in the Mandara Mountains (Cameroon)

The farming systems in the Mandara Mountains have been the subject of several studies (BOUTRAIS, 1973; PELISSIER and DIARA, 1978; ARGOULLON et al., 1981 b).

This is an area of dry montane agriculture where the populations, given the pejorative appellation Kirdi, in fact comprise seventeen different ethnic types. They have erected their family dwellings of pisé with conical roofs in an artificial environment of dry stone terraces, on which they grow millet.

The higher, unterraced ground serves as grazing for goats and sheep. It is subsistence farming in a particularly harsh environment and the people, deprived of resources, notably firewood, barely manage to survive.

The surrounding plain has been severely denuded of its forest by the Muslim settlers, who pushed the Kirdi up into the mountains. The 200 km retreat of the dense Cameroon rain forest's northern limit over the past century has brought advanced quantitative and qualitative degradation of the vegetation in southern Cameroon, accentuated in the last thirty years by ever-increasing human pressure, which is significant among forest populations but even more so on the savannas and pseudo-steppes. The farmer generally rotates his crops frequently because of the fragility and low fertility of the soil. But in the Mandara Mountains space is at a premium, the population dense; it is not possible to practise shifting cultivation.

Also, the soil deteriorates rapidly if it is not corrected physically and chemically, for example by adding manure. The Kirdi animists have developed a remarkable strategy which imposes constraint making it an impossibility to redescend the mountain to the plain, where other Islamized populations may exploit them. They have made a completely artificial landscape by maximum intensification of available land use for farming. For example, above Koza, where the population density is about 400 people per km², one can see a completely domesticated landscape:

- all slopes are converted into dry stone terraces; on the most gentle slopes, single stone cordons along contour lines prevent erosion;

- strings of small dry-stone dams (sometimes of masonry, because the Administration has been giving aid to this region) hold water and help it to infiltrate the few tiny alluvial plains bordering the major ravines; the ravine bottoms liable to flooding are planted with papyrus, *Aeschynomene* sp., *Sesbania Sesban* and *Mitragyne inermis* (see box), which can tolerate having their lower parts in water for several months;

- traditional pointed roof dwellings, grouped in 'saré' of a few units, are perched on granite boulders or artificial stone and clay platforms resting on several of these boulders. In this way, no cultivable space is sacrificed. The dwellings are often reached by stone steps or wooden ladders, or a combination of the two;

- the flocks, mostly goats and sheep, are not allowed to wander, the sign of an evolved agriculture. They are penned in circular clay enclosures built on granite boulders, again so as not to take up agricultural land, (contrast this with the wastage of rich land on airports such as Roissy, or the ill-considered extension of Cairo airport on irrigable alluvia able to yield up to four harvests a year!);

- close by the 'saré' there are always some fruit trees: mango, *Diospyros*, pawpaw, jujube, guava; others are scattered through the terraces, but the lower branches of all these woody plants are lopped off so as not to shade the crops which can then grow right up to their foot.

In this way, countless terraces maintained by low stone walls of meticulous construction retain the earth in cultivable planes, sometimes so small that only two or three plants of sorghum can be contained. Not a single inch is left uncultivated: the least depression holds a few rice plants, sorghum and millet cling to all the terraces and are even planted in rock fissures. A few *Faidherbia albida* grow on the rare projecting ledges, enriching the soil and providing forage for small ruminants. The jujubes are pruned so that they do not spread over the ground and take up the space for a few cereal plants – a few good vertical sap drawers are chosen on each clump and these are pruned to 1½ to 2 m so that they do not impede other crops; in this way, the bushes provide fruit, branches for fuel and saplings for timber or firewood. Grain legumes and, in late autumn, gourds are planted between the cereals. It is a veritable mountain garden.

A Multi-purpose Tree
Mitragyne inermis (Willd.) O. Ktze (Rubiaceae)

A tree occasionally reaching a height of fifteen metres or a bushy shrub favouring pond edges, water courses, drainage channels, hollows where water, even mildly saline, accumulates.

The foliage, including young branches, is much favoured by sheep, goats and camels. Bovines are not very partial to it but will eat it sometimes because the leaves stay green a long time during the dry season. According to LE HOUEROU (1979) the forage value is good:

net energy: 5.5-7.5 MJ/kg DM; DP/FU: 125-145; CP: 25-20%; P: 0.11-0.18%; DP: 10-12%.

The leaves and bark have febrifuge properties and numerous medicinal uses, against constipation, stomach pains, gonorrhoea, syphilis, leprosy, jaundice, dysentry, malaria, rheumatism, bilharzia, epilepsy and mental illness. An alkaloid, mitrinermine, is extracted from the bark. Some uses peculiar to the Hausa have been noted by ADAM *et al.* (1972: 282-283); for example, to make oneself loved by a woman, all one had to do was to apply to the body a liquid perfume mixed with powdered *M. inermis* seed and various other ingredients. Veterinary uses are also recognized, for example against sterility in cows.

The flowers, which appear from May to September, attract bees. The wood is used for making tablets on which to write the Koran and for various tools, even small items of furniture: it is resistant to termites, light brown, easy to work, water durable, not prone to splitting. It is also used as a fuel. A yellow dye is sometimes made from the bark. The branches are used for weaving mats or panel screens.

For several decades, efforts have been made to help the mountain-dwelling populations descend to the plain. Projects have been specifically set up for this purpose, such as the FAC Project for integrated rural development of the sub-prefecture of Guider (c. 1968). In the high plains above and to the west of Mora, large-scale land clearance and settlement programmes for farmers through the introduction of cotton growing have radically altered the landscape, which today is wide open and consists of vast fields with a few scrub copses and low galleries along the 'mayos' or temporary water courses, composed of bushes and shrubs rather than trees. A clue as to what the original vegetation was like can be found near Mozogo, in the listed (in 1934) forest of Gokoro: it covers more than 1,400 ha and was elevated to the status of National Park in 1976. It is a fairly dense forest comprising mainly *Acacia ataxacantha, A. sieberiana, Anogeissus leiocarpus, Sclerocarya Birroea* and a *Vitex (V. chariensis?);* also present are *Tamarindus indica, Daniellia Oliveri,* the Sudanian *Entada sudanica, Afzelia africana, Khaya senegalensis* – possibly introduced, *Terminalia avicennoides, T. Brownii* and, from the rocky mountains 1,400 m high to the west: *Celtis integrifolia, Sterculia setigera* and

Strychnos innocua. The principal animals include the grey duiker and the green monkey, the patas monkey and the dog-faced baboon.

One might talk of North Cameroon in terms of aridization, the passage from a semi-arid landscape and environment to an arid landscape and environment, and of aridification, or aridization caused by man. However, these phenomena are only clearly perceptible over small areas, so that it is preferable to talk of the degradation of the environment, of the landscape or natural resources, since this denotes a very generalized phenomenon affecting practically the whole region in question. This uncontrolled development is gathering momentum with the increased population pressure; although it began a long time ago, as reports from the beginning of this century and even from the last century attest, it has only periodically attracted attention, with the advent of the series of years of exceptional drought, such as around 1911, 1940 and 1970; but the ever greater gap in the ratio of available resources/resource demanders is now apparent to all, to governments as well as to individuals and to the international community. Uncontrolled development, through the lack of management which had not been felt too acutely until the last decade, results in soil erosion and the quantitative and qualitative reduction of natural cover without the creation of an agricultural landscape where resources and their consumption are in balance, and the impoverishment of the population.

It is noteworthy that in the Kirdi system natural vegetation has completely disappeared. Artificialization is total: even if local species are used, they are intensively managed: raised and treated as entirely domestic plants. Jujubes are a perfect example, pruned as they are in a manner which gives them an upright habit and fruits in an elevated canopy, whereas in nature they form a bushy shrub with a wide crown and numerous low branches. Beneath woody plants grown in this way, jujubes, acacias, figs, bastard mahogany, each ethnic group grows its crops, very finely adapted to the variations in the soil, as shown by HALLAIRE (1972, 1976) and BOULET (1975). In this way, the Matakam grow sorghum and millet in rotation every other year. The Ouldeme know several dozens of sorghum varieties, which they cultivate in succession and in mixes. Everywhere, cereals and woody perennials are intercropped with beans, okra, sesame, a few stands of tobacco, a little vouandzou and groundnuts. Each ethnic group is virtually tied to its mountain, from which it has succeeded in extracting enough to sustain life, despite a hostile environment.

6. The System among the Baoule (Ivory Coast)

BLANC-AMARD (1975) has studied the Baoule system, which has taken advantage of the patchwork arrangement of plant resources within the savanna/forest confines, and which utilizes a great variety of plants. For example, in only three villages, they have the use of 34 clonal varieties of yam. They also grow sweet potato, cassava, taro, xanthosoma, cowpeas, rice, groundnuts, maize and a little sorghum. Hunting plays an important role and is a prime source of meat. Oil and raffia palms and Palmyra are an important part of the economy and most often grown in close association with other crops, even with rice in shallow water. Elsewhere, on the forest margins, food crops including the banana are grown in conjunction with coffee and cacao. It is on the fringes of the savanna/forest areas that yields, especially of yam, are at their highest, and flavour at its best, hence the concentration of plots on these fringes. When the coffee and cacao plantations grow tall, food crops are relocated nearer the savanna. Whenever possible, they are placed near trees, the effect of which is considered so great that on the same yam mound the same varieties will not be used on the side facing the forest as on the side facing the savanna. Cotton is also grown; traditionally it was used to make loincloths and blankets, which were then sold. With the advent of industrialization, a cottage industry producing luxuries has replaced the manufacture of these articles.

Two aspects of this economy stand out as noteworthy. Firstly, the most refined agricultural practices – such as choice of varieties – are directly dependent on the presence of trees in general, and on such or such a species in particular. Secondly, the agricultural practices are in perfect harmony with the environment, fallow periods are often of long duration (9-11 years) and allow regeneration of the soil's fertility; the plant dynamics, so long as farming practices are not altered by excessive population density (more than 70 people/km^2), are evolving towards a forest climax. It has rightly been said that the success of Baoule agriculture is its mobility, for within the soils cultivated by each federation it is truly a long-cycle shifting cultivation system.

7. The gum gardens of Kordofan (Sudan)

Deforestation is practised everywhere in order to open up new land for farming. It is a weakness in the agriculture of developing African countries that they have not been able to develop a permanent and durable system of land use. Farming, instead of being sedentary, is largely shifting. Instead of staying with one piece of land and regenerating it in order to be able to do so, the farmer exhausts the soil and goes off to clear another patch of ground as soon as his field ceases to give a sufficiently good yield. This practice is a source of poverty.

As long as the population was sufficiently small, there was enough space for this kind of farming without too much damage being done. Each abandoned patch was left fallow for several years and the soil regained its fertility. A good example of this system was given by the famous 'gum gardens' of Kordofan in the Sudan Republic.

In this system, forestation is quasi-monospecific, consisting of *Acacia Senegal* Willd., or gum trees. These shrubs begin to produce gum in appreciable amounts around the age of 4 years and reach maximum production between 13 and 14 years, after which they begin to decline up to an age of 18 years. A system of rotation cropping was established, comprising one fallow patch with gum trees for about fifteen years and two cultivated patches, one rather intensive, the other less so and with grazing. After fifteen to twenty years the gum trees were cut down and that patch was cultivated intensively for 6-8 years, while the semi-cultivated semi-grazed patch in its turn became a gum garden.

With the population increase, it has become impossible to leave a patch planted with gum trees fallow for 20 or even 15 years: the rest period has been shortened ever further and, since the soil cannot regain its fertility, harvests have been in continuous decline.

One of the great advantages of this system was that the harvest took place in the dry season, while work on the farm was very slack. In addition, during the cultivated period of a patch, the old stumps sprout again, providing shoots to cut down for cattle feed; also, the gum groves adjacent to the cultivated patch produce seeds that fall on the field, others are carried, predigested, in the faeces of animals which, after the harvest, feed on the remains of the crops. These seeds germinate easily because the soil has already been tilled for crop-growing and cleared of weeds, so that, at the end of the cropping period there is already an appreciable quantity of young gum trees in place. This was an agro-silvi-pastoral type of system. It was balanced and permanent, thanks to the long fallow period which allowed the soil to recuperate. Fertility was also very often facilitated by spreading ash from the burnt chopped gum trees. The charcoal which resulted was partly consumed by the farmer, partly sold off, providing him with some income.

Attempts to reconstitute or create new gum gardens are being made in several countries, notably in Mauritania, Senegal and Sudan, where the *Acacia Senegal* have been hard hit in recent years by the exceptional drought, particularly in Mauritania. The gum gardens of Kordofan are being taken as the model. If one calculates that a gum plantation of 100 km^2 could produce all the gum arabic needed by industry, there is a risk that the price of the gum may drop if all the current projects succeed.

APPENDIX 4.

Woody agroforestry species for the dry regions of Africa

Below is a non-exhaustive list in table form of woody species for inclusion in the composition of the three main forestry system groups for the dry regions of Africa:

AS   agro-silvicultural
ASP agro-silvo-pastoral
SP   silvo-pastoral

These systems are indicated in column (3). The names in brackets indicate that the species are not very common in agroforestry.

In column (4) the form of agroforestry where the woody species is most used is marked with a cross: a dot indicates slightly less frequent use:

Column (5) indicates various uses:

A	apiculture	M	medicines
B	timber	N	food
C	dyes	NF	nitrogen-fixing
CS	soil conservation	O	oil
E	dendro-energy	P	trituration wood
EV	green manure	T	tannins
F	forage	V	ornamental
Fi	fibres	X	control of plant
G	gum, latex, resin		pests and diseases
H	hedges		

226

Woody agroforestry species for the dry zones of Africa

| (1) | (2) | (3) | (4) Applications | | | | | | | | | | | (5) |
Latin Name	Habitat	Agroforestry system	Mixed cropping	Fire-wood	Protein banks	House-hold gardens	Hedges or rows	Erosion control	Shelter or Shade	Stabil-ization	Trees/ Fields	Trees/ Pastures	Soil improve-ment	Principal Uses
Acacia ataxacantha	hedges, fresh alluvial sands, Southern, Western and Eastern Africa	AS		.			+				.			M
Acacia holosericea	Australia and arid zones East of Lake Chad to the Arab peninsula	SP			+							.		F,E
Acacia laeta	from Mali to the Red Sea	SP		.								+		G,M,F
Acacia macrostachya	Sahelo-Sudanian and Sudano-Sahelien zones	AP		.			+							N,F,M
Acacia mellifera	from Lake Chad to the Arabian Peninsula	ASP AS	.	+	.		+							A,E,F,Z
Acacia nilotica	Africa and the Indian peninsula	AS SP SP		+	+			.						B,G,A,T,S
Acacia pennata	Africa, semi-arid and humid	SP		+	+									A,M,Fi,T
Acacia polyacantha	sub-humid and semi-arid Africa on cool soils	SP		+					.			.		S,T,M,C
Acacia saligna	Australia	SP		.	+									F,E
Acacia Senegal	typically sahelian but also Eastern and Southern Africa	ASP SP	+	.	.						+		.	G,F,Fi,D,E, A,S
Acacia Seyal	semi-arid, particularly on clay	AS AS SP ASP		+	+		+	.	.			+		E,F,A,G,S
Acacia sieberiana	semi-arid, cooler areas	SP	+		+									A,S,M,B
Acacia tortilis ssp. raddiana	dry areas of Africa even North of the Sahara	SP					.		.	.				S,F,M,E
Acacia tortilis ssp. tortilis	arid and semi-arid Africa, and Arabian peninsula	SP AS	+	.	+							.		S,T,F,M,E
Adansonia digitata	sub-humid and semi-arid Africa, other species of the genus in Madagascar	ASP	+		.		+		.		+			N,Fi,M,F,A

Species	Habitat/Distribution	Type	1	2	3	4	5	6	7	8	9	10	11	Uses
Adenium obesum	dry, hardened, storny soils	ASP					+							M,V
(*Afzelia cuanzensis*)	dry Southern Africa	AS					+		·					E,H
Albizzia Chevalieri	Sudanian, sub-humid	SP	·	+										T,N,Fi,Z
Albizzia Lebbeck	semi-arid and sub-humid	SP			·	·	+							T,G,V,K,F,Z
		AS	·							+				
Anacardium occidentale	flexible for climate, soft or	AS				·				+				N,E,T,M
	permeable soils	ASP				+	·							
Annona senegalensis	semi-arid to semi-humid	SP		·							+			M,N,F,S
		AS								+	+			
		ASP		·						+	+			
Anogeissus leiocarpus	wide distribution but pre-fers cool soils	SP	·								+			T,S,C,N,G,M
Azadirachta indica	grown in many villages, of	ASP			+	·						·		V,M,F,O,Z
	Indian origin	AS			+			·						
Balanites aegyptica	arid and semi-arid zones,	ASP	+	·				·	·					F,N,T,S,O,M
	usually deep clay	SP		+			·			·				
		AS	+			·		·						
Bauhinia rufescens	Sahelian and Sudanian	SP	·	+			·							F,E,Fi,T,V,M
Bombax costatum	Sudanian	AS								+				Fi,N,M,F
Borassus aethiopium	semi-arid and sub-humid tropical Africa	AS	·							+	·			N,Fi,S,B,M
Boscia sp.pl. (on *Boscia senegalensis*, c.f. Baumer, 1981b)	Sahelo-Sudanian	SP	·						·		+			N,F,E
Butyrospermum Parkii	Sudanian and Sahelo-Sudanian	AS	·							+				N,B,E,C,M
Cadaba sp.pl.	dry Africa, Arabia, India	SP									+			F,N,M
Calliandra macrothyrsa	p.p.	ASP	·				·				·	+		F,E,S,Z
(*Calotropis procea*)	around all arid zones and/or damaged soils in Africa, Arabia and India	ASP					+							Fi,G,M,N (fer-ments),E
Capparis sp.pl.	Sahel, East Africa	SP					·				+			E,M,F
(*Cassia Siamea*)	Southern India, Burma, Sri Lanka, adaptable in sub-humid zones	ASP	+				·					·		E,V
Casuarina equisetifolia	Australia, Pacific, South East Asia	AS					·		·			+		Z,E,B,C
Celtis integrifolia	Arabia and from 3° to 15° lat. N and Africa	AS								+				N,F,M,Fi
Combretum aculeatum	Sahelian and even Sahelo-Saharian, but also Sahelo-Sudanian	SP	·				·				+			F,E,N,M

Woody agroforestry species for the dry zones of Africa

(1)	(2)	(3)	(4) Applications											(5)
Latin Name	Habitat	Agroforestry system	Mixed cropping	Fire-wood	Protein banks	House-hold gardens	Hedges or rows	Erosion control	Shelter or Shade	Stabilization	Trees/ Fields	Trees/ Pastures	Soil improvement	Principal Uses
Combretum glutinosum et C. cordofanum	Sahelian zone up to the Nile	SP				·						+		B,E,C,M,G
Combretum micranthum	very common in Sahel	ASP				·						+		N,E,S,Fi,M
Combretum nigricans	Sudanian and Guinean	ASP										+	·	N,E,M
Commiphora sp.pl.	tropical dry Africa	SP	·				+					·		G,S,F,M
Cordia sp.pl.	Sub-humid Africa	ASP									+			B,E
Crataeva Adansonii	Sahelo-Sudanian	SP	+									+		F,S,N,M,G
(Croton megalocarpus)	tropical Sub-humid Africa	AS	+											E,M
Dalbergia melanoxylon	dry Africa, humid soils	SP	+									·		B,S,M
Dichrostachys cinerea	semi-humid Sudanian zone and up to Southern Africa	ASP					+					·	·	Z,N,A
Dobera glabra	savanna and pseudo-steppe in East Africa	SP		+									·	N.E.F
Entada africana	dry zones of Africa, particularly North of the Equator	SP	·									+		F,Fi,T,M
Erythrina sp.pl.	widespread in all dry Africa	ASP					+							M,F
Euphorbia balsamifera	Canaries; acclimatized in the Sahel	AS					+							M
Euphorbia Tirucalli	India and tropical Africa	AS		·						·				M
Faidherbia albida	Senegal, Sudan, Mali, Niger, dry Africa	ASP			·		+				+			F,Z,A,M
Feretia apodanthera	Kenya, Sudanian Africa	SP									+			N,M,F
(Fiscus Thonningii)	tropical semi-humid Africa	ASP							+				·	Fi,M
Grewia bicolor	India, semi-arid and sub-humid Africa	ASP		+										N,E,F,M
Grewia flavescens	India, semi-arid and sub-humid Africa	ASP				·				+				M,N,E
Grewia mollis	Sudanian zone and East Africa	SP				+	+			·				N,Fi,N
Grewia tenax	circum-saharian zone, Iran, Arabia, India	SP	·			·	+							F,Fi,N

Species	Distribution		
Grewia villosa	West Africa and dry East Africa	SP	N,M,Fi,F
Guiera senegalensis	from Senegal to Niger	SP	M,F,N,E,A
Hyphaena thebaica	dry Africa	AS	Fi,N,S,E,M
Jatropha Curcas	India, acclimatized in all dry Africa	AS	M,X
(Khaya senegalensis)	Senegal and Sahel	AS	B,X,M,F
Leucaena leucocephala	tropical America and West Indies	ASP	E,F,N,A
Maerua sp.pl.	dry Africa	SP	F,N,M,V
(Mangifera indica)	Indian sub-continent	AS	N,E,A,V
Mimosa pennata	sub-humid and also semi-arid Africa	SP	F,A,T,M
Mimosa pigra	sub-humid Africa	SP	M
Mitragyne inermis	dry Africa but humid areas	SP	M,B,F,A,C,Fi
Moringa oleifera	India, Arabia	ASP	N,F,A,M
Parkia biglobosa	Sudanian zone	AS	N,B,V
Parkinsonia aculeata	dry tropical America	SP	F,E,M
Phoenix dactylifera	tropical and Mediterranean regions	ASP	N,B,Fi,A
Piliostigma reticulata	from Sahel to East Africa	SP	E,V,C,M,F
Prosopis africana	semi-arid, sub-humid West and East Africa	SP	B,E,T,F,M,A,Z
Prosopis juliflora	West Indies and tropical America	AS	F,E,A,Z
Psidium Goyava	tropical America	AS	N,M
(Pterocarpus lucens)	Sahelo-Sudanian	SP	N,F,M,E
Salvadora persica	Sahel, East and Southern Africa, India, Arabia, semi-arid zone	SP	F,M,S,E
Sclerocarya Birroea	Sahelian zone	SP	N,Fi,G,M,B,S
Sesbania grandiflora	Pacific	ASP	N,V,A,Z
(Sterculia setigera)	Sudanian zone	SP	E,G,N,M,Fi
Stereospermum kunthianum	Eastern and Western dry Africa	SP	A,M,B,V
(Tamarindus indica)	Madagascar and East Africa	AS	N,F,B,M,A,V
Tamarix sp.pl.	very large original habitat (cf. BAUM, 1978)	AS	M,E
Terminalia sp.pl.	dry Africa	SP	B,M,C,F
Ximenia americana	tropics	SP	N,F,E,S,M
Zizyphus sp.pl.	Africa and dry India	ASP	N,E,A,F

APPENDIX 5

List of tables, figures and maps

BIBLIOGRAPHY

ADAM, J. G., N. Echard & M. Lescot (1972). Plantes médicinales Hausa de L'Aden (République du Niger). *J.A.T.B.A.*, 19(8-9): 259-399.

AGGARWAL, R. K., J. P. Gupta, S. K. Saxena & K. D. Muthana (1976). Studies of soil physico-chemical and ecological changes under twelve years old 5 desert tree species of Western Rajasthan. *Indian Forester*, 102(12) : 863-872.

ALEXANDER, A. T. et al. (1982) *Projet de reboisements communautaires dans le Bassin arachidier du Sénégal (PRECOBA). Tableaux relatifs à l'étude sociologique (effectuée dans le département de Fatick),* Fatick (Sénégal), FAO project: FO: GCP/SEN D 28/FIN, Land Doc. no. 4, 40 p. unnumbered.

ALLAN, W. (1965). *The African husbandman.* Edinburgh, Oliver & Boyd.

ARGOULLON, J., M. Baumer & Ph. Enaud (1981a). *La relance de l'Opération 'Sahel vert' au Cameroun.* Saint Quentin en Yvelines (France), SCET-Agri, Report to UNSO, iv + 122 p. + 4 photos.

_____ (1981b). *L'opération 'Reboisements et correction des mayos' dans le cadre d'opérations coordonnées de protection de l'environnement au Nord-Cameroun.* SCET-Agri, Report to UNSO, iii + 130 p. + maps. Saint Quentin en Yvelines (France)

ARONSON, J. A. (1984). *Energy plants for desert agriculture: current state of knowledge. An Israeli perspective.* Beer-Sheva (Israel), Ben-Gurion University of the Negev, doc. BGUN – ARI-23-84, V+94 p.

ARONSON, J. A., A. Yaron & D. Pasternak (1984). *Evaluation of potential fuel crops for the Negev,* doc. BGUN-ART-25-84, 15 p.

ASAD, T. (1964). Seasonal movements of the Kababish Arabs of Northern Kordofan. *Sudan Notes and Records*, 45 :48-58.

_____ (1970). *The Kababish Arabs: Power, Authority and Consent in a Nomadic Tribe.* London, C. Hurst, XVI + 263 p.

AUBREVILLE, A. (1949a). *Climats, forêts et désertification de l'Afrique tropicale.* Paris, Soc. d'éd. géo., marit. et coloniales, 352 p.

_____ (1949b). Recherches et misères des forêts de l'Afrique noire française. BFT.

AUDRU, J. et al. (1966) *Etude des pâturages et des problèmes dans le Delta du Sénégal.* Maisons-Alfort, IEMVT, Et. agrostologique no. 15, 359 p.

BABIKER, Abdal (1983). Rural household energy in the Nuba Mountains, Republic of the Sudan. *Erdkunde*, 37(2) : 109-117.

BAGNOULS, F. & G. Gaussen (1953). Période de sécheresse et végétation. Paris, *C.R. Ac. Sc.,* 236 : 1076-1077.

_____ (1957). Climats biologiques et leur classification. *Ann. de géo.,* 355(66) : 193-220.

BARRAL H. (1968). *Tiogo, étude géographique d'un terroir Léla (Upper Volta).* Paris, ORSTOM, Atlas des structures agraires au sud du Sahara, 2; 72 p., 5 phot., 8 black and white and coloured annotated maps.

BAUMER M. (1962 a). *El Odaya Ecological Map.* Khartoum, Sudan Survey Dpt., 1 col. 1:15 000 map (topo. no.S. 1069-62)

_____ (1962 b). *Fire in Dar Maganin.* Khartoum, Sudan Survey Dpt, 1 col. 1:250,000 map (topo. no. S. 1070-62)

233

_____ (1968). *Ecologie et aménagement des pâturages au Kordofan (Rep. Sudan).*

_____ (1975). *Noms vernaculaires soudanais utiles à l'écologiste.* Paris, CNRS, 125 p.

_____ (1977), L'eau dans les zones arides: technologies appropriées d'approvisionnement. Paris. *Total info.* 70 : 17-25.

_____ (1978). L'eau dans les zones arides: technologies appropriées de conservation et d'utilisation. *Total info.*, 73 : 15-21.

_____ (1980). *Arbres, arbustes et arbrisseaux des régions arides et semi-arides. Données techniques.* Rome, FAO working doc. of the EMASAR Programme. xii + 318 p. roneo.

_____ (1981 a). *Aménagement de l'environnement et lutte contre la désertisation en Mauritanie; stratégie et propositions de projets.* Nouakchott, US-AID/ RAMS, v + 318 p.

_____ (1981 b). Rôle de *Boscia senegalensis* (Pers.) Lam. dans l'économie rurale africaine: sa consommation par le bétail. *Rev. élevage méd. vét. des pays tropicaux,* 34(3) : 325-328.

_____ (1983 a). *La recherche concernant le bois de feu au Cameroun, en Côte d'Ivoire et au Sénégal.* Montpellier, viii + 158 p. Consult. report to FAO.

_____ (1983 b). *Notes on trees and shrubs in arid and semi-arid regions.* Rome, FAO/UNEP, EMASAR Programme, Phase II, + 270 p.

_____ (1984). *Rapport sur une mission de consultation au Sénégal (7 juillet- 3 août 1984) et au Mali (4-16 août 1984) sur la production de bois de feu par l'agroforesterie.* Paris, Club du Sahel, v. + 77 p.

_____ (1985). *Candide et les oiseleurs.* Paper given at FAO seminar on *Quelea quelea,* Tsavo Park (Kenya), 21-25 Jan 1985, 12 pp typed.

BAUMER, M., T. DARNHOFER, D. HOEKSTRA & P. HUXLEY (1985). *Proposals for an Agroforestry Approach in the Jebel Marra Rural Development Project Area.* Nairobi, ICRAF, ii + 104 p.

BAUMER, M. & P. A. REY (1974). Pastoralisme, aménagement, cartographie de la végétation et développement intégral harmonisé dans les régions circumsahariennes. Genève, Institut d'étude du développement. *Genève-Afrique, Acta Africana,* 13(1) : 1-18.

BECHMANN, R. (1984). *Des arbres et des hommes. La forêt au Moyen Age.* Paris, Flammarion, 385 p.

BEETS, W. C. (1982). *Multiple cropping and tropical farming systems.* Gower/ Westview, xiv + 156 p.

_____ (1985). *The potential role of agroforestry in ACP States. A State-of-the-Art Study.* Wageningen, TCARC; ICRAF, xii + 259 p.

BELMONT, J. (1984). La participation, *Info-MAB* 2 : 1-2

BENE, J. G., H. W. BEALL & A. COTE (1977). *Trees, food and people: land management in the tropics.* Ottawa, IDRC.

BERNUS, E., with collab. of M. MAINGUET & I.C. CANNON-COSSUS (1980). Desertification in the Eghazer and Azawak region. Case study presented by the Government of Niger. *In* UNESCO, *Case studies on desertification.* Natural resources research, XVIII: 115-146.

BETTELHEIM, Ch. (1971). *Planification et croissance accélérée.* Paris, Maspero, Petite coll. Maspero No. 5, 192 p.

BILLE, J. C. (1978). *Rôle des arbres et arbustes en tant que sources de protéines dans*

234

la gestion des pâturages d'Afrique tropicale. Paper given at the 18th World Forestry Congress, Jakarta.

—— (1980). Measuring primary palatable production of browse plants. *In* LE HOUEROU (ed.) *Browse in Africa:* 185-195.

BLACT (1983). *Introduction à la Coopération en Afrique noire.* Paris, Karthala, 118 p. + appendices.

BLANC-PAMARD, C. (1975). *Un jeu écologique différentiel: les communautés rurales de forêt-savane au fond du 'V Baoulé' (Côte d'Ivoire).* Paris, Lab. de socio. et géo. afric.

BOGNETTEAU-VERLINDEN, F. (1980). *Study of impact of windbreaks in Majjia Valley, Niger.* Wageningen (Netherlands), Agric. Univ., 77 p. + app.

BOSCH, O. J. H. & J. J. P. VAN WIJK (1970). The influence of bushveld trees on the productivity of *Panicum maximum:* a preliminary report. *Proc. Grassl. Soc. S. Africa,* 5 : 69-74.

BOUDET, G. (1972). Désertification de l'Afrique tropicale sèche. *Adansonia,* 12(4) : 505-524.

—— (1976). *Les pâturages sahéliens. Les dangers de dégradation et les possibilités de régénération. Principes de gestion améliorée des parcours sahéliens.* Maisons-Alfort (France), IEMVT, 63 p. Also *in* FAO, *The Sahelian pastoral systems,* app. 4.

BOULET, J. (1975). *Magoumaz, pays mafa, Nord-Cameroun.* Paris, Mouton. Atlas des structures agraires au sud du Sahara, 11 p.

BOUTRAIS, J. (1973). La colonisation des plaines par les montagnards au nord du Cameroun (Monts Mandara). Paris. ORSTOM, *Trav. et Doc.*

BOYNES, B. M. (1940). *Composition and nutritive value of Sudan fodders.* Khartoum, Univ. Fac. of Agric., 189 p. (unpubl.).

BREWBAKER, J. L., D. L. PLUCKNETT & V. GONZALES (1972). *Varietal variation and yield trial of Leucaena leucocephala (Koa Hole).* Hawaii Agr. Expt. Station, Univ Hawaii Res. Bull. 166, 29 p.

BURKART, A. (1976). A Monograph of the genus Prosopis (Leguminosae, subfam. Mimosoidae). Harvard, Arnold Arboretum, *Harvard* 57: 219-249 and 450-525.

CALVIN, M. (1978). Green Factories. *Chem. Eng. News,* 56 : 30-36.

—— (1983). *Oil from plants.* Paper presented at BARC Science Seminar, USDA, Beltsville Md. Sept. 1982.

CARR, J. D. (1976). *The South African Acacias.* Johannesburg, Conservation Press.

CARREL, A. *L'homme, cet inconnu.* Paris, Plon, Livre de poche, 447 p.

CATINOT, R. (1974). Contribution du forestier à la lutte contre la désertification en zones sèches. *Techniques et développement.* p 11.

CATTERSON, T. M. (1984). *AID Experience in the Forestry Sector in the Sahel – Opportunities for the Future.* Paris. CILSS/Club du Sahel Steering Committee, OECD, 14-15 June 1984, 29 p.

CHAMBERS, R. S. (1979). Gasohol: Does it or doesn't it produce positive net energy? *Science,* 206 : 789-795.

CHANDLER, M. Y. (1979). Le Prosopis, une plante nuisible ou merveilleuse? *Sylva Africana,* 5 : 9-11.

CHARREAU, C. and F. VIDAL (1965). Influence de *l'Acacia albida* sur le sol, la nutrition et les rendements des mils Pennisetum au Sénégal. *Agro.trop.,*

20(6) and (7).

CHEEMA, M. S. Z. A. & S. A. QUADIR (1973). Autecology of *Acacia Senegal*. (L.) Willd. *Vegetatio* 27 : 131-162.

CHEVALIER, A. (1950). La décadence des sols et de la végétation en Afrique occidentale française et la protection de la nature. *Bois et forêts des tropiques*, 16 : 335-353.

CHILD, B. (1985a). *A Preliminary investigation of game ranching in Zimbabwe*, Thesis, Working paper.

—— (1985b). *Utilisation of Wildlife*. Paper given to the FAO Consultation on the role of forestry in combating desertification, Saltillo, (Mexico), 24-28 June 1985, 10 p.

CIDA (1984). *Stratégie matricielle d'intervention au Sahel: conception et programme de l'ACDI*. Paris, Meeting of the Club du Sahel, OECD, 14-15 June 1984.

CLAMAGIRAND, B. (1983). Technologies traditionnelles et modernisation. L'exemple de la fabrication du beurre de karité. In BLACT.: 77-83.

CLANET, J. C. & H. GILLET (1980). *Commiphora africana*, browse tree of the Sahel. *In* LE HOUEROU (ed.), *Browse in Africa*: 443-445.

Club du Sahel (May 1985). *Proposition de stratégie régionale de lutte contre la désertification*. Paris. OECD/Ouagadougou, CILLS, doc. Sahel D (85) 262, 19 p.

COMMONER (1975) *et al. The closing circle: nature, man and technology*. New York Alfred A. Knopf, x + 326 p.

COULIBALY, L. (Oct. 1983). *Note de réflexion sur le secteur forestier sahélien et son développement*. Ouagadougou, CILSS, 26 p. roneo.

CREES, J. (1984). Desertification in northern Kenya, Nairobi *Swara*, 7(5) : 30-34.

DANCETTE, A. (1968). Note sur les avantages d'une utilisation rationelle de l'*Acacia albida* au Sénégal. Bambey (Senegal), *Annales C.R.A.*, roneo.

DANCETTE, C. & M. NIANG (1979). *Rôle de l'arbre et son intégration dans les systèmes agraires du Nord du Sénégal. Le rôle des arbres au Sahel*. Colloque IDRC Dakar.

DARNHOFER, T. (1983). Microclimatic effects and design considerations of shelterbelts. *In* HOEKSTRA & KUGURU, *Agroforestry systems for small-scale farmers*: 95-111.

DEFFONTAINES P. (1933). *L'homme et la forêt*. Gallimard, Coll, géo.hum. no. 2, 187 p.

DELPECH, B. (1974 a). A Sim: un modèle de coopération agricole chez les paysans Sérér du Siné. Paris. *Trav. et doc. de l'ORSTOM*, 34 : 105-112.

—— (1974 b). Statuts sociaux, appartenances religieuses et relations interpersonnelles en milieu villageois Sérér. Paris. *Trav et doc. de l'ORSTOM*, 34 : 121-147.

DELWAULLE, J. C. (1977). *Le Gao (Faidherbia albida), Aspects forestiers du Projet Productivité de Dosso (Niger)*. C.T.F.T., 8 p. + 6 p. biblio.

—— (1978). *Plantations forestières en Afrique tropicale sèche*. Nogent-sur-Marne (France), C.T.F.T., 178 p.

DENEVE-STEVERLYNCK Th., A. ALEXANDER & O. KONE-NDIAYE (1982). *Projet de reboisements communautaires dans le bassin arachidier du Sénégal (PRE-COBA), Etude sociolologique: la motivation et les actions des populations à l'égard de l'arbre (Département de Fatick)*. Fatick (Senegal). FAO Project:

FO : GCP/SEN/023/FIN. Techn. report no. 1, vi + 95 p. + 3 apps.

DEPIERRE, D. & H. GILLET (1971). Désertification de la zone sahélienne du Tchad. *Bois et for. des trop.,* 139 p.

DEPOMMIER, D. (1983). *Aspects de la foresterie villageoise dans l'ouest et le nord Cameroun:2/L'arbre dans le paysage kapsiki et les besoins en bois des populations locales.* Yaoundé CTFT/IRA, 8 p. + annexes.

DIALLO, M. & A.M. JENSEN (1983). Projet de reboisements communautaires dans le Bassin arachidier du Sénégal (PRECOBA. Rapport semestriel, septembre 1982 à février 1983. FAO Fatick Project: FO: GCP/023/FIN, 18 p.

DORAN, J. C., D. J. BOLAND, J. W. TURNBULL & B.V. GUNN (1983). *Guide des semences d'acacias des zones sèches.* Rome, F.A.O. (ix) + 116 p.

DOSSO, D. *et al.* (1981). *Enquête sur la consommation de combustible ligneux dans un village du nord de la Côte d'Ivoire (zone dense de Korhogo).* Bouaké, Inst. agric. Mém. de fia d'études (4 ème promo) approx. 120 p.

DOURAT, A. (ed.) (1983). *Fodder production and utilisation by small animals in arid regions.* Beer-Sheva (Israel), Ben-Gurion Univ. of the Negev, doc. BGUN-15-83, 32 p.

DUGAIN, F. (1959). *Rapport de mission au Niger.* Dakar, ORSTOM.

DUMONT, R. *Le Burkina Faso n'est pas 'en voie de développement' mais 'en voie de destruction'.* Typescript, 114 p. dated April 1984.

DUPIRE, M. (1962). Trade and Markets in the Economy of the Nomadic Fulani of Niger (Bororo). *In* BOHANNAN, P. & G. DALTO (ed.), *Markets in Africa:* 335-362. Evanston, N.W. Univ. Press.

DUPRIEZ, H. & Ph. DE LEENER (1983). *Agriculture tropicale en milieu paysan africain.* Dakar, ENDA/Paris, L'Harmattan/Nivelles (Belgique), Terres et Vie, 280 p.

DUVIGNEAUD (1974), *La synthèse écologique.* Paris. Drouin, 296 p.

DYSON-HUDSON, N. (1972). The Study of Nomads. *J. Asian and Afr. St.,* F (1,2) : 30-47.

EHRLICH, P. (1971, 2nd. ed.) *The population bomb.* New York, Ballantine.

EHRLICH, P., A. H. EHRLICH & J.P. HOLDREN (1977, 3rd ed.). *Ecoscience. Population, resources, environment.* San Francisco, Freeman, xv + 1051 p.

ELAMIN, H. M. (1975). Germination and seedling development of the Sudan acacias. *Sudan Silva,* 3(20) : 23-33.

ELGUETA, S. & S. CALDERON (1971). *Estudia del tamarugo como productor de alimento de ganado lanar en la Pampa del Tamarugal.* Instituto Forestal (Peru), Inf. tecn. no. 38, 36 p.

EMBERGER, L. (1960). *Les végétaux vasculaires.* Tome II. 1539 p. in 2 vols. by CHADEFAUD & EMBERGER. *Traité de botanique (systématique).* Paris, Masson.

ENABOR, E. F. & S. K. ADEYOJU (1975). *An appraisal of departmental taungya as practised in the South-eastern State of Nigeria.* Ibadan, Federal Min, of Forests.

EVENARI, M., L. SHENAN & N. TADMOR (1971). *The Negev: the Challenge of a Desert.* Cambridge (Mass.). Harvard Univ. Press.

EVENARI M., U. NESSLER, A. ROGEL & O. SCHENK (1975). *Faire revivre le désert. Expériences d'agriculture en zones arides.* Zurich, Entr'aide protestante suisse, 38 p.

FAO. *Integrating crops and livestock in West Africa.* Rome. FAO Animal Prod. and

Health Paper 41, vi + 112 p.

_____ (1974 a). *Méthodes de plantation forestière dans les savanes africaines.* FAO Collection: Mise en Valeur des Forêts no. 19 : 185 p.

_____ (1974 b). *Rapport de la troisième session du Groupe FAO d'experts des ressources génétiques forestières.* Rome, FAO FO/FGR/3/Rep.

_____ (1976). *Rapport mensuel des activités (mai-juin 1976).* Nouakchott, FAO, Project RAF/74-301, Amélioration des pâturages et de la production animale, 15 p.

_____ (1977). *Les systèmes pastoraux sahéliens. Données socio-démographiques de base en vue de la conservation et de la mise en valeur des parcours arides et semi-arides.* Rome, FAO, FAO Study: Production végétale et protection des plantes no. 5, xiii + 389 p.

_____ (1980). *Conservation des ressources naturelles en zones arides et semi-arides.* Rome, FAO, Conservation des sols, no. 3, xii + 135 p.

_____ (1981 a). *Carte de la situation du bois de feu dans les pays en développement.* Rome, FAO. Explanatory note in 4 langs. (48 p.) and a map in colour, scale 1 : 25 000 000.

_____ (1981 b). *Projet d'évaluation des ressources forestières tropicales (dans le cadre du GEMS).* Rome, FAO. *Les ressources forestières de l'Afrique tropicale,* 2 vol., vii + 118 p. and iv + 586 p.; *Los recursos forestales de la America tropical,* vi + 343 p.; *Forest resources of tropical Asia,* ix + 475 p.

_____ (1984). *Protéger et produire. Conservation des sols en vue de développement.* Rome, FAO. Illustrated booklet, 40 p.

_____ (1985 a). *Rapport de la consultation technique sur la recherche et le développement dendro-énergétiques en Afrique, Addis-Ababa,* 27-30 Nov. 1984 ii + 228 p.

_____ (1985 b). *Rapport sommaire sur la consultation d'experts sur le rôle de la foresterie dans la lutte contre la désertification, Saltillo (Mexico),24-28 juin 1985,* 47 p.

FAO/UNEP (1984). *Map of desertification hazards.* Explanatory note + 1 sheet at 1 : 25 000 000 scale with 6 maps.

FAO/UNEP/UNESCO (1980). Méthode provisoire pour l'évaluation de la dégradation des sols. Rome, FAO, 1 vol., xi + 88 p. + 1 portfolio with 6 maps in colour at 1:5 000 000 scale, 3 on 'current rate and position', 3 on 'hazards'.

FELKER, P. (1978). *State of the art: Acacia albida as a complementary permanent intercrop with annual crops.* Univ. of Riverside (Calif.), Ph.D thesis, 133 p.

FERNANDES, E. C. M., A. OKTINGATI & J. MAGHEMBE (1984). The Chaga homegardens: a multistoried agroforestry cropping system on Mt. Kilimanjaro (Northern Tanzania), *Agroforestry Systems,* 2 : 73-86.

FERLIN, G. (1981). *Techniques de reboisement dans les zones subdésertiques d'Afrique.* Ottawa, C.R.D.I., 46 p. illus.

FERRARIS, R. (1979). Productivity of *Leucaena leucocephala* in the wet tropics of North Queensland. *Trop. Grassl.,* 13 (1) : 20-27.

FFOLLIOTT, P. F. & W. P. CLARY (1972). *Selected and annotated bibliography of understorey-overstorey vegetation relationships.* Univ. of Arizona, Agric. Exp. Sta., Techn. Bull. no. 198, 32 p.

FIELD, C. R., H. F. LAMPREY, S. M. MASHET & M. NORTON-GRIFFITHS (1983). Household, livestock and wildlife numbers and distribution in Marsabit district: population size, densities and habitat selection of fixed environmental variables. In LUSIGI (ed.) *Proc. of the IPAL Seminar:* 101-125.

FORTI, M. (1971). *Introduction of fodder shrubs and their evaluation for use in semi-arid areas of the North-western Negev.* Beer-Sheva, The Negev Inst. for Arid Zone Res., 11 p.

FORTI, M., S. MENDLINGER, J. A. ARONSON & A. YARON (1984). *New crops for arid lands. Second annual report, February 1983 – January 1984.* Beer-Sheva (Israel), Ben-Gurion Univ. of the Negev. doc. BGUN-ARI-18-84, 18 p.

FORTMANN, L. & D. ROCHELEAU (1985). Women and agroforestry: four myths and three case studies. *Agroforestry systems,* 2 : 253-272.

FOURNIER, F. (1960). *Climat et érosion.* Paris, Presses Univ. de France, viii + 201 p.

FRANCO, A. A. (1982). Fixaçao de N_2 atmosférico en *Prosopis juliflora* (Sw.) DC. *In* Empresa de Pesquisa Agropecuaria do Rio Grande do Norte SAA, Document 7, *Simposio Brasileiro sobre Algaroba, Natal 1982, Conferência e Trabalhos Apresentados,* 407 p.

FRISCH, D. (1985). *Allocution prononcée à la cérémonie d'inauguration du Centre technique de coopération agricole et rurale ACP-EEC, Ede/Wageningen, 6 fév. 1985.*

GALLAIS, J. (1965). Le paysan dogon (République du Mali). *Cah. d'Outre-Mer* 70 : 123-143.

——— (1972). Essai sur la situation actuelle des relations entre pasteurs et paysans dans le Sahel ouest-africain. *In Etudes de géographie tropicale offertes a Pierre Gourou.* Paris, Mouton.

GALLAIS, J. & A. H. SIDIKOU (1978). Stratégies traditionnelles, prise de décision moderne et aménagement des ressources naturelles dans la zone sahélo-soudanienne. *In* UNESCO: *Aménagement des ressources naturelles en Afrique . . .*: 11-33.

GARCIA, R. (1981). *Nature pleads not guilty: A Report of the IFIAS Project on Drought and Man.* Oxford, Pergamon.

——— (1984). *'Food Systems and Society', A Conceptual and Methodological Challenge.* Geneva, UNRISD, 73 p.

GASTELLU, J. M. (1974). L'organisation du travail agricole en milieu Sérér. Paris, Trav. et doc. d'ORSTOM no. 34 : 13-104.

——— (1981) *L'égalitarisme économique des Sérér du Sénégal.* Paris, Work. Doc. ORSTOM no. 120, 808 p.

GEERLING, C. & S. DE BIE (1985). *Wildlife Utilisation as a Type of Landuse: An Approach to Implementation.* Paper presented at the Experts' Consultation on the role of forestry in combating desertification. Saltillo (Mexico), 23-28 June 1985, 3 p.

GIFFARD, P. L. (1964). Les possibilités de reboisement en *Acacia albida* au Sénégal. *Bois et forêts des tropiques,* 95 : 21-33.

——— (1971) Recherches complémentaires sur *Acacia albida* Del. *Bois et forêts des tropiques,* 135 : 3-20.

——— (1972). *Rôle de l'Acacia albida dans la régéneration des sols en zone tropicale aride.* Buenos Aires. Paper given at 7th World Forestry Congress.

——— (1974) *L'arbre dans le paysage sénégalais. Sylviculture en zone tropicale sèche.* Dakar, CTFT, 431 p.

——— (1975). Les gommiers, essences de reboisement pour les régions sahéliennes.

Bois et Forêts des Tropiques, 161 : 3-21

GILLET, H. (1973). Tapis végétal et pâturages du Sahel. *In* UNESCO, *Le Sahel: bases écologiques de l'aménagement:* 21-27.

GIRI, J. (1985). La technique peut-elle venir au secours du Sahel? In I.S.F., *L'ingénieur et le développement:* 11-12.

GLOYNE, R. W. (1955). Effect of a windbreak on the speed and direction of wind. *Meteor. Magazine*, 84 : 272-281.

GOLDING, D. L. (1970). The effects of forests on precipitation. *Forestry Chronicle*, 46(5): 397-402.

GORSE, J. (1984). *La désertification dans les zones sahélienne et soudanienne de l'Afrique de l'ouest*. Washington (D.C.), World Bank. Report 5210 (confidential), vii + 69 p. + 1 map sheet.

GOUDET, J. P. (1984). *Equilibre du milieu naturel en Afrique tropicale sèche. Végétation ligneuse et désertification*. Nogent-sur-Marne (France), CTFT, 19 p.

GOUDET, J. P. & D. DEPOMMIER (1983). *Agroforesterie: foresterie et systèmes de production, étude de cas*. Nogent-sur-Marne (France), CTFT Working Doc., ii + 71 p. + 31 p. biblio.

GOSSEYE, P. (1980). Introduction of browse plants in the Sahelo-Sudanian zone. *In* LE HOUEROU (ed.), *Browse in Africa:* 393-397.

GROUZIS, M. (1979). *Structure, composition floristique et dynamique de la production de matière sèche de formations végétales sahéliennes (Mare d'Oursi, Haute Volta)*. Ouagadougou, ORSTOM, 56 p. roneo.

GUISCAFRE, J. (1961). Conservation des sols et protection des cultures par bandes brise-vent: cantons Doukoula, Tebtibali et Wina (Cameroon). *Bois et Forêts des Tropiques*, 79.

GUPTA, J. P., G. G. S. N. RAO, Y. S. RAMAKRISHNA & B. V. RAMANA RAO (1984). Role of shelterbelts in arid zone. *Indian Farming*, 34(7) : 29-30.

HALEVY, G. (1971). A study of *Acacia albida* in Israel. *La-Yaaran*, 21(3-4) : 89-97.

HALL, N. & J. W. TURNBULL, M. I. H. BROOKER (1975). *Acacia cambagei* R. T. Bak. Australia Acacia Series Leaflet CSIRO no. 1.

HALL, N. & J. W. TURNBULL, J. C. DORAN (1979). *Acacia aneura* F. Muell. ex Benth. Australia Acacia Series Leaflet CSIRO no. 7.

HALL, N. & J. W. TURNBULL, P. N. MARTENSZ (1981 a). *Acacia victoriae* Benth. Australia Acacia Series Leaflet CSIRO no. 14.

―――― (1981 b). *Acacia pruinocarpa* Tindaale Australia Acacia Series Leaflet CSIRO no. 16.

HALLAIRE, A. (1972). *Hodogway (Cameroun nord)*. Paris, Mouton, Atlas des structures agraires au sud du Sahara, 6.

―――― (1976). Problèmes de développement au nord des Monts Mandara, Paris, *Cah. ORSTOM, Ser. Sc. hum.*, 13(1) : 3-22.

HARBISON, F. (1962). La planification du développement des ressources humaines dans les économies en cours de modernisation. *Rev. int. du travail.*

HARE, F. K. (1977). Climate and desertification. *In* UNEP *Desertification int. de librairie.:* 63-167.

HARROY, J. P. (1944). *Afrique, terre qui meurt*. Brussels, Hayez & Off.

HAUCK, R. D. (1971). Quantitative estimates of nitrogen cycle process; concepts and review. *In* IAEA *Nitrogen in Soil Plant Studies:* 65-80.

HAWKINS, M. W. (1972). *Observations on indigenous and modern forestry activities in West Africa.* UNU Workshop on Agroforestry, Feiburg, May 31-June 5, 1982, 12 p.

HENRY, P. M. (1975). *La force des faibles.* Paris, Ed. Entente, 156 p.

HERLOCKER, D. (1983). Range ecology programme: past and present activities. *In* LUSIGI (ed.) *Proceedings . . .: 263-279.*

HIERNAUX, P., M. I. CISSE & L. DIARRA (1978 and 1979). *Rapports annuels d'activités de la section d'écologie.* Bamako, CIPEA, 200 p. each.

HJORT, A. (1975). Mise en valeur traditionnelle des terrains dans les terres sèches marginales. *In* RAPP *et al.* (ed.), *Peut-on arrêter . . .:* 45-55.

HOEKSTRA, D. A. (1983). An economic analysis of a simulated alley cropping system for semi-arid conditions, using micro-computers. *Agroforestry Systems,* 1(4) : 335-345.

―――― (1985). Choosing the discount rate for analysing agroforestry systems/technologies from a private economic viewpoint. *Forest Ecology and Management,* 10 : 177-183.

HOEKSTRA, D. A. & F. M. KUGURU (1983). *Agroforestry systems for small-scale farmers.* ICRAF, Proc. of an ICRAF/BAT Workshop held in Nairobi, September 1982, xxi + 283 p.

HOEKSTRA, D. A. *et al.* (1984). *Agroforestry systems for the semi-arid areas of Machakos District, Kenya.* Nairobi, ICRAF, Working Paper 19, (i) + 28 p.

HOROWITZ, M. M. (1972). Ethnic Boundary Maintenance among Pastoralists and Farmers in the Western Sudan (Niger). *In* IRONS, W. & N. DYSON-HUDSON (ed.), *Perspectives on Nomadism:* 105-114. Leiden, E. J. Brill.

HOSKINS, M. (1982). Agroforestry extension: Communications for action. Communic. at the Africa Forestry Workshop, Mombasa (Kenya). May 1982, 14 p.

HUBERT (1921). Le désséchement progressif en Afrique Occidentale Française. *Bull. Comm. Etud. Hist. Scient. AOF,* no. 4.

HUMBERT (1937). La protection de la nature dans les pays intertropicaux et subtropicaux: Contribution à l'étude des Réserves naturelles et des Parcs nationaux. *Mém. Soc. Biogéogr.:* 159 ff.

HUXLEY, P. A. (1983 a) (ed.) *Plant research and agroforestry.* Nairobi, ICRAF, xv + 617 p. + 15 photogr.

―――― (1983 b). Comments on agroforestry classifications: with special reference to plant aspects. *In* HUXLEY (ed.) *Plant research and agroforestry:* 161-171.

―――― (1983 c). The role of trees in agroforestry: some comments. *In* HUXLEY (ed.) *Plant research and agroforestry:* 257-270.

ICRAF (1983 a). *Guidelines for Agroforestry Diagnosis and Design.* Nairobi, ICRAF, Working Paper no. 6, 25 p.

―――― (1983 b). *Resources for Agroforestry Diagnosis and Design.* Nairobi, ICRAF, Working Paper no. 7, 383 p.

IONESCO, T. (1970 a). *Remarques méthodologiques concernant l'étude des ressources pastorales du Maroc.* Rabat, D.R.A. 28 p. roneo.

―――― (1970 b). Méthodologie marocaine de la cartographie de la végétation. *Al Awamia,* 19

JAHN, S. A. A. (1981). *Traditional water purification in tropical developing countries. Existing methods and potential application.* Eschborn, GTZ. Schriftenreihe 117, 284 p.

―――― (1985). *Better water in the tropics by technology transfer from the laboratory to* rural houses. *Experiences from a pilot project with natural coagulants in the Sudan.* Eschborn, GTZ.

JAHNKE, H. G. (1982). *Livestock production systems and livestock development in tropical Africa.* Kiel, Kieler Wissenschaftsverlag Vang.

JUNG, S. (1969). *Influence de l'Acacia albida (Del.) sur la biologie des sols dior.* Dakar, ORSTOM. Internal Report. 63 p. + 3 p. biblio.

KANG, B. T. & B. DUGUMA (1984). *Nitrogen Management in Alley Cropping Systems.* Paper given at the Int. Symp. on the management of nitrogen in tropical prod. systems, IITA (Nigeria), 23-26 Oct. 1984, 7 pp.

KANG, B. T., G. F. WILSON & L. SIPKENS (1981). Alley cropping maize (*Zea mays* L.) and leucaena (*Leucaena leucocephala* Lam.) in Southern Nigeria. *Plant and Soil,* 63 : 165-179.

KARSCHON. R. (1975). *Seed germination of Acacia raddiana Savi and A. tortilis Hayne as related to infestation by bruchids.* Bet Dagan Israel. Agricultural Research Organization, Leaflet no. 52.

KAUL, R. N. & B. N. GANGULI (1963). Studies on economics of raising nursery seedlings in the arid zone. *Annals of Arid Zones,* 1(2) : 85-105.

KAUL, R. N. & M. S. MANOHAR (1966). Germination studies on arid zone tree seeds I. *Acacia senegal* Willd. *Indian Forester* 32 : 199-503

KEITA, J. D. (1967). *Les problèmes forestiers du Mali. La menace fondamentale: la désertification du continent.* Bamako (2nd ed. 1973). Tech. publ. by Serv. des Eaux et Forêts, vol. 1, 47 p.

—— (1983). La Direction des Eaux et Forêts, animateur et conseiller technique dans la lutte contre la désertification, an interview with Mr Nampaa Sanogho. Bamako, *L'Essor,* no. 9075: 4.

KENNARD, D. G. (1973). Relationships between the canopy cover and *Panicum maximum* in the vicinity of Fort Victoria. *Rhod. J. of Agric. Res.,* 11 : 145-153.

KING, J. M. & B. S. HEATH (1975). Game Domestication for Animal Production in Africa. Experiences at the Galana Ranch. *World Animal Review,* 16: 23-30.

KUMAR, P. & B. K. PURKAYASTHA (1972). Note on germination of the seeds of lac hosts. *Indian J. Agric. Sci.* 24 : 430-431.

LABAN, P. (ed.) (1981). *Proceedings of the workshop on land evaluation for forestry.* Wageningen, ILRI Publ. no. 28, 355 p.

LAKHNO, E. S. (1972). *The forest and Man's health.* (in Ukrainian). Kiev, USSR. Zdorov'ya, 143 p.

LAMPREY, H. E. (1963). Ecological separation of the large mammal species in the Tarangire Game Reserve, Tanganyika. *E. Afr. Wildl. J.,* 1: 63-92.

—— (1964). Estimation of the large mammal densities, biomass and energy exchange in the Tarangire Game Reserve and the Maasai steppe in Tanganyika. *E. Afr. Wildl. J.,* 2 : 1-46.

—— (1978). Le projet intégré sur les terres arides. Paris, UNESCO, *Nature et ressources,* 14(4) : 2-12.

—— (1981). Kenya: seeking remedies for desert encroachment. UNESCO's Integrated Project in Arid Lands (IPAL) reviewed. *Span,* 24(2) : 4 p.

—— (1983). Pastoralism yesterday and today: the over-grazing problem. *In* BOURLIERE (ed.) *Tropical Savannas:* 643-666 (Chap. 31).

—— (1983). IPAL Woodland Ecology Programme: summarized account, Nov.

1981. *In* Lusigi (ed.) *Proc. of the IPAL Seminar:* 280-319.

Landsberg, H. E. (1974). Man-made climate changes. *In* WMO *Proc. of the Symp. on Physical and Dynamic Climatology:* 282-303. Leningrad, Gidrometeoizdat publ. WMO no. 347.

Lanly, J. P. (1983). *The nature, extent and developmental problems associated with shifting cultivation in the tropics.* Rome, FAO, Paper Expert Consult. on Educ. Training and Res. Aspects of Shifting Cultivation, 12-16 Dec. 1983.

Lavigne, J. C. (1977). Bilan de dix ans de révolution verte. *Economie et humanisme,* 238 : 14025.

Leakey, R. E. & B. Lewin (1979). *Les origines de l'homme.* Paris, Arthaud, 264 pp.

Lebret, J. *et al.* (1951). *Dynamique concrète du développement.* Paris. Economie et humanisme, Ed. sociales et ouvrières, 550 p.

Lefort, J. (1984). An integrated research and development approach for rural areas of the less developed countries. *Int. J. for Dev. Techno.,* 2 : 87-91.

Legris, P. (1963). *La végétation de l'Inde: écologie et flore.* Pondichery, Inst. français, Trav. Section Scient. et Techn., vol. VI.

Le Houerou, H. N. (1977). Rangelands Production and Annual Rainfall Relations in the Mediterranean Basin and in the African Sahelo-Sudanian Zone. *J. of Range Man.,* 30(3) : 181-189.

―――― (1978). *Le rôle des arbres et arbustes dans les pâturages sahéliens.* Addis Ababa. Communic. to Working Group on the role of trees in the Sahel, 33 p. typed.

―――― (1980 a). Agroforestry techniques for the conservation and improvement of soil fertility in arid and semi-arid zones. *In* Le Houerou (ed.), *Browse in Africa*: 433-435.

―――― (1980b). *Browse in Africa: The current state of knowledge.* Addis-Ababa, ILCA, Papers presented at the Int. Symp. on Browse in Africa, Addis-Ababa, April 8-12, 1980, and other submissions, 491 p.

―――― (1980 c). Composition chimique et valeur nutritive des ligneux fourragers en Afrique de l'ouest. *In* Le Houerou (ed.), *Browse in Africa*: 261-289.

Le Houerou, H. M. & G. F. Popov (1981). *An eco-climatic classification of intertropical Africa.* Rome, FAO, Plant prod. and prot. Paper no. 31, i + 40 p. + 3 map sheets.

Lericollais, A. (1972). *Sol, étude géographique d'un terroir Sérér (Sénégal).* Paris, Mouton, Atlas des structures agraires au sud du Sahara, 7: 110 p. + x photogr. plates.

Levang, P. (1978). *Biomasse herbacée de formations sahéliennes. Etudes méthodologiques et application au bassin versant de la mare d'Oursi.* Ouagadougou, ORSTOM, 29 pp. roneo + app.

Lipinsky, E. S. (1978). Fuels from biomass: Integration with food and materials systems. *Science,* 199 : 644-651.

Lundgren, B. (1981). Land qualities and growth in the tropics. *In* Laban: 237-252.

Lundgren, B. & J. B. Raintree (1983). Sustained Agroforestry. *In* ISNAR, *Agricultural Research for Development:* Potentials and challenges in Asia, The Hague: 37-49.

Lusigi, W. J. (1981). *Combating desertification: rehabilitating degraded production systems in Northern Kenya.* UNESCO, IPAL Techn. Rep. A-4, v + 141 pp.

―――― (ed.) (1983). *Proceedings of the IPAL Scientific Seminar, Nairobi, 1-2 Dec.*

1981. UNESCO/MAB Integrated Project on Arid Lands, 355 p.

Mabbutt, J. A. & C. Floret (ed.) (1980). *Etudes de cas sur la désertification,* Paris, UNESCO, Recherches sur les resources naturelles XVIII, approx. 300 pp.

Maghembe, J. A., E. M. Kariuki & R. D. Haller (1983). Biomass and nutrient accumulation in young *Prosopis juliflora* at Mombasa, Kenya. *Agroforestry systems,* 1(4) : 313-321.

Mainguet, M. (1982). Désertification et crise des oasis. Définition des traumatismes pour un traitement approprié. *In* Gallais, J. (ed.) *C. R. du Sém. sur la gestion des terres arides en Afrique de l'ouest:* 38-39. Tokyo, U.N.U.

Malassis, L. (1973). *Agriculture et processus de développement. Essai d'orientation pédagogique.* UNESCO, Educ. and rural devpt. no. 1, 308 p.

Malcolm, C. V. (1982). *Programme for plant production on salt-affected wastelands and rangeland in Iraq.*

Mann, H. S. & S. K. Saxena (ed.) (1981). *Khejri (Prosopis cineraria) in the Indian desert.* Jodhpur (India), CAZRI, Monograph 11.

Manshard, W. (1982). Alternativen der Energieversorgung in Entwicklungslandern. *Geogr. Rundschau,* 34(12) : 430-435.

Martonne, F. de (1955) (3rd ed.) (1st in 1928). *Géographie physique, vol. III: Biogéographie.* Paris, A. Colin.

Maydell, H. J. von. (1979). *Modellproject der Agroforstwirtschaft im Arrondissement Sebba (Haute Volta).* Hamburg, B.F.H. 16 p.

―――― (1982). *Agroforestry in the Sahel. A contribution to solving problems of rural development in semi-arid regions.* Hamburg. Inst. for World Forestry, 34 p. + 2 p. biblio. + 4 p. tabl. appendix.

―――― (1983). *Trees and shrubs of the Sahel. Their characteristics and uses.* Eschborn, German Techn. Coop. Service (GTZ), no. 196, 525 p.

―――― (1984). *Agroforestry Systems and Practices in the Arid and Semi-Arid Parts of Africa.* Nairobi, ICRAF, Agroforestry Systems Inventory, Report of consultant (unpubl.)

Merryman, J. (1979). Ecological stress and adaptive response: a study of drought-induced nomad settlement in Northern Kenya. *Pan-Africanist,* 8 : 6-16.

Milleville, P. (1982) (new ed.). *Etude d'un système de production agro-pastoral sahélien de Haute-Volta, 1ère partie: le système de culture.* Ouagadougou, ORSTOM, (ii) + 66 p.

Molard, R. (1948). *Afrique occidentale française.*

Monjauze, A. & H. N. Le Houerou (1965). Le rôle des *Opuntia* dans l'économie agricole nord-africaine. Tunis, *Bull. Ec. nat. sup. agric.* 8-9 : 85-164.

Monod, Th. (1950). Autour du problème du déssèchement africain. Dakar, *IFAN Bull.* 12(2) : 514 ff.

―――― (1973). *Les Déserts.* Paris, Horizons de France.

―――― (ed.) (1975). *Pastoralism in tropical Africa.* London, Int. African Inst., Oxford Univ. Press.

Montalembert, M. R. & J. Clement (1983). Disponibilités de bois de feu dans les pays en développement. Rome, FAO, Stud. For. no. 42, viii + 119 p.

Mourgues, G. (1950). Le nomadisme et le déboisement dans les régions sahéliennes. *C. R. Première Conf. int. des Africanistes de l'Ouest,* 1 : 138-167.

Muthana, K. D. (1974). *Improved techniques for tree plantation in the Arid Zone.* Jodhpur, Central Arid Zone Research Inst., Tech. bull. no. 2.

MYERS, H. (1983). *A Wealth of Wild Species: Storehouse for Human Welfare.* Colorado, Westview press.

NAIR, P. K. R. (1980). *Agroforestry species. A crop sheets manual.* Nairobi, ICRAF, ix + 336 p.

―― (1983). Multiple land use and agroforestry. In *Better Crops for Food: Ciba Foundation Symposium 97,* London, Pitman Books Ltd.: 101-111.

―― (1985). *Classification of agroforestry systems.* Nairobi, ICRAF Working Paper 28, (ii) + 59 p.

NAIR, P. K. R., E. C. M. FERNANDES & P. N. WAMBUGU (1984). Multipurpose leguminous trees and shrubs for agroforestry. *Agroforestry Systems,* 2: 145-163.

NAJADA, I. (1980). Analyse du secteur forestier. *In* Club du Sahel, *Analyse du secteur forestier et propositions: le Niger. Vol. II: annexes 1-9:* 107-140.

NAS (1979). Tropical legumes: Resources for the Future. (Nat. Academy of Sciences: Washington, D.C.). (1980). *Firewood Crops: Shrub and Tree Species for Energy Production.* Washington, D.C. Nat. Ac. of Sc., xi + 237 p.

―― (1983). *Agroforestry in the West African Sahel.* Washington, D.C., National Academy Press, ix + 86 p.

OKIGBO, B. N. & D. J. GREENLAND (1977). Intercropping systems in tropical Africa. *In* STELLY (ed.), *Multiple Cropping,* ASA Special Publ. 26 : 63-101.

―― (1977). Neglected plants of horticultural importance in traditional farming systems of tropical Africa. The Hague, *Acta hortic,* 53 : 131-150.

PARDY, A. A. (1953). Notes on indigenous trees and shrubs of Southern Rhodesia: *Acacia albida* Del. Mimosaceae. *Rhosesian Agric. J.,* 50(4) : 325.

PARTRIDGE, I. J. & E. RANACOU (1973). Yields of *Leucaena leucocephala* in Fiji. *Trop. Grassl.,* 7(3) : 327-329.

PATHAK, P. S., S. K. GUPTA & R. D. ROY (1980). Studies on seed polymorphism, germination and seedling growth of *Acacia tortilis* Hayne. *Indian Forester,* 3 : 64-7.

PEDLEY, L. (1986). Derivation and dispersal of *Acacia* (Leguminosae), with particular reference to Australia, and the recognition of *Senegalia* and *Racosperma. Bot J. Linnean Soc.,* 92: 219-254.

―― (1987a). *Racosperma* (Leguminosae, Mimosoideae) Queensland: a checklist. *Austrobaileya,* 2(4): 344-357.

―― (1987b). *Racosperma* Martius (Leguminosae, Mimosoideae) in New Zealand: a checklist. *Austrobaileya,* 2(4): 358-359.

PELISSIER, P. (1953). Le rôle d'*Acacia albida* en Pays Sérér. Les paysans Sérères. Essais sur la formation d'un terroir au Sénégal. *Cahiers d'Outre-Mer,* 6 : 106-127.

―― (1966). *Les paysans du Sénégal.* Paris. CNRS, 939 p.

PELISSIER, P. & S. DIARRA (1978). Stratégies traditionnelles, prise de décision moderne et aménagement des ressources naturelles en Afrique soudanienne. *In* UNESCO, *Aménagement des ressources naturelles:* 35-57.

PENMAN, H. L. (1948). Natural evaporation from open water, bare soil and grass. London, *Proc. Roy. Soc.,* 193 : 120-145.

PENNING DE VRIES, T., F. W. & M. A. DJITEYE (1982). *La productivité des pâturages sahéliens.* Wageningen, PUDOC, 292 p.

PEYRE DE FABREGUES, B. (1963). *Etude des pâturages naturels sahéliens. Ranch du*

Nord-Sanam (Rep. du Niger). Maisons-Alfort. IEMVT, Agrostol. Stud. no. 5, 136 p.

―――― (1967). *Etude agrostologique des pâturages de la zone de Zinder, Rép. du Niger*. Maisons-Alfort. IEMVT, Agrostol. Stud. no. 17, 188 p.

―――― (1970). *Pâturages naturels sahéliens du Sud Tamoana (Rep. du Niger)*. Maisons-Alfort, IEMVT, Astrolog. Stud. no. 28.

PEYRE DE FABREGUES, B. & J. P. LEBRUN (1976). *Catalogue des plantes vasculaires du Niger*. Maisons-Alfort. IEMVT, Bot. Stud. no. 3, 433 p.

PLAISANCE (1961). *Les formations végétales et paysages ruraux. Lexique et guide bibliographique*. Paris, Gauthier-Villars, *424 p.*

PORTERES, R. (1957). Un arbre vivant à contre saison en Afrique soudano-zambézienne: *Faidherbia albida. Science et nature*, 19 : 24.

POULSEN, G. (1972 a). Les gousses de Prosopis, une ressource sous-utilisée. *Sylva africana*, 4 : 8.

―――― (1979 b). Réflexions sous un Prosopis, *Sylva africana*, 5 : 1-4.

PREECE, P. B. (1971). Contributions to the biology of mulga. II. Germination *Aust. J. Bot.* 19 : 39-42.

PRESCOTT, J. A. & J. A. THOMAS (1949). *Proc. R. Geogr. Soc. of Australia, S. Austr.* Br., 50 : 42.

PRINCEN, L. H. (1979). New crop developments for industrial oils, *J. Am. Oil Chem. Soc.* 56: 845-854.

―――― (1982). Alternate industrial feedstock from agriculture. *Econ. Bot.* 36(3) : 302-312.

―――― (1983). New oilseed crops on the horizon. *Econ. Bot.* 37(4) : 478-491.

QURESHI, A. H. (1978). *Sustained yield from tropical forest: a practical policy for resource and environmental management*. Honolulu, E.-W. Centre, E.-W. Environment and Policy Institute.

RADWANSKI, S. A. & G. E. WICKENS (1967). The ecology of *Acacia albida* on mantle soils in Zalingei, Jebel Marra, Sudan. *J. Appl. Ecology*, 4 : 569-579.

―――― (1981). Vegetative Fallows and Potential Value of the Neem Tree (*Azadirachta indica*) in the Tropics. *Econ. Bot.*, 35(4) : 398-414.

RAINTREE, J. B. (1983 a). *A Diagnostic approach to agroforestry design.* Paper submitted to the Int. Symp. on Strategies and Designs for Afforestation, Reforestation and Tree Planting. Hinkeloord, Wageningen (Holland), Sept. 19-23, 1983.

―――― (1983 b). Strategies for enhancing the adoptability of agroforestry innovations. *Agroforestry Systems*, 1(3) : 173-187.

RAPP, A., H. N. LE HOUEROU & R. LUNDHOLM (ed.) (1976). *Peut-on arrêter l'extension des déserts?* Stockholm, NER, Ecology Bull. 24, 248 p.

REY, P. A. (1962). *Les fondements biogéographiques de l'aménagement des montagnes*. Comm. au Congrès de la Féd. fr. d'économie montagnarde, Lacaune 1962. Toulouse, CNRS, Service de la carte de la végétation, Notes & doc. 3, 11 p.

RICHARDS, P. (1985). *Indigenous Agricultural Revolution: Ecology and Food Production in West Africa*. London, Hutchinson.

RIQUIER, J. R. (1978). Land Resources Degradation, Brussels, Europ. comm. *The Courier*, 47 : 47-50.

RIQUIER, J. R. & Ch. ROSSETTI (1976). *Considérations méthodologiques sur l'établissement d'une carte des risques de désertification*. Rome, FAO, report of a technical consultation.

RITTER, W. (1983). *The Fuelwood Crisis: Reemergence of an Old Problem.* Nurnberg Univ. 23 pp. roneo.

ROBINSON, P. (1983). The role of sylvopastoralism in small farming systems. *In* HOEKSTRA & KUGURU. *Agroforestry systems for small-scale farmers:* 147-169.

ROCHETTE, R. M. (1985 a). *Proposition d'orientations pour l'application de la stratégie régionale de lutte contre la désertification au Sahel.* Paris, OECD/ Ouagadougou, CILSS, doc. Sahel D (85) 257, iii + 28 p.

—— (1985 b). *Stratégie de lutte contre la désertification au Sahel.* Synthesis of the regional seminar on desertification of the Sahel, Nouakchott, 29 Oct-4 Nov. 1984. Paris. OECD/Ouagadougou, CILSS, doc. Sahel CR (85)48, iii + 90 p.

ROGERS, E. M. & F. F. SHOEMAKER (1971). *Communication of innovations.* New York, The Free Press.

SACHS, I. *et al.* (1980), *Initiation à l'ecodéveloppement.* Toulouse, Privat, 365 pp.

SAHLINS, M. (1972). *Stone Age Economics.* Chocago, Aldine-Atherton.

SAID, A. N. & H. J. SCHWARTZ (1983). Progress report on the nutrition studies on goats and camels and preliminary results of the studies in goat nutrition. *In* LUSIGI (ed.): 136-156.

SARDAN, O. DE (1983). Les paysans africains face au développement. *In* B.L.A.C.T., *Introduction à la coopération:* 9-36.

SCHUMACHER, E. F. (1974). *Small is beautiful: A study of economics as if people mattered.* London, Sphere Books, 255 p.

SETE EL DIN, Ab. (1984). Agroforestry practices in the dry regions. Khartoum, *At Tasahhur,* 2 : 7-11.

SHANKAR, V. (1981). *Interrelationships of tree overstorey vegetation in silvipastoral systems.* Jodhpur (India), CAZRI. Lecture given at the Summer School 'Agroforestry in arid and semi-arid zones', 15 June-14 July 1981, 14 p.

SIDIKOU, A. H. (1974). Sédentarité et mobilité entre Niger et Zgaret. *Etudes nigériennes,* 34:

SINGH, K. S. & P. LAL (1969). Effect of Khejri (*Prosopis spicigera* Linn.) and Babool (*Acacia arabica*) trees on soil fertility and profile characteristic. *Ann. Arid Zones,* 8(1) : 33-36.

SPEARS, J. S. (1980). Can farming and forestry co-exist in the tropics? *Unasylva,* 32 : 128.

—— (1984). *Review of World Bank Financed Forestry Activity for year 1983.* Washington, World Bank. 37 p.

SRIVASTAVA, J. P. L. (1978). Lopping studies on *Prosopis cineraria. Indian Forester,* 104(4) : 269-274.

STEINHEIL, P. DE (1941). L'euphorbe résinifère, plante à caoutchouc, résine et vernis. *Rév. gén. caoutch. plast.,* 18(2) : 55-59.

STEPPLER, H. A. & J. B. RAINTREE (1983). The ICRAF research strategy in relation to plant science research in agroforestry. *In* HUXLEY (ed) *Plant Research and Agroforestry:* 297-304.

SYNOTT, T. J. (1979). *A report on prospects, problems and proposals for tree planting.* Nairobi, UNESCO, IPAL Technical Report D-26.

TAPP , O. (1984. *Desertification in North East Africa and the role of agroforestry as a means of its counteraction in Sudan.* Edinburgh, M.Sc. thesis, 100 p.

THOMSON, J. T. (1984). *Agroforestry and natural forest management: possibilities and conditions for participation*. Lome (Togo), paper presented to USAID Africa Bureau Forestry Conference. May 7-11, 1984.

TIMBERLAKE, I. (1985). *Africa in crisis. The causes, the cures of environmental bankruptcy*. London, I.I.E.D./Earthscan. 233 p.

TOKIN, B. P. (1946). Phytoncides (in Russian). Moscow, USSR Academy of Sciences.

―― (1963). Results of the 4th conference on phytoncides (in Russian). *Zh. obstr. ch. Biol.*, 24(3) : 230-235).

TOLBA, M. K. (1985a). *Desertification control: moving beyond the laboratory*. Paper presented to the Conf. 'Arid Lands: today and tomorrow', Tucson (Arizona), 20-25 Oct. 1985.

―― (1985 b). *Heads in the sand. A new appraisal of arid lands management*. Paper presented to the Conf. 'Arid lands: today and tomorrow', Tucson (Arizona), 20-25 Oct. 1985.

TORRES, F. (1983). Role of Woody Perennials in Animal Agroforestry. *Agrofor. Systems*, 1(2) : 131-163.

TOTHILL, J. D. (1954). *Agriculture in the Sudan*. Oxford Univ. Press, 974 p. + 1 map sheet + several maps in colour.

TOUTAIN, G. (1974). La micro-exploitation phoenicicole saharienne face au développement. Rabat, *Al Awamia*, 52.

―― (1977). Eléments d'agronomie saharienne. De la recherche au développement. Paris, INRA, xi + 277 pp.

TOUTAIN, G. & G. DE WISPELAERE (1977). *Pâturages de l'O.R.D. du Sahel et de la zone de délestage du nord-est de Fada N'Gourma*. Maisons-Alfort (France), IEMVT, Agropast. Study no. 51.

TOWNSHEND, G. M. (1952). Agri-silviculture. Note to the Editor. *Emp. For. Rev.*, 31(3).

TROPICAL INSTITUTE, AMSTERDAM. Bulletin 303. *Agroforestry, Proceedings of the 50th 'Tropische Landbouwdag'* (Symposium on tropical agriculture): 11-24.

UDVARDY, M. D. F. (1975). *A Classification of the Biogeographical Provinces of the World*. Morges (Switzerland), IUCN, Occasional Paper no. 18, 48 p.

UNCOD (1974). *Technology and desertification*. (Preparatory) Background Document, UN Conf. on Desertification, doc. A/CONF/74/6, 122 p.

UNEP (1977). *Desertification: its causes and consequences*. Oxford, Pergamon, 448 p.

―― (1984). *L'état de l'environnement en 1984. L'environnement dans le dialogue entre pays développés et pays en développement et entre ces deux groupes de pays*. Nairobi, UNEP/GC.12.11. v+ 40 p.

UNEP/FAO/UNESCO/WMO (:1977). *Carte mondiale de la désertification, à l'échelle du 1:25,000,000*. UN Conf. on the desert, Nairobi, 29 Aug.-9 Sept. 1977, doc. A/CONF. 74/2, 1 note of 11 pp. and 1 map in colour.

UNESCO (1973). *Le Sahel: bases écologiques de l'aménagement*. Paris, Tech. notes of MAB, 99 p.

―― (1978). *Aménagement des ressources naturelles en Afrique: stratégies traditionnelles et prise de décision moderne*. Tech. notes of MAB 9, 83 p.

―― (1979). *Carte de la répartition mondiale des régions arides*. Paris, UNESCO, Tech. notes of MAB 7, 1 note of 55 p. + 1 colour map of scale 1:25,000,000.

UNIDO (1985). Cash from the desert. *Development and cooperation* (publ. G.T.Z.), 2 : 33.

VASCONCELOS, M. (1985). *Alternativas technologicas para a agropecuaria do Semi-Arido*. Sao Paulo. Nobel, 171 p.

WALTER, H. & H. LEITH (1967). *Klimadiagram Weltatlas*. Iena, Fisher Verl., 200 pp.

WEISZ, P. B., W. O. HAAG & P. G. RODEWALD (1979). Catalytic production of high grade fuel (gasoline) from biomass compounds by shape selective catalysis. *Sciences*. 206 : 57-58.

WEST, O. (1950). Indigenous tree crops for Southern Rhodesia. *Rhod. Agric. J.* 47 : 204-217.

WICKENS, G. E. (1969). A study of *Acacia albida* Del. (Mimosoideae). *Kew Bulletin* 23 : 181-202.

WIERSUM, K. F. (1985). *Trees in agricultural and livestock development*. Mexico, 9th World Forestry Congress, Theme I.3, invited paper.

WINCKLER, G. (1982). *La désertification dans les pays du Sahel*. Eschborn, GTZ, Sahel Info 4, iv + 55 p. + 15 p. illustr.

WINDHORST, H. W. (1979). Neuere Versuche der Bestimmung der Primarproduktion des Walder und forstlicher Ertragspotentiale. *Erdkunde,* 33 : 10-23.

WOOD, P. J. (1984). *Mixed Systems of Plant Production in Africa, Past, Present and Future*. Nairobi, ICRAF, Working Paper 20, 15 p.

World Bank (1981). *Développement accéléré en Afrique au sud du Sahara,* Washington. (9 Oct. 1984). *La désertification dans les zones sahélienne et soudanienne de l'Afrique de l'ouest*. Washington, IBRD, report 5210.

WORMALD, T. J. (1984). *The management of the natural forests in the arid and semi-arid zones of East and Southern Africa*. UK. A report for ODA (iii + 83 p.).

YANDJI, E. (1982). Traditional agroforestry systems in the Central African Republic. *In* MacDONALD, L. H. (ed.), *Agroforestry in the African Humid Tropics:* 52-55, Tokyo, UNU.

ZAROUG, M. G. (1984). *Fodder trees and shrubs and their role in improving forage supply from arid and semi-arid lands in the Near East Region*. Report presented at the Int. Round Table on Prosopis. Arica (Chile), 11-15 June, 1984, ii + 23 p. + 2 p. ref.

The International Council for Research in Agroforestry (ICRAF) was established in 1977. ICRAF is an autonomous, non-profit-making International Council governed by a Board of Trustees.

The objectives of the Council are to increase the social, economic and nutritional well-being of peoples of developing countries through the promotion of agroforestry systems to achieve better land use in developing countries without detriment to their environments, to encourage and support research and training relevant to agroforestry systems, to facilitate the collection and dissemination of information relevant to such systems and to assist in the international co-ordination of agroforestry development.

The Technical Centre for Agricultural and Rural Co-operation (CTA) was set up in 1983 under the Second ACP-EEC Lomé Convention. The Centre is at the disposal of the ACP (African, Caribbean and Pacific) States' authorities responsible for agricultural development in order to provide them with better access to information, research, training and innovations in the fields of agricultural and rural development.

The International Council for
Research in Agroforestry (ICRAF)
P.O. Box 30677
Nairobi
Kenya

Technical Centre for Agricultural
and Rural Co-operation (CTA)
P.O. Box 380
6700 AJ Wageningen
The Netherlands

250